THE QUEST FOR LIBERATION
AND RECONCILIATION

J. Deotis Roberts

THE QUEST FOR LIBERATION
AND RECONCILIATION

*Essays in Honor of
J. Deotis Roberts*

Edited by
Michael Battle

WESTMINSTER
JOHN KNOX PRESS
LOUISVILLE · KENTUCKY

Scripture quotations from the New Revised Standard Version of the Bible are copyright © 1989 by the Division of Christian Education of the National Council of the Churches of Christ in the U.S.A. and are used by permission.

Chapter 3, Norbert M. Samuelson's essay "Science and Spirituality," is reprinted by permission of The International Institute for Secular Humanistic Judaism. (Secular Spirituality: Passionate Journey to a Rational Judaism, proceeding of Colloquium '01, published by The International Institute for Secular Humanistic Judaism/Milan Press, Farmington Hills, MI, M. Bonnie Cousens [ed], 2003, pp. 110–136.)

Book design by Sharon Adams
Cover design by Lisa Buckley

First edition
Published by Westminster John Knox Press
Louisville, Kentucky

This book is printed on acid-free paper that meets the American National Standards Institute Z39.48 standard. ∞

PRINTED IN THE UNITED STATES OF AMERICA

05 06 07 08 09 10 11 12 13 14—10 9 8 7 6 5 4 3 2 1

Library of Congress Cataloging-in-Publication Data

The quest for liberation and reconciliation : essays in honor of J. Deotis Roberts / Michael Battle, editor.
    p. cm.
  Includes bibliographical references and index.
  ISBN 0-664-22892-5 (alk. paper)
  1. Black theology.   2. Race—Religious aspects—Christianity.
  I. Roberts, J. Deotis (James Deotis), 1927–   II. Battle, Michael, 1963–

BT82.7.Q47 2005
230'.089'96073—dc22
                              2004056957

Contents

Foreword

With this book, the reader is invited into the enduring contributions of J. Deotis Roberts. With essays from nationally and internationally recognized theological figures, this book attests to the powerful impact of Roberts's theological vision, one that remains instructive for how we still navigate liberation and reconciliation in the world.

As a first-generation African American theologian, Roberts was a pioneer of black theological discourse in the late 1960s and early 1970s. As one can imagine, such work contained the adventure of creating and training generations of scholars at both historically black theological schools and schools composed predominantly of white scholars and students. Such an adventure required courage amid the largely white, European theological and academic communities in which black theological discourse was either unintelligible or insignificant. It was within these contexts that black theology was introduced and finally launched as a vital academic discourse. In this regard, much is owed to J. Deotis Roberts for maintaining hope that black theologians could be taken seriously.

As the reader engages the symphony of voices in honor of Roberts, some of the foremost theologians in the United States and beyond provide their particular interpretations of Roberts's scholarship and theological pilgrimage. The wonderful emergence out of this is that one learns how Roberts challenged black theology to move beyond bifurcation to a reconstructive discourse in which a diversity of people could seek God in common.

ARCHBISHOP DESMOND TUTU

Introduction

We are afflicted in every way, but not crushed; perplexed, but not driven to despair; persecuted, but not forsaken; struck down, but not destroyed.
2 Corinthians 4:8–10

In many ways Saint Paul's words to the Corinthian people are fitting to begin this volume in honor of J. Deotis Roberts (b. 1927), who turns seventy-eight years old in July 2005. To reflect on the life and witness of Roberts makes us ask the question: What is it that keeps us hoping against hope? What is it that keeps us going, even when we see our hopes crushed? Especially in the African American community, we have seen our hopes dashed many times. What keeps us reaching for the things we do not yet have? J. Deotis Roberts provides the answer in that the promises and ideas of the Christian faith inspire us to keep "questing." Indeed, a Christian dies in the faith quest. It is the promises of the Christian faith that keep our faith in the quest for understanding. We are promised that though we are afflicted, we will not be crushed; though we are perplexed, we will not be driven to despair; though we are persecuted, we will not be forsaken; though so many of us have been struck down, we will not be destroyed. Christian hope will never die. Instead, bolstered by the promises of faith, we boldly proclaim our hope that one day all of God's children will live in peace. Often, it feels like despair, a hope against hope, but it is this hope, this reaching for Christ's just peace in the world, that pushes us forward. As Paul says in Romans 8:24, "For in hope we were saved."

Faith in the quest of understanding must include an emphasis on reconciliation among all persons, without which such faith ceases to be Christian (Eph. 2:14ff.). Roberts's faith is in the quest for "reconciliation that brings black [people] together and of reconciliation that brings black and white [people] together."[1] Roberts says, "It is my belief that true freedom overcomes estrangement and heals the brokenness between peoples."[2] However, Roberts argues, "reconciliation can take place only between equals. It cannot coexist with a situation of Whites over Blacks."[3] Therefore the goal of our faith quest, genuine reconciliation with both God and our neighbor, can come only if there is the commitment to see all people as created in the image of God (Gen. 1:26) and of infinite value to God (1 Cor. 6:20; 1 Pet. 1:18).

Roberts provides the context for black theology to move beyond any deadlocks between white and black people. Much of Roberts's work in epistemology, comparative study of religions, philosophy, and theology, as well as ethics, seeks comprehension and interdisciplinary results. As the South African theologian Tinyiko Samuel Maluleke attests in his essay in this volume, "We are honoring Deotis Roberts at a time when all radical theologies are facing great challenges." Such interdisciplinary work also includes ecumenical work as Kosuke Koyama's essay invites. To respond to these times, this volume demonstrates the power of interdisciplinary work that Roberts has pursued throughout his esteemed life. One can see such interdisciplinary pursuit not only through Roberts's academic work but through his community outreach as well, including his board memberships (e.g., Albert Schweitzer Fellowship, Plowshare Institute, Ecumenical and Cultural Institute, and International Bonhoeffer Society). During the height of black theology, Roberts continued this broader study of black theology. For example, his book on philosophical theology, *A Philosophical Introduction to Theology*, indicates a wider vision and competence for black theology.[4] And yet, Roberts maintains his particularity as a black Baptist.[5]

Roberts's continued life and witness to the enduring gospel that is not destroyed must be celebrated. It is my conclusion that as one of the primary architects of black theology, he has not been celebrated sufficiently as a major North American theologian. As important a figure as Roberts has become in the theological world, his work has limited visibility among the wider audience to whom his theology has much to say and teach. Contributors to this volume attribute this undervaluation mainly to the contexts in which Roberts taught, African American theological institutions lacking Ph.D. programs, and to his more confessional theology. The latter was often deemed difficult for academicians to locate as theory per se. This misinterpretation and lack of recognition can end with this volume, as well as with his recently released collected essays in David Goatley's edited volume *Black Religion, Black Theology: The Collected Essays of J. Deotis Roberts*.[6] Although Goatley's volume focuses more on Roberts's work in black theology, my edited volume engages and extends the seminal and enduring theological contributions of J. Deotis Roberts. This volume before you seeks to be more inclusive of a diversity of contexts and covers a broader context of a lifetime of scholarship for Roberts.

Roberts received his Ph.D. degree in 1957, at which time he began his teaching and research. The decade of 1958–1968 was a developmental period that helped establish black scholars, just as Roberts established himself in epistemological research regarding questions of faith in relation to knowledge. The crucial question early on for Roberts was: What can we know and still believe? With this question in the volatile period of Roberts's work, he was led to explore existentialism and other religions and cultures to seek an answer for his times. Such a quest was not just in theory, as he engaged extensive travel and study in Europe, Asia, and the Middle East. Egypt was the only African country he was able to explore during this time. From this time of extensive travel Roberts developed his book *A Theology of Dialogue*, which concerned interfaith and cross-cultural dialogue. This meant that for Roberts the Christian perspective must always include ecumenical dialogue. Howard University became an ideal setting for Roberts to explore and develop these ecumenical and international themes. Also, Howard University was involved in the legal phase of the Civil Rights struggle in which Roberts entered into dialogue with lawyers and Civil Rights advocates. For example, Roberts was a council observer of the church phase of Martin Luther King Jr.'s movement, but he did not march with King. Since Roberts was deeply involved in the life of the church as a theologian, however, he was drawn into the theological phase of the black power movement through the National Council of Black Churches. Related groups met at Howard University and the Interdenominational Theological Center (ITC) and drew Roberts deeper into the Civil Rights movement. This turbulent period merged Roberts's temperament as a theologian (philosophical and exploratory) and a practitioner (church leader and expositor of church dogmatics). Roberts states, "I had also reached a certain maturity as a thinker, through teaching, research and experience into my engagement with other religious scholars at that juncture."[7] Roberts's relationship with James Cone enters at this time.

As a first-generation African American theologian, Roberts was a pioneer of black theological discourse in the late 1960s. The dialogue that developed between Cone and Roberts could be said to have generated from the youthful catalyst behind the black power movement. Roberts states:

> As Dean Lawrence Jones put it: I was drawn into this movement by the ministers and theological students not as a dialog partner with Cone. In fact the pressure was so great that I need time and space to decide if I should get involved and on what terms. Fortunately, my college work at Johnson C. Smith and Shaw University and my ministry in black congregations had prepared me to build upon what I already knew as a native of North Carolina, having much experience in black congregations in North Carolina, Hartford and the D.C.-Baltimore corridor prepared me to relate to both black intellectuals and black ministers and lay persons.[8]

Roberts continues to tell of two of his books that were crucial for him to enter into the movement to empower black people: *Quest for a Black Theology* and *Liberation and Reconciliation: A Black Theology*.[9] The latter book was written during a leave from Howard when Roberts went to teach at Swarthmore College. Resulting from a series of lectures and a year of retreat, *Liberation and Reconciliation* was written with an awareness of what was going on in the black power/black consciousness movement. The year at Swarthmore was a personal intellectual struggle for Roberts with these social justice issues swirling around in his head and heart, especially those issues concerning racial justice. Upon his return from Howard University, Roberts knew what his position should be regarding the black power dynamic, and this is when his dialogue with Cone first began. "My position should be seen," writes Roberts, "as a mediation between the position of King and Cone rather than a response to Cone. More than that, what I had to say can only be appreciated in the context of all that I had developed in this intellectual and experiential experience that made me who I was as a thinker."[10]

As a result, his work contains the adventure of constructing and training generations of scholars not only at historically black theological schools but now at educational institutions around the world. Being among the first black theological agents required courage amid largely white, European theological and academic communities, in which black theological discourse was either unintelligible or insignificant. It was within these contexts that black theology was introduced and finally launched as a vital academic discourse that has impacted a whole field of what is considered, today, contextual theology (liberation theology, feminist and womanist theology, etc.). Delores Carpenter's essay in this volume demonstrates why such contextual theology remains vital. As colleague, conversation partner, and mentor of some of the foremost theologians in the United States and the world, Roberts still deeply influences theological discourse in a variety of ways. It is my contention as editor, however, that Roberts's particular contribution of scholarship and theological pilgrimage is in his challenge to black theology to move beyond bifurcation in its construction of a world stricken with racism to a world of reconciliation. In other words, Roberts opened many people's eyes, in a very dangerous and fragile period for black identity, to see how to proceed beyond violence and an "us against them" worldview. Roberts's genius was his pursuit beyond the options of either radical black nationalism or the conservative black "cheap grace."

A number of scholars have been invited to write original essays for this volume from their area of expertise and engagement with Roberts's theology. They have been chosen on the basis of (1) their authority and passion for the subjects that J. Deotis Roberts wrote on and taught, (2) their relationship with Roberts, and (3) their articulation of a synthesis between reflection and action. At the core of Roberts's thought and passion is the striking harmony between the quest for liberation and the need for reconciliation, not only in black–white relations but in all human relations. In such a context, Roberts's voice became a prominent response to the other pioneer of black theological discourse, James Cone, especially Cone's work *Black Theology and Black Power*.[11] In his text, Cone maintained that the black power movement was the prophetic example of God's liberating presence within the crucible of racism in United States, and that black theology was the logical extension of this trend in the religious realm. In his book *Liberation and Reconciliation*, Roberts also advanced the thesis that, given the racist nature of the United States as a society, black theology was needed to articulate the manner of how God liberates the oppressed.[12] Roberts, however, was critical of Cone's liberationist proposal. Any student of black theology must be careful in the quest for understanding Roberts's critique of Cone.

In response to Cone, Roberts examined various biblical and theological themes from the perspective of the black experience and concluded that along with liberation, nonviolent reconciliation between black and white people in the United States was the appropriate response to racial oppression. The critique really became dialogue. The dialogue between Roberts and Cone is important for understanding the historical context of the emergence of black theology. In 1969, James Cone suggested in *Black Theology and Black Power* that black power is essential in understanding Christ's central power of liberating the oppressed in twentieth-century America. Few could anticipate the tremendous impact of Cone's publishing this book. A year later, Cone's book *A Black Theology of Liberation* appeared.[13] In this next book, Cone argued for how Christianity is a religion of liberation for the oppressed; that blacks in America are the oppressed of today; and that, therefore, if theology is the "rational study of the being of God in the world in light of the existential situation of an oppressed community," then Christian theology *must* be black theology. This book began to elicit the serious attention that black theology and James Cone have come to deserve and require.

Cone's central thesis is that "one's social and historical context decides not only the questions we address to God but also the mode or form of the answers given to the questions." Cone has deeply inspired J. Deotis Roberts to formulate a mediating response to the tragic situation of race in America. When a definitive history of the black church is written, Cone and Roberts will be credited with heating up a lively debate on perennial and substantial theological issues within ecclesiastical, scholarly, and critical circles. Such debate follows from the character of black theology's quest to understand God's presence in a world "afflicted in every way, but not crushed; perplexed, but not driven to despair; persecuted, but not forsaken; struck down, but not destroyed." Both Cone and Roberts seek to see God in such a world, and their theological debate is indicative of such pursuit. There was no malicious or destructive criticism between the two scholars. If the critic does not take the route of internal and external criticism, he or she becomes guilty of begging the question being debated. Roberts and Cone remind America that the purpose, if not the actual effect, of theological discipline is to call into question the ultimacy of the norms settled upon by those in power. Consequently, the norms set by the powerful cannot be enlisted as the critical apparatus for evaluating theology. To put the issue in another way: it became controversial for black theologians such as Roberts and Cone to argue for the legitimacy of the black voice in "Ivy League" theology. Often they were dismissed by "established" theologians as offering an inherent form of racism, whereby the critic evaluates with a prior conclusion of the inherent superiority of black people. But the authenticity of Roberts and Cone must be regarded in their own duty to construct a critical language in which the powerful could see that is was often the situation or context in which other theological voices could not be heard or even understood. To show the integrity of Roberts's and Cone's enterprise, one can simply notice how they engaged one another.

The criticisms of Roberts regarding Cone's work pertain essentially to Cone's theological method. In Roberts's *A Black Political Theology*, he argues that Cone's radical christocentric view hinders conversations between black American and African theologians. In Cone's later work, he acknowledges along with Roberts that black Americans are not the only oppressed group in today's world. Feminist and southern theologians have begun to articulate an analysis of the oppressed, the oppressor, and oppression that enlarges what Cone and Roberts initiated. This is the great legacy that both Cone and Roberts will leave behind—namely, that theology's relevance must always be understood in the systemic restoration of human relationships gone awry. This points to my personal debt to the pioneering work of Cone and Roberts. All contextual scholars are indebted to their prowess in making black theology relevant to all oppressed and liberated peoples.

Black theology is fairly recent, approximately four decades old. Although it is fairly new to religious studies, it has attracted the attention of the religious scholar. It has become a crucial theological discourse that informs foundational understandings of theology per se. Christian black theology was a product of the hostility between races in the United States, which took place throughout the sixties and seventies. During this time religion played a vital role, a political role, to the liberation of certain groups. Throughout the sixties, black religious leaders such as Malcolm X and Dr. Martin Luther King Jr. were influential in the public sphere. In response, from the black Christian church Cone and Roberts systematized Christian black theology for the first time, transferring the experience of black Christians to the classroom and the study of religion.

During the sixties and seventies, black religious leaders played an active role in mediating and separating the two races while fighting racism. Although Malcolm X began his work in opposition to other human identities, he later changed his perspective. As minister in the Nation of Islam in New York, he started as an advocate of segregation and black nationalism because of his loyalty to Elijah Muhammad, founder of Nation of Islam. During this time he was primarily known for his opposition to white people, calling them "blue-eyed devils." Malcolm had an experience that changed his perspective on life and race when he journeyed to Mecca to take part in a *hajj*—a trip to Mecca required of all Muslims if one can afford to take the trip. During the *hajj*, Malcolm encountered a number of Muslims who where racially different from him. He then realized that not all whites were racist or "blue-eyed devils" and came with this renewed perspective into the States.

In contrast, Martin Luther King Jr. used an integrationist perspective during the Civil Rights movement. Dr. King, a minister of a Baptist church in Georgia, believed in his concept of the "Beloved Community" spacious enough to contain all people, even those called enemies. King articulated nonviolence into the Civil Rights movement, which was differentiated from the black militant's slogan "by any means necessary." While King advocated a nonviolent approach, he was adamant that racism must be rooted out, as a disease must systemically healed.

This background of integration versus separation influenced and molded Christian black theology. According to much of African American religious thought today, black theology is no longer a gift of a generic Christian gospel dispensed to slaves; rather, the Christian gospel has become an appropriation by black slaves of the gospel given by their white oppressors. Black theology was different from other Christian theology because black slaves could not use standard, white Christian theology, as Christian theology was oppressive to slaves. Henceforth, slaves were forced to develop a theology that spoke to their current situation and circumstance. As a result, black theology is a product of the black Christian perspective, which is rooted in slavery, struggles for justice, and liberation from oppression.

According to many, black theology is nurtured, sustained, and passed on in the black Christian churches in their various ways of expression.[14] Black theology has always had a home in the Christian church; however, the views of the Black Panthers and the Nation of Islam's nationalistic talk did not comply with the church's position on reconciliation. Currently, the black militancy/black power and the Nation of Islam identities have hinted at the wisdom of a position directed toward reconciliation. The genius of the Truth and Reconciliation Commission in South Africa especially has helped many to see the pragmatism and relevance of reconciliatory approaches to conflict.

To compare black Christian theology and black power movements today, we need to understand the social, political, and religious context of black theology. James Cone, in formulating black theology, meshes it with the controversial term of *black power*, which, according to Cone, is an attitude, an inward affirmation of the essential worth of blackness. Black power goes against the misconception of others about black people; according to Cone, black power goes against anything that dehumanizes the black person. Hence, Cone forms black theology to articulate a black perspective in theology, yet he clearly uses "black power" to thrust his argument forward. However, in doing this Cone is criticized by some as conforming his theology to the separatist black power movement.

Roberts, also influenced by black power movements, the Civil Rights movement, and the view that ends and means are organically one, disagreed sometimes with Cone's more radical rhetoric. Cone's black power rhetoric was often interpreted (rightly and wrongly) in the nationalism/separation category, while Roberts can be placed in a number of different categories, as illustrated by the headings of this book. I think, however, that their similarity outweighs their differences, as both Cone and Roberts describe black power in a more positive light and use the term in a systematic way to describe a discourse for disenfranchised persons. For example, Roberts describes black power as black consciousness, black pride, black self-determination.[15] Cone believes that Black Power is not the antithesis to Christianity, . . . and it is Christ's central message to the twentieth-century America.[16] One could conclude that both Roberts's and Cone's usage of the phrase "black power" in black theology does not necessarily promote violence or hatred but can become a heuristic device by which to describe struggle of black people in oppressive conditions to become human, self-conscious, and liberated. Roberts states, [God] *speaks* savingly to [humanity] in a particular historical and cultural setting. Black Theology must concern itself with the manner of God's address to . . . the context of the black presence or the black experience of being a black [person] who seeks to confess faith in God . . . in the racist society in which [that person] is victimized.[17]

This honorary volume contributes to the understanding of black theology not only for scholars but for people all over the world. With essays from nationally and internationally recognized theological figures, this volume attests to the breadth of Roberts's theological vision, one that is expansive yet ever negotiating the concussive tensions between liberation and reconciliation. No longer can the black perspective in theological and religious discourse be taken for granted. Any academic theological pedagogy that does not acknowledge the intellectual aspect of black theology enough to implement black theology in the curriculum can no longer be seen as systematic. This was always the focus of Cone and Roberts. They emphasized the need for theology to be authentic to the reflector.

Although today black theology still struggles to penetrate the academy, Cone and Roberts prepared a way for the second generation of theologians and the generations to follow. Black theologians today not only are concerned with preserving the "message" of Cone and Roberts but seek to be empowered by them to articulate theology that matters to nonacademically trained persons and to those "sitting in the pews." Dwight Hopkins, Cone's former student, summarizes the goal of black theology today as being that the second generation of black theologians have to integrate a gospel of full humanity, a critical acceptance of African American religious history, and an understanding of theological, cultural, and political power in the United States.[18] Hopkins is a vital voice, as he indicates a future direction and expansion of Cone's project. Today, black theologians like myself have enjoyed the fruits of the labors of the first black theologians who made black theology part of the curriculum.

Cone and Roberts are architects for a theology that seeks resolution in a seemingly irreconcilable world. They propose that black theology and Christian theology have a communicative relationship, where both sides come to an agreement about what God is saying to all humanity. Roberts's chief contribution is in his perennial argument that Christian theology should not be ostracized and cast away in black theology today. His genius is in his affirmation that Christian theology has always been about both liberation and reconciliation. Roberts also insists that one must distinguish between two mutually exclusive positions in black religion: Afro-American Christianity and the religion of black power. Thus, Roberts intends his work to be the expression of a black theology that is at the same time authentically Christian. Part 1 of this volume probes the meaning of the relationship between liberation and reconciliation that constituted much of the dynamic between Roberts and Cone. The chapters by Jürgen Moltmann and John Macquarrie accentuate an interpretation of the gospel that emphasizes both liberation from structural evil and reconciliation among all of God's creation.

Dwight Hopkins reaches into the African heritage and the African American cultural resources in the quest for what truly constitutes culture in the journey toward true freedom and justice. This seems most appropriate to honoring Roberts, who constantly utilized the "chosen people" motif as it applies to the destiny of black culture and the role of the black church. Later in the volume, Janice Hale, Edward Wimberly, Delores Carpenter, and William Brackney all articulate Roberts's desire to encourage perceiving the destiny of all people as an extended family, and the black family in particular, and even as a nuclear fellowship toward centers of healing and sustenance within the grace of God.

In Part 1, Norbert Samuelson, Frederick Ferré, and Alistair Kee honor Roberts's work in philosophical theology, especially concerning the problem of God-talk (as *logos* about *theos*) within the context of the black understanding of salvation history, revelation, providence, and theodicy. Turning back to theological anthropology, Hopkins provides a challenge for human dignity in light of the black experience. Many of the writers emphasize the necessity of human dignity in response to present problems such as drugs, violence, and the growing black underclass. They also give attention to the meaning of liberation in overcoming sin and experiencing salvation, both of which are multidimensional.

One of the challenging themes of Roberts's theology grew out of his Christology, in which there was dialogue with and rejection of the thesis for a "literal only" understanding of the black Messiah. Instead, Roberts searches for a broader definition of the black Messiah as liberator and reconciler within a multicultural, global, and gender-inclusive context. The comment has been made, for instance, that much of black theology is not ontological or theological analysis and corroboration but simply black history. Roberts would advance another interpretative principle: an interim assessment must first be a descriptive analysis, and only then can it move to a critical appraisal. Roberts moves on to discuss the doctrines of Christian hope and eschatology as they pertain to both the present and the future. From a black perspective, the resurrection event becomes the focal point for empowering present acts for both the personal and social goals of salvation and eternal life. In the final chapter, Roberts attempts to address some of the ethical implications of his work, such as the ongoing legacy of racism in light of his thesis on liberation and reconciliation. He concludes by suggesting pragmatic applications of this exegesis to the present struggle.

This volume honors the expansion of all of Roberts's original work. It (1) represents a greater sensitivity to the larger audience of poor and oppressed people, (2) retains a balance between liberation and reconciliation within a pluralistic society, (3) emphasizes the relevance of black theology for the global human family, (4) utilizes inclusive language, and (5) underscores the need for a definitive theology of ministry out of the black church tradition. This volume merits reading as a vital text on black theology and interdisciplinary studies that has laid the foundation for a new generation of African American religious scholars. Along with persons such as Charles Curran and Peter Paris, Roberts has been instrumental in providing the moral space for new ways of doing theology, within both the church and the academy.

Instead of seeing Roberts's work as disparate and unlocated due to its breadth and scope, it is our hope that this collection becomes regarded as a serious engagement of his scholarship, as well as a long overdue gesture to express gratitude for

Roberts's invaluable contribution to the academy, the church, and the world. As editor of this volume, I can attest to this invaluable contribution, having known him as a valued colleague at Duke Divinity School and as a mentor. My own affinity for Roberts's work has to do with his love for the church. Roberts has spent much of his distinguished career doing theology in the service of the church. His desire has always been to influence church, academy, and world so that not only black people are liberated but all may participate in the kingdom of God. He creates a *via media* between the self-serving metaphysical approach of some theology and the sometimes vapid pragmatism of black religious studies that focus only on social relevance instead of the difficulty of Jesus' gospel. It is a profound honor to edit this collection of essays in honor of such a respected and influential figure in modern American theology.

This book gathers important essays from some of the most well-known theologians in the world, arranged to show the development of Roberts's thought. They reveal his commitment to the church and to his theological model of liberation and reconciliation. Theology is free, Roberts writes, because it moves one toward a fuller realization of what God is calling one to do; Christian theology is reconciling because Christians are reconciled to God through Christ and are called to a ministry of reconciliation. In the end, the reader may see the whole picture of the volume as comprising four sections determined by the primary contours of Roberts's scholarship: (1) theological reflection, (2) faith in dialogue, (3) shaping family ministry, and (4) theological education. These four areas are further subdivided by the expertise of the essayists. The reader is now invited to feast on the rich essays that follow, as the tone is set for the breadth of Roberts's theological vision.

PART 1
THEOLOGICAL REFLECTION

SYSTEMATIC THEOLOGY

Chapter 1

Religious Dialogue
or Social Justice?

Jürgen Moltmann

Psalm 82
YHWH stands in the assembly of the gods,
In the midst of the gods he pronounces judgment.

"How long will you judge unjustly
And favor the wicked?
Give justice to the weak and the orphans,
Uphold the rights of the wretched and the destitute,
Free the weak and the poor,
Deliver them from the power of the wicked!"

They have neither understanding nor insight,
They walk about in darkness.
All the foundations of the earth are shaken.

"I say: 'You are gods
And sons of the Most High, all of you!
Yet truly you shall die like human beings,
And fall like one of the princes.'"

Arise, YHWH, judge the earth,
For all the peoples belong to you!

THE ASSEMBLY OF THE GODS

Here at last we have a real interreligious dialogue where something happens! Not a "parliament" of the world religions, not a United Nations assembly of "religious leaders," not an ecumenical multifaith program. No, the old gods and the new ones, and those who think they are "sons of the Most High," gather together— I suppose in heaven—and dispute about their lordship over the world. A fantastic idea: let the gods finally get on with it themselves, and do what we on earth are trying to achieve with so much effort, but so fruitlessly!

This assembly of the gods is not concerned about peace. What the gods are concerned with is justice, because it is justice alone that is the foundation for the earth, and justice is what the poor yearn for.

Let us now imagine that we find ourselves in this assembly of the gods. Whom do we see round us, in this congregation of the immortals? Over there in the right-hand corner I can see Zeus, the father of the gods, turning up with his wonderful Greek gods from Mount Olympus. He is surrounded by countless gods and goddesses. The young Ganymede is fanning him, to give him fresh air.

Over there in the left-hand corner I can see the Indian gods appearing, with Brahma, Vishnu, and Shiva—and of course they have their goddesses too, and a throng of enchanting temple dancers in the bargain. But over there in the corner at the back, near the organ, it is a really solemn affair: Marduk and Ishtar are just entering, coming from Babylon, of course followed by a great procession of the whole Assyrian court.

And in the fourth corner, beside the organ—yes, it really is the great Egyptian gods Ammun and Ra, Isis and Osiris, with Nut and Tot and with them the godlike beasts. What a glorious sight! But no—I haven't forgotten them. They're not here yet, but I can already hear the hoofbeats of their wild herd as it comes thundering up. That is Wotan, the Germanic god, one-eyed but carrying a tremendous spear, and beside him Thor with his mighty hammer, which strikes lightning from the clouds. They have come to us directly from Valhalla. Oh yes, "How bright those glorious spirits shine!"

But down here is a whole throng of pretty unpleasant gods too, gods who don't want to be overlooked. These gods "walk in darkness." There is the horrible Moloch of the Phoenicians, who devours little children with an insatiable hunger. There is Kali from Calcutta, who prefers fresh young boys, whose skulls she then wears on a chain round her neck. The other sinister figure is called Mammon. Long before Karl Marx, Martin Luther thought that he was the most despicable idol on earth. What is he doing over there in his dark corner? I expect he is just planning the next "hostile takeover" of some firm or other and is collecting floating money in order to destabilize the smaller nations in Asia, so as to thrust down even more people into poverty. The last in this horrible alliance is Mars, the god of war, who taught us in school that *dulce et decorum est pro patria mori*—it is a sweet and proper thing to die for one's country—and who then rejoiced over the mass graves in Verdun and Stalingrad, or wherever the nations are forced to go on sacrificing the flower of their youth to him. Truly an illustrious assembly, these gods and demons, who are the real judges and rulers of our world!

But suddenly someone stands up in this exalted ecumenical assembly and pronounces judgment. No one knows him, and he has an unpronounceable name. We say YHWH, but we know that this is not what he is called. He comes forward in the form of a little mountain god from Sinai. What does he look like? I imagine him looking like John the Baptist, poor and ragged, dressed only in camel hair, and with a leather girdle; for not much else is to be had on his desert mountain. But he has a flaming passion in his heart—passion for the poor and the oppressed, and for the righteousness that brings them justice. His very appearance is a provocation, and what he has to say about "interreligious dialogue" is nothing other than a shattering call to repentance out of the depths, addressed to these illustrious gods and goddesses in their diverse Olympian paradises, palaces, and temples.

YHWH CALLS THE GODS TO REPENT

"How long will you reign unjustly and favor the wicked?" That is his indictment. Is it meant morally? Is it directed against the risqué doings of some of the gods, which the sagas of the different peoples describe so amusingly? I don't think so. The gods are certainly capricious—Homer was right about that. But they are only capricious as is chance in personal or political history—contingent, that is to say incalculable, capricious, as the fate that we are subject to is "blind." To ward off the evil whims of chance and the blind raging of fate, men and women bring the gods sacrifices, to keep them in a good mood and so that they will look favorably on them. *Do ut des*—I am giving you something so that you will give me something back. That was the old Roman commercial principle for sacrificial dealings with the gods. But not just in Rome. How was it with Cain and Abel? "And the Lord had regard for Abel and his offering, but for Cain and his offering he had no regard" (Gen. 4:4–5). Why? No one has ever been able to say, down to the present day.

But there is more still behind the sacrificial cults. Because the gods rule unjustly, favoring the wicked but disregarding the poor, "all the foundations of the earth are shaken," asserts YHWH. It is not just the caprices of chance and the blindness of human destiny that depend on the will of the gods. It is the order of the cosmos itself too. The system of the earth itself depends on them. It is not just life *within* these orders that is contingent. The orders themselves are contingent as well. They are so fragile that human beings have to implore the goodwill of the gods. Why do the gods of the harvest demand the first fruits of the field? Why must the firstborn children be sacrificed to the people's gods? Why did the Aztecs offer to their gods the still quivering, bloody hearts of their slaughtered enemies?

It is because there is this nameless, fathomless fear that perhaps one day nothing will grow in the fields anymore, that one day no more children will be born, that one morning the sun might not rise above the horizon. The judging and ruling of the gods dominates personal biography, the political history of the world, and the history of the cosmos. If the gods are as "blind" as chance, if they have "neither insight nor understanding," then they will bring the whole structure of the world to destruction; then nothing is certain anymore; then you can no longer rely on anything. Everything threatens to sink into chaos. Life and blessing can issue from the gods, but equally, they can bring devastation and destruction on the world. That is why the Indian gods and goddesses always have a sunny side and a shadow side. Shiva creates the world through his fiery dance—and also destroys it again. Parvati manifests herself as the mother of life—and as Kali she devours her own children and sticks out her bloodthirsty tongue.

Is YHWH right when he asks accusingly: "How long will you favor the wicked?" That is indeed a question of life and death for human beings, and a question about the being or nonbeing of the earth.

We don't know what Zeus, Marduk, Brahma, Mammon, or Mars answered, or if they saw and heard the little mountain God from Sinai at all. But we can imagine what their reply was, for we ourselves are always still given over to the caprices of chance and to blind fate, and we sense how the foundations of the earth "are shaken" by the ecological wickedness of unjust human economic systems, crimes that are actually favored by their gods—Mammon, for instance.

What does YHWH advise his fellow gods?

> Give justice to the weak.
> Maintain the rights of the wretched and the destitute,
> Free the poor
> And deliver them from the power of the wicked.

Looking at the gods, with their greed for sacrifice, he says in simple, familiar words: You gods, don't ask what human beings must do for you; ask what you can do for them! Don't demand sacrifice—bring about justice! But with what justice are they to judge? And justice for whom?

YHWH'S RIGHTEOUSNESS THAT BRINGS ABOUT JUSTICE

According to Israel's experience of God, YHWH, unlike the other gods, is one who "maintains the cause of the needy, and executes justice for the poor" (Ps. 140:12). He "raises the poor from the dust, and lifts the needy from the ash heap" (Ps. 113:7). He does not just lay down what justice and injustice are, like human judges, so as to reward and to punish; he creates justice for those who suffer violence and frees the helpless from the hand of the wicked. The book of Job therefore calls him the hope of the poor (5:16). So YHWH is not a judge who judges without respect of persons, like Justitia, with her bandaged eyes. He is quite explicitly the advocate, who takes the part of people without rights and puts to rights the unjust.

Again we come face to face with sacrifices. But here we are looking at the victims. The little unimportant people, the poor and the wretched, are the victims of the wicked, who feel that they are the darlings of their gods. The victims are the losers in our success-orientated society. They are humiliated by the winners because "they haven't made it," or so the judgment goes. In all societies, ancient, modern, or postmodern, we find these victims on the downside of history. But we have to look for them; for people sitting in darkness cannot be seen. They are the people crippled by debt, the impoverished, the homeless, the HIV-infected, and the abandoned children. Today these people are not sacrificed to the gods on bloody altars: they are the surplus people whom others tread underfoot so as to get to the top of the ladder themselves.

Bring about justice for the poor; liberate these wretched men, women, and children; save them from the power of the wicked, who have everything going for them: that is the righteous rule of the saints in Israel. The righteous God knows the rights of the unimportant, but the gods of the wicked have no insight. They demand sacrifices, but the Righteous One is concerned about the victims.

YHWH is righteous because—but also only insofar as—he gives their rights to the people who have no rights. More than that: the Godness of God is to be perceived from this righteousness that sees those without rights righted. Where this justice-creating righteousness does not exist there are no gods, whether they let themselves be called gods or not. God or idols: it is righteousness and justice that makes the difference. God and the gods: it is the salvation of the poor that brings them together. For this is what YHWH expects of the high gods: the liberation of the oppressed.

THE POOR AND THE EARTH

Why does YHWH love the little unimportant people and not the rich; the losers, not the achievers; the ugly, not the beautiful? If he found pleasure in their misery he would not be just. But it is the very reverse that is true. The young Luther hit the nail on the head when he said that sinners aren't loved because they are lovely; they are lovely because they are loved. Being loved really does make the ugly beautiful, and in the same way the salvation that brings about justice makes those without rights righteous, and the nearness of God makes the poor rich.

"Poor and needy": that is what the psalmists continually call themselves when they cry out to God "out of the deep" (*de profundis*). They are then crying out to the God who had mercy on Israel's prisoners in Egypt, because he saw their affliction and came down to them. Every day the poor struggle with death through hunger, sickness, and discouragement. They have nothing more to which they can appeal in order to achieve justice. God is their last hope. But they do not have to whimper for grace and beg for mercy.

No, they actually have a right to God's help, for he has promised it to them in his covenant, promised it on his honor. This legal entitlement is not based on what they have but on what they don't have. In their poverty and despair they have a right to God's saving justice. Through God's "preferential option" for the oppressed, these people vouch for him in a violent world of the wicked, because they are his, whether they know it or not.

The poor and the earth: YHWH's justice-creating righteousness has a saving significance not just for the poor in the world of human beings but for the foundations of the earth in the world of nature too. Social justice and ecological wisdom correspond, just as social injustice and crimes against nature go hand in hand. So whoever gives rights to people without rights also saves the earth, which sustains the life of us all. This modern insight is really as old as Israel's psalms:

> God has established the earth and it stands fast.
> He judges the people with equity.

The human order is destroyed by crimes committed by the wicked against the poor; the cosmic order is destroyed by the gods who favor the wicked. Consequently the one, single justice-bringing righteousness must rule in the human world, in the cosmic world, and in the world of the gods, if the foundations of the earth are not to be shaken.

THE MORTALITY OF THE GODS

YHWH's judgment on the gods who favor wickedness is unequivocal: "You are gods and sons of the Most High, all of you! Yet truly you shall die like human beings and fall like one of the princes." That means they really are "gods" and are called to their godlike responsibility. But they haven't judged justly. They have ruled capriciously, and by doing so they lose their immortality. They fall like the political powers-that-be, whose wickedness they have favored. They have become "mortal gods," as Thomas Hobbes called his Leviathan.

The unheard-of thing is this psalm is not the absolute claim with which YHWH judges his "fellow gods" in this remarkable divine assembly. In this psalm Israel identifies the idea of the righteousness that saves the poor and brings about justice for the oppressed with the divinity of the gods, and therefore judges all gods—the God of Israel too—according to the standard of justice for those who have no rights. The poor have authority over the gods. The suffering of the oppressed is made the supreme standard—and that means the standard for "the sons of the Most High" too. That is incredible, for it makes gods mortal and human beings immortal. Which God measures up to this righteousness? Who judges the little people, brings about justice for the wretched, saves the poor from the hand of the wicked?

The great gods of the dazzling rulers and victorious nations "walk in darkness," we are told. So is the God of Israel the only one who stands in the light of this saving righteousness?

No, not even the God of Israel; for he has first to be exhorted to "rise up":

> Arise, YHWH, judge the earth,
> for all the peoples belong to thee.

Is he sleeping, as another psalm assumes? Or has he gone away? Or is he deliberately "hiding his face"? Who knows?

I suppose that up to then he had showed himself to the shepherd Moses, and through him to the poor people of Israel, only as the little mountain god from Sinai; but now his uprising from this little people and this tiny country between Egypt and Babylon is to take place in judgment on all the nations and the whole earth. Justice and righteousness will then go forth from Zion and liberate all nations, say the prophets. If YHWH in his whole greatness as the Creator of heaven and earth rises up, then "with righteousness he shall judge the poor, and decide with equity for the meek of the earth" (Isa. 11:4). "Then justice will dwell in the wilderness, and righteousness abide in the fruitful field" (Isa. 32:16). Then the whims of chance will vanish, and fate will no longer be blind, for righteousness and justice will put everything to rights: the gods and human beings, heaven and earth. Because today we are hoping for this divine uprising; we too, with all our powers and potentialities, are rising against the wickedness that humiliates the poor and favors the violent, and are crying to the rulers and forces in power: "How long will you judge unjustly and favor the wicked?"

So let our contribution to dialogue be the righteousness that raises up the unimportant, and gives justice to the poor, and liberates the wretched. Let it be this, which we bring to the dialogue with our own religion and with the gods of other religions, and with the powers of this godless world.

Amen.

Chapter 2

The Problem
of Religious Knowledge

John Macquarrie

It was in 1962 that I arrived in the United States from Scotland to take up the
position of professor of systematic theology in Union Theological Seminary, New
York. The seminary had arranged for me to make visits to other seminaries and
colleges in the eastern parts of the country, so that I might meet colleagues working in the field of systematic theology and have an exchange with them.

So it came about that in the spring of 1963 I went to Washington, D.C.
Among the institutions that had invited me there was Howard University, at that
time a virtually all-black community. I was kindly received, and among those
whom I met was Professor James Deotis Roberts, then still in the early part of his
career. We struck up a friendship that has lasted ever since, renewed from time
to time by meetings in both the United States and the United Kingdom. So let
me begin by saying how pleased and honored I am to have been invited to contribute a chapter to his *Festschrift*, and to celebrate his outstanding public achievements as a man and a theologian and, at the same time, almost forty years of
personal friendship.

During the course of that visit, Professor Roberts presented me with a copy
of his early book, *Faith and Reason: A Comparative Study of Pascal, Bergson and
James*. It was inscribed on the flyleaf: "To Prof. John Macquarrie with the com-

pliments of the Author. May 23, 1963." We made the interesting discovery, too, that during a period of study at the University of Edinburgh, Deotis had at weekends served a church very close to my hometown.

Later he was to gain fame through his contributions to black theology, but in those days black theology had not yet begun to have the influence it was destined to attain. But I think it is important to remember that before he wrote his books on black theology, Professor Roberts had wrestled with one of the most stubborn problems in what we may call fundamental theology. In an age of science, there is a widespread view that unless beliefs can be substantiated by arguments analogous to those used by natural scientists, they cannot qualify as "knowledge." They are dismissed as mere "opinions" or even, by some extreme critics, as "nonsense," emotional utterances without any cognitive content. One of the most challenging questions that can be addressed to any theologian or preacher is "How do you justify your claim to have knowledge of God, or of Christ, or of human destiny?" Just as the everyday applications of mathematics in our technological civilization depend on more basic work in what is called "pure" mathematics, so the application of theology to social questions presupposes a prior engagement with what I have called "fundamental" theology.

That explains why I have claimed importance for Professor Roberts's early engagement with the problem of religious knowledge, and why in this chapter I concentrate attention on his book *Faith and Reason*. The subtitle of the book informs us that Roberts will consider three important figures from the history of philosophy—Blaise Pascal, Henri-Louis Bergson, and William James. These three thinkers are very different from one another, but they are all agreed that truth has forms that are neither attainable nor testable by the logical procedures of abstract reasoning.

Pascal appeals to the "heart." Admittedly, this is a vague word, which we associate more with romanticism than with science. When Pascal declares that "we know the truth not only by means of reasoning, but also by means of the heart, and it is in the latter way that we know first principles. . . . The heart has its reasons, of which reason does not know,"[1] he is claiming some kind of intuition or direct knowing. We shall come back to ask further about this. Meanwhile, we should also note that Pascal was very far from being antiscientific. He was, on the contrary, one of the leading scientists and mathematicians of his time, but he strongly believed that not all our knowing is rational and scientific. There are other important forms of knowing, but these too have a rightful claim to be considered knowledge.

Bergson, who belonged to the Jewish community, had a scientific background, though his interests were in biology rather than physics. It was the phenomenon of time that first led him to break out of a mechanistic background. He made a sharp distinction between clock time and lived time. Clock time quantifies time and thereby spatializes it, depriving it of that which is essentially temporal in its mode of being. Like a cinematograph, it breaks up the sequence of events into a series of static pictures. Only in our experience of time as duration, time as a flowing stream, so to speak, do we begin to understand something of the essence of time. Bergson has been called "the first process philosopher," and certainly we can regard him as one of the pioneers of that brand of philosophy. He used his conception of time to defend the freedom of the human will and then, in a broader application, to distinguish between the material and the spiritual realms. In his most famous book, *Creative Evolution*, studies led him to emphasize the importance of instinct as contrasted with intellect, and he claimed to discern a driving force, or *nisus*, in evolution (he called this *nisus* the *élan vital,* or "impulse to life"), in opposition to the widely held view that the changes of evolution come about primarily or even exclusively through chance mutations. In later writings, the somewhat vague notion of an impulse to life approaches nearer to the traditional thought of God. When he made his will in 1937, he included in it the words: "My reflections have led me closer and closer to Catholicism." But he saw clearly the wave of anti-Semitism that was already beginning to flood Europe at that time, and he loyally stood by the Jewish people in their time of persecution.

Different again from both Pascal and Bergson is William James. His philosophy is often called "pragmatism," but this is a word that has deteriorated in recent years. It is now often applied to the actions of politicians who care little about moral or philosophical principles and are interested only in practical measures that will realize their ends. That was not the case with James. Certainly, he believed that thought and action go together, but he was at the opposite extreme from those (including many scientists) who believe that thought must be "value-free," that is to say, uninfluenced by moral or religious considerations. By contrast, James believed that our thinking is true (though this can never be more than a matter of degree) when it enriches human life. "Any idea upon which we can ride, so to speak; any idea that can carry us prosperously from one part of our experience to any other part, linking things satisfactorily, working securely, simplifying, saving labor, is true just for so much."[2] The truth of religion, therefore, is not to be settled by intellectual arguments but only by the test of committing ourselves to what James calls the "religious hypothesis," namely, that human lives are somehow continuous with a larger life from which they derive help. Here he is, one must say, stretching beyond pragmatism to something like a metaphysical speculation, though the test of its truth remains pragmatic. He speculates that the unconscious reaches of the self may form the link with this larger spiritual world. He writes: "The further limits of our being plunged, it seems to me, into an altogether other dimension of existence from the sensible and merely 'understandable' world. Name it the mystical region or supernatural region, whichever you choose. The unseen region in question is not merely ideal, for it produces effects in this world. But that which produces effects within another reality must be termed a reality itself; 'God' is the natural appellation for the supreme reality, so I will call this higher part of the universe by the name of God."[3] I am not entirely convinced by this argument, which seems to be a departure from James's pragmatic method. But he could defend his position on purely pragmatic grounds, if indeed religion and its acknowledgment of God have been shown historically to be an enrichment of human life.

Professor Roberts states in his preface that his three chosen exemplars "make a radical break from the position to which they object (the autonomy of the rational method) and the swing to the opposite view (the affirmation of intuition). The 'reasons of the heart' of Pascal are basic to all three philosophers."[4] I suppose these "reasons of the heart" are much the same as what Paul calls "spiritual discernment" (1 Cor. 2:14). But this does not mean that, for Roberts, his three mentors are on an equal footing. He awards the primacy to Pascal and gives a good reason for his choice. All three write positively and appreciatively of mysticism as a direct or intuitive way of knowing God. The difference is that Pascal was himself a mystic, and his utterances about mysticism are based on his own experience, whereas Bergson and James have learned about mysticism from others, from reading the works of the great mystics, men and women who have known this experience in all the major religions of the world. In Roberts's judgment, Pascal's treatment of mysticism has an authority which that of James or Bergson has not, for they know as a *probability* what Pascal knows as a *certainty*. That certainty is perhaps nowhere more apparent than in Pascal's overwhelming claim that "Jesus Christ is the goal of everything, and the center to which everything tends. He who knows him knows the reason for all things."[5]

This is such a bold claim that one is perhaps initially put off by it. Is this not pure subjectivism? Can it be accepted on the strength of individual experiences, or must it be subjected to public scrutiny, as the findings of science are?

By the very nature of the case, it would seem that no amount of argument could possibly either prove or disprove the mystical claim. If one has had the experience, one lines up with Pascal. If one has not had it, like Bergson and James, then one may be sympathetic to the claim. Pascal is more than sympathetic—he identifies with the claim and compares his own mystical experience to that of Augustine.

I think it is becoming clear that if there is a religious *knowledge* that is more than mere opinion, then there must be valid ways of knowing or modes of cognition other than the rational and scientific mode. There must be experiences such as mysticism or revelation or other "high" moments when there takes place an encounter between divine and human. The well-known book of W. T. Stace, *Mysticism and Philosophy*, supports my remark that no amount of argument will settle the matter. The author, though sympathetic to mysticism, never reaches the point where he can establish the mystic's claim to be in touch with a "supernatural" reality. Indeed, if mysticism and analogous experiences are like perception, direct experiences, then they are simply not amenable to adequate discussion through discursive argument. We can only listen to the mystic with sympathy, look in the same direction, and we either see or do not see. But it would be wrong to set what we may broadly call the "mystical" in opposition to reason. Those who claim a mystical experience believe rather that they have deepened the powers of reason or in some respect gone beyond its normal reach. So the first step in making such experiences more credible is simply to show that there are limits to rational inquiry. As Søren Kierkegaard put it, reason comes to a point where it makes a "collision" and can go no further on its present course. Either it turns away or else seeks a different way of knowing.

Here I think it may be worthwhile to look again at one of the greatest figures of the Enlightenment, Immanuel Kant. Surely there could be no greater champion of reason than Kant. Yet we often forget that when Kant wrote his *Critique of Pure Reason*, his intention was not that the book should celebrate the powers of reason but that it should expose its limits. For instance, he sought to show that the traditional arguments for the existence of God are invalid, and this is seized upon by some as a validation of agnosticism. But much of Kant's subsequent work modifies the apparently negative results of his first critique.

In his *Critique of Practical Reason*, the standpoint of pure reason, that is, value-free reason, is abandoned in favor of practical reason: that is, reason illuminated by conscience and moral values, which for Kant are not subjective but directly perceived aspects of reality making an ineluctable claim upon a rational person. He implicitly rejects the "value-free" stance.

Even in the *Critique of Pure Reason*, he had given an important place (often underestimated) to the role of the imagination, which plays an essential part ("secret art of the soul") in rendering the natural world intelligible. The point about imagination is that it departs from the "clear and distinct" ideas of rational discourse into a coded language in which the meanings of words are stretched beyond their normal usage.

But it is in the *Critique of Judgement* that Kant goes furthest in acknowledging a mystical or, if you prefer, revelatory type of experience. He introduces the notion of the "sublime." The sublime "is the name given to that which is absolutely great, what is beyond all comparison great."[6] The word is used by Kant in the context of aesthetics. There are works, in music and in the visual arts, that simply "bowl us over," so to speak. They do not call for argument; they simply impress themselves upon us as "absolutely great," beyond comparison. Such would be the plays of Shakespeare or the "Passions" of Bach or Leonardo's *Last Supper*. We recognize something ultimate, something going beyond the bounds of ordinary experience, the place where reason makes a collision and is replaced by wonder. If this is true in art, it is true also in religion, for aesthetic and religious experiences are closely related. It was, if you like, the sublime in Jesus Christ that caused Pascal to say that Christ is the center of everything.

It is interesting to note that Kant's idea of the sublime has been resurrected by some thinkers, both philosophical and theological, who claim the name "postmodernists." The French philosopher Jean-François Lyotard was among them. He did not use the idea in defense of religion but hailed it rather in the negative sense that it sets a limit to the narrow rationalism of modernism.[7] The English theologian John Milbank has also appropriated the idea of the sublime, though he finds it exemplified in Kierkegaard, Nietzsche, and Heidegger, rather than in Kant. More precisely, Kant represents (according to Milbank) a first phase in discourse about the sublime. For Kant, "the sublime or the indeterminable, was safely off-limits for the proper exercise of theoretical reason, which is confined to notions that can't be 'schematized' within space and time. In the second phase sublimity is perceived to 'contaminate' what is deceptively taken for finitude."[8] As Milbank says, philosophers are not content to remain silent on the sublime or the mystical. They have searched desperately for ways to talk about that which lies beyond both reason and ordinary language. Even Jacques Derrida, for all his skepticism, seems to find a place for the sublime in his elastic concept of *différance*. These recent recoveries of the sublime add to the suspicion that postmodernism, in some of its aspects, is a return to premodernism, which would mean a recognition of the rights of reason together with a curbing of its more exclusive demands.

It would be interesting to inquire how far Professor Roberts's early book influenced his better-known volumes on black theology, but that would be too large an inquiry to begin here. But what can be said is that Professor Roberts, in that early book, was touching on problems that still remain high on the theological agenda and that seem to be calling for a rehabilitation of the notion of revelation.

PHILOSOPHICAL THEOLOGY/ PHILOSOPHY OF RELIGION

Chapter 3

Science and Spirituality

Norbert M. Samuelson

Rabbi Sherwin Wine invited me to speak at the 2001 Conference of the International Institute for Secular Humanist Judaism on the question "Can Albert Einstein's life and thought serve as a model for Jewish spirituality within the framework of a secular humanist Judaism?" This paper is my answer to the question. It is divided into two main sections. The first section is a summary of Einstein's biography set within the context of the science, the Jewish civilization, and the European civilization of his lifetime. The second section uses the generalizations from the first to deduce answers to the following questions: Was Einstein Jewish? (The answer is yes, with qualifications.) Was he secular? (The answer is yes and no, depending on what you mean by "secular.") Was he spiritual? (The answer is yes and no, depending on what you mean by "spiritual.") Finally, was he a humanist? (The answer is no.) The conclusion of this paper uses the answers given in the second section to answer directly Rabbi Wine's initial question.

THE NARRATIVE—EINSTEIN'S LIFE AND WORLD

1879–1894: Education in Science and Religion

Albert Einstein was born on March 14, 1879, in Elm. Elm was a small city in southwestern Germany, situated on the Danube River, near Lake Constance and the Swiss border, somewhat south of the major industrial city of Stuttgart. His father, Hermann Einstein, was at that time a reasonably prosperous featherbed merchant. Both he and his wife, Pauline (Koch), were openly Jewish but were totally nonobservant. Albert was their first child (a sister, Maja, was born one year later) and their only son.

Albert's formal schooling began in 1885, at the age of six, when his parents enrolled him in a Roman Catholic *Volksschule* (more or less the equivalent of an American private grade school) called the Peterschule. The choice was made because of the school's academic reputation. No consideration was given to its religious affiliation. However, to compensate for the school's required courses in religion (i.e., Roman Catholicism), Albert's parents added to his private violin lessons home instruction in what Albert referred to as "the principles of Judaism." The teacher was a distant relative.

We have little idea what the relative taught the young Albert. Moses Maimonides tells us in his *Mishnah Torah* that if the father himself knows nothing about Judaism, he may hire a teacher who does.[1] What the young child should be taught is "written Law" and "grammar," which seems to mean to read the Hebrew text and to understand its plain meaning (*peshat*) in the vernacular.[2] In any case, the "religion" lessons in school and/or the "Judaism" lessons at home did stimulate an active interest in Albert in religion, for he constantly reflected on the concepts he weaned from the biblical text and he expressed a desire to be trained for bar mitzvah.

Just what interested him in religion is difficult to say. My guess is that the fascination was limited to religious ideas about metaphysical questions such has what the universe looks like, how it began, and how will it end. I do not think he had any particular interest in religious ritual.

I think religion was for the young Albert precisely what science was for the older Albert—a textual setting that allowed free speculation about the truth of the "higher things," namely, the meaning and value of the universe in general. In this sense Einstein never changed. For his whole life, almost from birth and on continuously to his death, life was about trying to discover the truth about humanity's ultimate questions of physical meaning. Again, he spent almost every waking moment of his life thinking about these ultimate metaphysical questions. Because he was a human being, he did other things as well—he ate, drank, played, had sexual relations, and slept—but all of these "worldly" or "physical" activities were secondary.

Maimonides said (again) in the *Mishnah Torah* that a man should devote his entire life to the contemplation of God, which he does by spending all of his time studying. The education begins at birth and runs continuously until the moment of death. More specifically, you should work at your job no more than three hours a day and devote another nine hours each day to studying what the tradition says and deducing from its words conceptual knowledge.[3] Certainly this is how Einstein led his life. However, the focus for his study on Jewish texts ended in 1891, when Albert was thirteen years old, when a twenty-three-year-old Polish Jewish medical student named Max Talmud rented a room in Albert's home.

From Talmud (Max, that is, and not "the" Talmud), Albert learned something about Immanuel Kant and his *Critique of Pure Reason*. He also learned that God did not compose the Torah and hand it to Moses on Mount Sinai. In other words, Talmud taught Einstein that what the Torah literally says need not be true, and this discovery so disenchanted Albert from religion that he called off his bar mitzvah. More than the bar mitzvah itself, Albert lost interest in religion in general and Judaism in the particular.

For Albert, the only thing that mattered was the pursuit of truth. He cared about anything that and anyone who supported his interest, and he was disinterested in anything that and anyone who had nothing to contribute. At the age of his transition into physical maturity, he experienced his first major disenchantment. The second would be his first marriage. However, we are not yet at the point of our narrative to discuss Albert's "love life."

At the age of fourteen Albert was sent in 1892 to live in Munich, in the southeast of Germany, in order to attend school at the Luitold Gymnasium (which was more or less the American equivalent of a private high school). Although Munich itself was largely a Roman Catholic city, the school Albert attended was interdenominational and included in its curriculum of required courses special classes in religious studies for Jewish students. The teachers hired for the class were, like Albert's first teacher Heinrich Friedmann, educated and committed heterodox Jews. It is at this stage that Albert learned almost everything he would ever learn about Jewish civilization, and it is likely that he received his introduction to the only form of contemporary Jewish ideology that ever attracted him—Zionism.

It is not altogether clear what it was about Zionism that attracted him, since in every other respect Albert was antinationalist. I suspect that at least in part this affirmation was an act of rebellion against his anti-Semitic classmates. Albert handled his "difference" by openly affirming rather than secretly concealing it. To so act would not have been unusual in a central European Jewish community of his day, composed of Jews whose primary commitment to Judaism was their gentile neighbors' denial of their right to be purely "people" and who found in Zionism an acceptable, Jewishly heterodox way to resist European hatred of the Jew as Jew.

1894–1900: Electrodynamics, Sex, and the Importance of Light

Shortly thereafter, in 1894, Albert's father changed businesses and became the manager of a factory that manufactured dynamos. Albert himself was supposed to remain in Munich until he completed his studies at the gymnasium. However, schoolwork (as opposed to self-directed study) did not hold Albert's attention. More than in school, Albert took a great deal of interest in his father's factory. There he learned everything he could about how to run and make the machines his father's factory built, as well as the physical principles that made the running and the manufacturing of the machines possible. The physical principles were the cutting edge of late-nineteenth-century physics, principles formulated in 1873 in James Clerk Maxwell's *Treatise on Electricity and Magnetism* that unified the

two seemly different forces of electricity and magnetism into a single electrody-
namic force.

It is this unification that made his father's dynamos possible. The young
Albert, like almost any teenage boy, was fascinated by the machines themselves,
but Albert's fascination extended beyond the machines to their underlying physical principles. It is this deeper intellectual curiosity that distinguished Albert
from his peers. The fascination never ended (for Albert never really "matured"
emotionally beyond his teens), as he moved from understanding the unification
of electricity and magnetism to attempting to understand the unification of all
the other forces—the weak force (which causes unstable fundamental particles to
decay despite their electromagnetic tendency to attract each other), the strong
force (which holds together nuclei despite the electromagnetic tendency of their
atoms to repulse each other), and, most elusive of all, gravity (which causes every
macroscopic thing in the universe to move in space relative to every other macroscopic thing).

In 1895, at the age of seventeen, Albert left Munich without graduating to
join his parents, who had moved first to Pavia, Italy (near Milan), and then to
Aarau. There Albert's father Hermann struggled (in vain) to recover his fortunes
after the financial failure of his dynamo factory. It was in this year that Albert
renounced his German citizenship, so he could not be drafted into the army, and
he first asked the central question that would direct his speculation in theoretical physics for the rest of his life: What would it be like to ride on a beam of light?
His search for an answer to this question led first to his special and then to his
general theory of relativity.

Einstein brought together all that he had ever learned about both religion and
physics into this single line of speculation. The real question was, just what is
light? and the answer to that question was the foundation of all scientific and religious speculation as it had developed at the end of the nineteenth century.

In terms of religion, there has always been a close association, if not an identity,
between God, truth, and light. For example, according to the literal interpretation
of the Genesis story of creation, the first (and possibly the only) thing that God
creates is light. The waters, the dark, and the earth already exist, independent of
God. God's creation of light enables the distinction between day and night, and it
plays a central role (at least in medieval rabbinic philosophical commentaries on
Genesis 1) in the formation of the firmament by which God shapes the world into
dry land and seas as well as earth and sky. Add to this description the later rabbinic
dogma that God created the universe "out of nothing," which these rabbis interpreted to mean "out of nothing other than himself." What follows logically is an
identity claim between the eternal God and his (primordial) light.

In terms of modern science, the premier science has always been physics. It is
premier in terms of logical or foundational priority over other sciences, in the
sense that ultimately the causal principles of explanation of all macrocosmic phenomena must be somehow dependent on the causal principles of explanation of
microcosmic phenomena, so that in more general terms the "large and complex"

is causally dependent on the "small and simple"—and the smallest and simplest things in the universe are the subject matter of fundamental physics. In general, the smaller the component, the more fundamental. In terms of any atomic or particle conception of the universe, no entity is smaller or simpler than the photon, and photons (or "quanta") are the bundles of energy transmitted in light waves.

Let me say the same thing in a slightly different way. The physical universe can be thought of either in terms of discrete objects (that classical philosophers called "substances") or discrete movements (that modern philosophers call "processes"). Physics claims that both ways of understanding everything are true. When the universe is looked at in terms of motion, it is seen as sets of waves, and the simplest of these waves is light. When the universe is looked at in terms of substances, it is seen as bundles of photons, and these photon packets also are light. From both perspectives, it is the principles of light that are the most fundamental principles of everything that is. To discover the truth about these principles is the only thing that ultimately ever mattered to Einstein in his entire life, from early childhood to his death at the age of seventy-six.

Having skipped graduation from high school, Albert went on to college at the age of eighteen in 1896 at the Federal Institute of Technology (called the ETH) in Zurich, Switzerland. There he continued his normal life pattern of ignoring almost everything that had nothing to do with his driving main interest in life— to understand the fundamental nature of the physical universe. I say "almost" everything, because the generalization includes all his formal academic studies but not his adolescent interest in women. In 1898, at the age of nineteen, Albert met and fell in love with a Greek Orthodox fellow student from Hungary named Mileva Marie. His relationship with Mileva would affect the rest of his life, but perhaps not as much as his friendship with a Jewish student mathematician at the ETH named Marcel Grossman. It was Grossman's notes that enabled Einstein to pass courses at the ETH that he never attended. And it was Grossman's skill as a mathematician—skills that Einstein himself never really mastered with sufficient excellence to help him demonstrate what his thought experiments enabled him intuitively to grasp—that enabled Einstein years later to demonstrate his special theory of relativity and discover that gravity is a curvature of space-time that is caused by matter.

The year 1898 was critical for Einstein's life and thought in yet another way. It was the time that Einstein rejected the idea of "ether," a rejection that enabled him to decide that the speed of light is an absolute, which is the cornerstone of his special relativity theory. Aristotle had asserted that light is a product of a change in the medium between the seeing eye and the seen object. He also believed, like Parmenides, that between two positive objects there must be something positive, because there cannot exist nothing; hence space must contain something, not nothing; hence, there can be no such thing as a real or actual vacuum (*viz.*, an existent space occupied by an actual nothing). By Newton's time a different, more mathematical account was suggested to explain sight, but Newton no less than Aristotle believed that there cannot be an actual nothing, so that space must be occupied by something. This something that filled the seemingly empty space was hypothesized by Newton to be the "eyes of God," through which God could sense and therefore feel everything that happens in his created universe.

This traditional Western scientific belief in an invisible something occupying all space was not dismissed until the time of Einstein. In fact, that insight lay behind Einstein's special theory of relativity. Failed attempts to determine experimentally the nature of the ether led Einstein and other physicists like him to conclude that it did not exist. However, Einstein went one step further than the best of his peers to infer that if the velocity of light cannot be affected by its medium, it cannot be affected by anything. Hence, the speed of light in a vacuum is an absolute. In fact, it may be the only absolute in the universe. Furthermore, speed is a measurement of space traversed over a period of time, so that if the speed of light is a constant, but the appearance of its speed is different relative to the location of an observer, then the difference must be due either to the space covered or the time in which it is covered. The space itself is no less constant than the speed of light; hence, Einstein concluded, it is time that is inconstant. Time is not an absolute; it is different depending on who is measuring it when and where.

At this stage Einstein's theory was only that, a theory. However, technological advances were occurring in physics that would enable Einstein to make a much stronger claim about the veracity of his thesis. Nine years earlier, in 1889, George Ellery Hale had invented a spectroheliograph that made it possible to photograph the sun by the light of a single determined spectral line. This technique would make it possible for astronomers to make measurements of the velocity of even very distant celestial objects with far greater precision than had ever been possible in the past. These observations and measurements would play a critical role in verifying Einstein's theory.

In general, Einstein was a participant in an age of great scientific progress—the end of the nineteenth and the beginning of the twentieth centuries—that possibly was greater than any other earlier time in history, with the exception of the seventeenth-century construction of the telescope for research in astronomy by Galileo at the start of the century and the formalization of calculus as the modern language of physics by Isaac Newton and Gottfried Wilhelm Leibniz at the century's end. In 1899 the mathematician Gottlob Frege published his *Foundation of Arithmetic* that made it possible for Alfred North Whitehead and Bertrand Russell to revolutionize logic and philosophy. In 1900, Johann Gregor Mendel's laws on the transmission of hereditary characteristics were rediscovered by Hugo de Vries, Carl F. J. E. Correns, and Erich Tschermak von Seysenegg, which supplied Darwin's earlier theory of genetic evolution with a solid scientific and mathematical foundation, changing forever the field of biology and the way we think about the relationship between humans and other life forms. And in that very same year, 1900, Albert graduated from the ETH, and Max Planck announced the quantum hypothesis for determining the black body spectrum, a hypothesis that would play a central role in Einstein's contribution to quantum mechanics and in his winning a Nobel Prize.

Graduation opened no doors for Einstein's life or career. He was unable to find work as a physicist, and Mileva Marie became pregnant. He got a job as a traveling substitute teacher in Switzerland and then a job tutoring in Zurich. Neither was enough to support a wife and a child. Marie dropped out of the university and returned to her parents' home in Hungary to have their child, whom they named Lieserl. The girl was given up for adoption. We know that the child became seriously ill, but we do not know what became of her. The assumption is that she died.

1900: European Anti-Semitism

Why could Einstein not find work as a physicist? There are several answers to this question. The most important one is that he could not receive good recommendations from any of his teachers. They did not recommend him and universities did not want him because, as his academic record shows, Albert never was, by conventional academic standards, a good student. However, it is also true that he was a Jew with gentile professors, and he was applying for work in gentile universities in a gentile Europe that was increasingly anti-Semitic.

European Christian attitudes toward Jews changed in what can be described by the curve of a sine function. There were highs and there were lows. Albert was born at the time of a high. In 1815 the Congress of Vienna created a union of German states to replace the Holy Roman Empire, but that union was dissolved in 1866 after the Austro-Prussian War. That dissolution enabled former member states to act on their own, which resulted in the emancipation of the Jews in Switzerland in 1866, and in Austria-Hungary in 1867. In 1870 the Jews were emancipated in Italy and the ghetto of Rome was abolished. Then, just eight years before Albert was born, in 1871, William I of Prussia became the emperor of the then reunified German states, under a new constitution that granted full rights to Jews. It was the first time that Jews had ever really been treated under law as equals in a Christian European nation. However, 1871 was also the time that the term *anti-Semitism* was introduced. The year was the high point of European Christian philo-Semitism (an irrational love of the Jew as a Jew), but it also marked the beginning as well of the decline of Europe into anti-Semitism (an irrational hate of the Jew as a Jew).

Clearly these changes were reflected in both the secularity of Albert's parents and in Albert's own lack of loyalty to any nation-state. These general political-cultural trends also reflected themselves in the academic scientists. As the nineteenth century ended, Jews were welcomed into universities, both as students and professors. However, by the end of the first decade of the twentieth century, European universities were already reconsidering their earlier "generosity." People began to talk about something that they called "Jewish science." Jewish science is what Jews rather than Christians do. It is flashy and smart, but it is also shallow and superficial. Jews rejected Christ because they could not understand God as a compassionate being. They could not understand it because Jews by their very nature are lacking in compassion. Their intelligence is a compensation for this emotional deficiency.[4] But the intelligence itself was inherently limited.

The intellect has no data of its own to analyze. The data come from the senses, and Jews, because of their emotional deficiencies, have deficient senses to inform their reasoning. Hence, Jewish intellect is necessarily shallow by comparison with Christian intellect. The proof of this, Germans argued in the 1920s and 1930s, is that Jews like Einstein created abstract and obtuse theoretical kinds of physics such as relativity theory that have a certain kind of conceptual elegance but no practical consequences, whereas good Christian physicists, even theoretical ones like Niels Henrik Bohr, could invent quantum mechanics that is anything but "elegant" but has enormous practical consequences for modern life. Even though Einstein played a role in discovering quantum mechanics, his Jewish soul kept him from taking it seriously. In this defect he was no better than the other Jew pseudo-scientist Sigmund Freud, who invented a form of psychology that had no lasting healing effects, despite its theoretical elegance, unlike the mundane but most helpful behaviorist psychology of the good Christian neo-Darwinian social evolutionists.

1901–1920: The Ascent of Einstein as a Scientist

The low point of Albert Einstein's personal life was in 1901, when he was separated from his wife and child because of poverty and his father, Hermann, died. After 1901, as Europe deteriorated in the direction of the world war and its aftermath, and anti-Semitism continued to rise to levels of hatred never before experienced by Jews in their collective history, Albert's own fortunes began to improve. In fact, his career began an ascent that lasted the remainder of his life.

From 1902 to 1909, Einstein worked as an examiner in a patent office in Bern. It was a job that paid enough for him to marry Mileva and leave him with more than enough time (both at work and at home) to do physics. They had two children—Hans Albert and Eduard—whom Albert basically ignored as he spent almost all his waking hours thinking out issues in theoretical physics with his academic friends in what they called the "Olympia Academy." Mileva had started out as a physicist too. However, she failed to pass her exams, became pregnant, married, and now, with two children, became transformed from a bright and promising female theoretical physicist into what Albert and his Academy undoubtedly considered to be just another *Hausfrau*.

Albert and Mileva grew more and more apart. In the end Albert had an affair with his cousin, Elsa, whom he married in 1919 after Mileva divorced him. However, Elsa meant little more to Einstein than did Mileva. Albert's sole passion was for thinking.

He received his Ph.D. from the University of Zurich in 1905 for postulating photons (*viz.*, light quanta) to explain what was known as the photoelectric effect. In the same year he also proposed a quantum theory to explain specific heat, explained the so-called Brownian movement of solid particles suspended in either a gas or a liquid, and developed his special theory of relativity. Now he moved on to a new, more philosophical question, about his speculative physics. He asked: Could God have created a universe any different than the one he created? The question opened the door for Einstein to move from the special to the general theory of relativity, a move that became possible once he determined that acceleration and gravity are equivalents.

Four years after he received his Ph.D., in 1909 at the age of thirty years, Einstein received his first academic appointment—as an adjunct professor at the University of Zurich. One year later he became a regular professor at the University of Prague. One year later, 1911, he began his intimate relationship with his cousin Elsa on a trip to Germany, and he astounded the physics world at a conference at the University of Brussels, where he asserted that his special theory of relativity entails that gravity and inertia are equivalent.

Einstein was becoming famous, both in the world of physicists, because of his work as a theorist, and in the popular press, because he was a *Jewish* famous physicist in a world of anti-Semites. In 1912 he accepted a chair in theoretical physics at the Federal Institute of Technology in Zurich, where, with the help of a friendly mathematician, he concluded that gravity is a curvature in space-time caused by matter. In 1913 he became a professor of physics at the Prussian Academy of the Sciences in Berlin, as well as the director of theoretical physics at the Kaiser Wilhelm Institute, and his long-estranged wife Mileva took her sons and left Albert.

In 1914 the First World War began. Whereas other German Jews, including Jewish philosophers—for instance, Hermann Cohen, Martin Buber, and Franz Rosenzweig—were active supporters and even participants in the war out of their sense of German patriotism, Einstein virtually ignored the war, for he was a committed pacifist who found no value in any form of nationalistic patriotism. What most concerned him was his close work with his old school friend Marcel Grossman in figuring out the geometry of the curved surfaces that his proposed identity of gravity and inertia entails. The work in physical geometry enabled him, in 1916, in the middle of the world war, to complete his general theory of relativity, whose central feature was an identity equation between two ratios: the ratio of matter to energy and the ratio of space to time. In other words, matter is related to energy as space is related to time. ($G_{\mu\nu} = 8T_{\pi\mu}$).

In 1919, Arthur Stanley Eddington's expedition of the Royal Society in the Gulf of Guinea observed a solar eclipse and recorded a small shift in the orbit of the planet Mercury. This observation confirmed the deflection of starlight in the vicinity of the sun predicted by Einstein's general theory of relativity, which provided Einstein's theory with the empirical basis to claim that his imaginative theory is a physical law of the universe. In that same year Mileva divorced Albert, Elsa married Albert, the world war ended for a while, and Albert became a media star. He was forty years old, and it was the high point of Einstein's life, both professionally and personally.

1921–1932: Einstein and Spinoza

In 1921, while on mental vacation from thinking about physics, Albert read Spinoza's *Ethics* for the first time. He read it in a German translation that F. Meiner published in Leipzig in 1910.

Also in 1921, Einstein received the Nobel Prize in physics for his work on the photoelectric effect. In 1923 he visited Palestine on a return trip from Japan and began a brief correspondence with the Ashkenazi chief rabbi of Tel Aviv, Abraham J. Kook. In 1927 he participated in a famous conference on quantum mechanics with Werner Heisenberg and Niels Bohr, where Einstein attempted to dissuade his peers from this new physics to which Einstein himself had made contributions in his earlier years. He failed to mount a convincing argument, but he himself remained convinced that this view of the universe could not be correct. The conviction had more to do with philosophy than with science.

There were two features of Spinoza's philosophy that appealed to the author of the theories of relativity. First, Spinoza rejected the duality of mind and matter. For him, neither had ultimate reality. Rather, they were two perspectives on a single reality. Second, Spinoza was a strict determinist, who believed that the only sense in which an individual can be said to be free is that the immediate cause of his or her action is a determination of the will, but that act of self-determination is itself determined by a chain of other causes and reasons. Einstein incorporated this view of reality into his theories of relativity. In regard to the duality of mind and matter, relativity theory explains reality in terms of a ratio between three terms—energy (E), mass (m), and the speed of light (c)—such that $E = mc^2$. Mass is not matter and energy is not spirit or mind. Rather, mass is a ratio of energy and the speed of light ($m = E/c^2$), as energy and speed are defined by the same ratio. The fundamental reality is the ratio that defines the terms of the ratio. In that sense this ratio is, for Einstein, what absolute substance was for Spinoza. (In effect, both Einstein's ratio and Spinoza's substance are definitions of God.)

It was his affirmation of Spinoza's philosophical commitment to determinism that made it impossible for Einstein to accept quantum mechanics. In quantum mechanics the ultimate equations that explain the most basic dynamics of the simplest building blocks of the universe are all probability equations: for example, "$\Delta p_y a \geq h$", where "$p_y a$" expresses a momentum a particle along an axis y at a position a, "$\Delta p_y a$" expresses the probability that the particle is at the position ay, and "h" is a constant between 0 (impossibility) and 1 (necessity). The equation says that the probability of a particle being at a specific position in space is equal to or greater than a specific number, and that number can be either probability extreme—0 (impossibility) or 1 (necessity)—only if the position or the momentum is measured. Otherwise the particle's location is indefinite. These equations apply to all subatomic entities, that is, all the particles that make up an atom. This means that atoms do not at all look like little solar systems with fixed-in-space nuclei (à la the sun) and fixed-in-orbit electrons (à la the sun's satellites). Rather, atoms look more like spherical gas clouds within which the composite particles may be anywhere. More accurately, they are anywhere in the cloud until they are measured, and then and only then does their position become definite. Now, if this is the case, then ultimately nothing is precisely anywhere, and if the ultimate causal principles are determinations of particle motions in space-time, then nothing is determined.

That the mathematics of quantum mechanics entails such a picture, if in fact quantum mechanics reflects the way reality is, meant for Einstein (but not Heisenberg and Bohr) that this kind of physics did not describe reality. It was nothing more than a useful mathematical trick that enabled us in our ignorance to manipulate physical reality, but it did not describe the way the reality is. It is at this point that Einstein said that God does not play dice with the universe, which meant that God would not create a universe that is indeterminate, which for him entailed that it is ultimately unknowable, even by God.

Einstein's judgment at this point is philosophical rather than scientific, and the philosophy is Spinozistic. A perfect being will know everything, but only what is completely determinate is in principle knowable. Hence the universe must be perfectly determinate, or, which is to say the same thing, every event has a cause.

From his faith in the truth of determinism, Einstein moved away from studies in quantum mechanics and looked deeper into his relativity theory. In 1929 he announced that he had found the key to formulating a unified field theory that would unite the forces determining subatomic phenomena with gravity and electromagnetism in a way that would unite relativity and quantum mechanics into a single, more fundamental theory. He spent the rest of his life trying to work out the equations.

1933–1955: The American Years

In 1933, Einstein received an appointment at the Institute for Advanced Studies in Princeton. Elsa died in 1936. In 1939 he wrote to Franklin Delano Roosevelt about the possibility of the Germans developing an atomic bomb. In 1940 he became a U.S. citizen. In 1949, Mileva died. However, all these events had relatively little importance for Einstein in the last decades of his life. For Einstein, what was important was his progress in understanding absolutely everything. In 1950 he announced that he had discovered a mathematical expression of an unified field theory, an expression whose value for physics is still being debated by intellectual historians. It was his last major act. He died of a heart attack on April 18, 1955, in a Princeton hospital. His purported final words were a request for paper and a pencil in order to make some calculations. Following his instructions, his body was cremated and scattered without any ceremony.

QUESTIONS AND ANSWERS

That, in brief, is a summary of Einstein's life and thought. It is, if you will, the data from which we will extrapolate an answer to our question: Can Einstein serve as a model for Jewish spirituality within the framework of secular humanist Judaism? In constructing an answer let us first consider, Was he in fact Jewish, secular, or a humanist?

Was Einstein Jewish?

Let us first deal with the question of his Jewishness. Note that it is our question, not his. After Einstein died, friends suggested that a chair of Jewish studies be established at Princeton University in his name. His estate directors opposed the decision. A chair in physics or mathematics would be an appropriate way to honor his memory, they argued, but not in Jewish studies, which were of no importance to him whatsoever. I think their judgment was accurate.

Einstein certainly was Jewish in the minimal popular senses of the term. He (like Spinoza) was born of Jewish parents, he never denied that he was Jewish, and he never converted to Christianity. However, he was not Jewish in any deeper sense of the term.

In this connection, it is of interest to note the November 28, 1919, London *Times* article on Arthur Stanley Eddington's experimental confirmation of Einstein's theory of general relativity. Eddington told Einstein, "All of England is talking about your theory. It is the best thing that could have happened to scientific relations between England and Germany." Einstein replied, "Here is an interesting application of the principle of relativity. Today in Germany I am called a German man of science and in England I am reported as a Swiss Jew. If I come to be regarded as a 'bête noir,' the description will be reversed, and I shall become a Swiss Jew for the Germans and a German for the English."[5] Of course, Einstein's joke about being Jewish was more than a joke. Einstein often used humor to deal with issues that emotionally meant a great deal to him (e.g., his biographical comments on his personal failures as a husband and as a father; the play of serious thinkers rarely is mere play). This particular joke makes it clear that he unqualifiedly affirmed his ethnic identity as a Jew, but he no more valued being Jewish than he valued being German or any nationality. Einstein accepted that he was Jewish as a biographical fact of his birth, but that was all.

If Einstein's thought was in any sense Jewish, it was not orthodox.[6] As we have seen, he chose not to participate in any form of Jewish ritual, including the traditional rites of passage (for he refused to be bar mitzvahed and he chose to be cremated). Similarly, it is probably inappropriate to call his thought in any sense Jewish.

Philosophers are called "Jewish philosophers" if their philosophy was to some significant extent formed by their study of Jewish texts. It is in this sense that Spinoza, for example, is called a Jewish philosopher. However, the same cannot be said for Einstein. Some people have suggested that Einstein's thought was influenced by the Talmud, but to my knowledge the only Talmud that influenced him was Max Talmud, whose learning led the youthful Einstein to lose interest in the Bible and decide against a bar mitzvah.

It is true that Einstein's beliefs were close to Spinoza's. However, Spinoza's writings played no apparent role in the way that Einstein formulated his world and life view, since he read Spinoza for the first time when he was forty-one years old, well after he fully formulated his deepest beliefs about almost everything.

Einstein certainly did express respect for Jewish philosophers, notably Moses Maimonides and Baruch Spinoza. However, his knowledge of them was entirely superficial, as he himself admitted.[7] The only major Jewish belief that Einstein clearly affirmed was in Zionism. However, Zionism is something he came to fairly late in life, as a result of his experience of German anti-Semitism. In fact, Ben Gurion offered Einstein the first presidency of the newly formed modern state of Israel, which Einstein (to the probable relief of both men) refused. Einstein affirmed being Jewish because his world made being Jewish something negative. It was both an act of defiance against an ignorant world and his own personal joke. As the earlier quote illustrated, the two motives for affirming his Jewishness were not separate. Perhaps the single most "Jewish" thing about Einstein's thought was his use of humor as a way to handle what mattered most to him emotionally.

Was Einstein Secular?

Since the question of Einstein's beliefs about religion and God have already been introduced, it would be best now to consider whether or not Einstein was "secular." In this case I think the answer is clearly no. However, this absolute negation needs some qualification.

Einstein made a number of popular-press-level statements about God, two of which stand out in my mind as having particular significance. The first is the famous statement, mentioned above, that Einstein's reason for rejecting quantum mechanics was that God does not play dice with the universe. The second is a statement recorded by D. Brian.[8] On April 12, 1930, Einstein attended a concert of the Berlin Philharmonic Orchestra, with Bruno Walter as the conductor and Yehudi Menuhin as the soloist. After the concert he went up to Menuhin and said, "Now I know there is a God in heaven."

Both statements conform to what we said above about Einstein's religious beliefs. First, they expressed an understanding of theology that, although uninformed by reading Spinoza, closely reflects Spinoza's worldview. Second, God-talk functioned for Einstein as a way of expressing experiences that deeply moved him emotionally, whose depth so embarrassed him that he had to say them with humor in a way that attempted to conceal the emotion he revealed.

So, was Einstein secular? No, if "secular" means not believing in God. Clearly Einstein believed in God, and that belief played an important role in all his thought, including his physics. However, his deity was a Spinozistic deity far more than he was Maimonidean. Einstein's God was a deity who is served best through the study of science, and not a deity who is served at all through communal and private religious liturgy. So, if living a secular life means to live a life in which religion plays little or no role, then in this sense Einstein definitely was secular.

Was Einstein Spiritual?

If Einstein was secular in the sense that he had no use for religious ritual in his life, can we then say he was spiritual? The answer is an equivocal yes and no, depending on what we mean by "spiritual."

Some people use the term *spiritual* to mean "religious," without the associations of involvement in any form of institutional religion. I believe Einstein himself used the term this way. In a 1948 essay entitled "Religion and Science: Irreconcilable?" for the Liberal Ministers' Club of New York City, Einstein asserted that science depends on a "religious attitude" but not on any form of institutional religion. Einstein considered himself religious in this sense, a sense in which to be religious meant to study science. Einstein would be most comfortable with the use of the term *spiritual* as the emotion associated with what drives a human being like Einstein to spend his entire life attempting to understand the nature of light as a foundational conception of the nature of the universe. It is an emotion akin to what Spinoza called "the intellectual love of God" (*amor Dei intellectualis*).

Some people use "spiritual" to describe the quality of a person's life of great excellence in the pursuit of the good of others. In this sense a person is spiritual if he or she lives a life that is what religious people call "saintly." The early rabbis might call this quality *middot chasidut*, which literally means the characteristics of the state of the life of a true *chasid*, where a *chasid* is understood to be a person who wants to go beyond the mere letter of the law (*halacha*), beyond what merely is good and not bad, in order to do simply for its own sake what is the best. In this sense of the term, Einstein's total dedication to theoretical physics, to the near exclusion of everything else in life, including human relations, could qualify as spirituality if we were willing to affirm, as the classical Jewish philosophers did, that to study nature is to study God, and that this form of activity is the highest form of worship. However, others would claim that "excellence" in this sense of the term *spiritual* means moral excellence, that is, excellence in interpersonal human relationships, and in this sense clearly Einstein was not spiritual. A man who abandons a child for the sake of a career move and who destroys two marriages because of sexual lust is, they would argue, no "saint."

How then can a man like Einstein be saintly/spiritual in one sense but not in another? The question is more than linguistic. The ambiguity is not so much about the meaning of the term as it is about the nature of spirituality itself. Spirituality describes a way of being, but it is not being in isolation. It is being in relationship to another. The question is who that other is. The answer turns on our answer to the last of our initial questions in this section, namely, was Einstein a humanist?

Was Einstein a Humanist?

If a humanist is someone who values humanity more than anything else in reality, then clearly Albert Einstein was not a humanist. Whether we base our judgment on his life or on his thought, the answer is the same. In terms of his thought as a physicist, Einstein's understanding of the universe in general was very much like Spinoza's. For Spinoza, ultimate reality is a single, simple, absolute substance that, in the imaginative language of religions, is called God. The universe of multiple thoughts that we think and the physical states of affairs that we perceive through our senses are all manifestations of or perspectives on (depending on how you interpret the relationship between substance, attributes, and modes in Spinoza's thought) what in absolute terms is a single, simple thing. In Einstein's case ultimate reality is a single, absolute set of mathematical equations through which all forces in all force fields are strictly determined, which in turn determine all motions in space-time, which in reality are the components of perceived reality (energy and mass). Hence, human beings—like every other material physical object—are reducible to their motions in time-space that are determined by a beautiful-in-their-mathematical-simplicity set of laws that we could imaginatively (if we are so inclined) call God, just as Spinoza called the "absolute substance" God, the author of the *Zohar* called "the Infinite" God, and Maimonides called "the Unmoved Mover" God. It is this scientifically hypothesized absolute reality that purportedly transcends the so-called plastic world of the objects of human sense perception that Einstein, no less than his relatively unknown and unread Jewish philosophic predecessors, valued most highly.

By comparison to these purported creator deities, humanity was of little value. In fact, humanity is by comparison so little valued that all the Jewish philosophers struggled to find a conception of a compassionate deity of revelation in relation to humanity that could complement their harsh and just deity of creation in relationship to physical reality. For Einstein, however, there was no such struggle. He was not an atheist in the sense that he affirmed there was no deity at all. On the contrary, he not only "believed" in a deity; he believed that physics demonstrates that this deity exists. He (or better, it) is the ultimate set of mathematical principles by which absolutely everything can be rendered intelligible. Einstein dedicated his entire life to finding and understanding this deity, and in his absolute devotion to the search, he had relatively little time for anything or anyone else. In this practical sense as well, Einstein may have been spiritual and a saint, but he was no humanist.

The following two statements by Einstein, I think, highlight this view of his nonhumanistic spirituality. The first is about ethics, which he understood to be sets of rules about how human beings ought to relate to each other. He said (in his *The World as I See It*) that "there is nothing divine about morality; it is a purely human affair." It is quite clear from its history and from nature that human beings play a very minor role in the universe. First, human morality is irrelevant in the laws of nature. If, for example, both Jesus and Hitler had been standing in

Hiroshima on the day that an atomic bomb exploded there, both men would have been reduced to their molecular components by strict laws of thermodynamics. Their demise would have been the same, and the relative good of the one and the relative evil of the other would have made no difference. Second, the spatial location of human beings is utterly insignificant. They are minor inhabitants (given the age of the planet) of a minor planet in a minor solar system in a minor galaxy. Third, the universe existed for billions of years without human beings, and the universe will continue to exist for billions of years after humanity disappears (which will happen, if not sooner, when our particular star reaches middle age, becomes a supernova, and gives off sufficient heat that all of its satellites will be incinerated). Hence, ethics and morality are of no concern to a deity such as Einstein's, who is (in imaginative language) the master of the universe.

The second statement is in Einstein's essay "What I Believe." Having explained that he does not "believe in human freedom in the philosophical sense," he added that the "most beautiful experience we can have is the mysterious. It is the fundamental emotion which stands at the cradle of true art and true science." This emotion was for him his sense of religiosity or, as we today would say, his "spirituality." He said that this "knowledge of [the] existence of something we cannot penetrate" is the content of "true religiosity," and he added that "in this sense, and in this sense alone, I am a deeply religious man."[9]

CONCLUSION—WHAT CAN WE LEARN?

Our conclusion is that Einstein's life and thought constitute a modern example of spirituality, which can be interpreted to be Jewish and secular but not humanist. Can this example teach us anything about living a Jewish secular humanist spiritual life? I think it can. To see how, we need to contextualize Einstein's thought more carefully within the wisdom or virtue tradition of Jewish ethics.

There is a continuous tradition of Jewish ethics that runs from the biblical book of Proverbs, through the theology of Moses Maimonides, through the philosophy of Baruch Spinoza. At the heart of the tradition is the early rabbinic judgment that there are three ways to serve God (Torah, worship, and good deeds), and that the latter two are intended as preparation for the former. We do good deeds and perform liturgy so that we may be trained to understand who and what God is. The most rigorous presentation of this "way of Torah" in rabbinic tradition is given in Maimonides' *Mishnah Torah*. There he tells us in the very first book that the ultimate commandment is to believe in the oneness of God, that no one can fulfill this commandment who does not understand the belief, and that it is impossible to understand what it means to say that God is one without a thorough knowledge of what we today would call physics and astronomy. The rest of the code, which encompasses the entire system of Jewish law, is a relatively detailed account of how you prepare yourself for this level of understanding. The final goal of human existence is to understand the nature of God, and everything else in life is to be judged strictly in terms of whether it leads to or detracts from this goal.

The ethical principles that underlie Maimonides' account of the "life of Torah" are Aristotelian. Maimonides, like Aristotle, assumed that there is a strict connection between morality and understanding, the former being a necessary preparation for the latter. Spinoza perpetuated this same tradition, but did so by claiming not that morality is a prerequisite for knowledge but that true morality is identical with true knowledge. By equating knowledge with the good, he in effect dismissed any claim of there being a constructive relationship between ethics (in the sense of values of human interaction) and wisdom (in the sense of values of human knowledge). In this way as well, Einstein followed in Spinoza's steps.

It is at this point that Jewish secular humanists would have to separate themselves from Spinoza as well as from the tradition of Jewish virtue ethics. No matter how spiritual Einstein was in his reasonably successful pursuit of divine wisdom, that in no sense pardons his great failure in almost all human relationships. In truth, to know is in itself a great human moral value. This judgment is the truth of the Jewish moral wisdom tradition. However, that does not mean that knowledge is an ultimate value, and it does not mean that a mere life of wisdom can be called a morally good life. There is no causal connection between the two, and this judgment entails that there is something deeply and fundamentally wrong with the tradition of virtue ethics as it developed in Jewish philosophy.

How then are we to lead, or at least try to lead, a moral life? The most important lesson is that morality is a relationship between human beings, and that relationship is what is most critical in leading the good life. However, the lesson from Einstein's life is no less significant. A life devoted to the pursuit of knowledge—all kinds of knowledge, from physics to rabbinic texts—is also something of intrinsic value.

The Aristotelians were wrong to believe there is a necessary connection between morality and wisdom. However, the two are not totally disconnected. To know is inherently good; to lead a life in the pursuit of knowledge is a spiritual life; and to lead a life in this pursuit in the context of a community of fellow human beings who share a common sense of moral commitment to each other is the highest sense of spirituality.

Some people ask, which is better—to observe the *mitzvot* or to do good deeds? The common answer is, why not do both? We have reached the same conclusion. To study nature and to be morally responsible for your neighbor (literally "neighbor," *viz.*, the one who is closest to you) are both inherent goods, and there should be no reason to choose between them, for to do both is to be preferred over either in isolation.

References

Bohr, Niels. *Physics and Philosophy.* New York: Harper and Row, 1958.
Craig, William Lane, and Smith Quentin. *Theism, Atheism, and the Big Bang Cosmology.* Oxford: Oxford University Press, 1996.

Davies, Paul C. W. *The New Physics.* Cambridge: Cambridge University Press, 1989.

Ellis, George F. R., and R. M. Williams. *Flat and Curved Space-Times.* New York: Oxford University Press, 1988.

Fine, Arthur. *The Shaky Game—Einstein, Realism and the Quantum Theory.* Chicago: University of Chicago Press, 1986.

Fox, Marvin. *Interpreting Maimonides: Studies in Methodology, Metaphysics, and Moral Philosophy.* Chicago and London: University of Chicago Press, 1990.

Heisenberg, W. *The Physicist's Conception of Nature.* Translated into English by Arnold J. Pomerans. Westport, Conn.: Greenwood Press, 1970.

Jammer, Max. *Einstein and Religion.* Princeton, N.J.: Princeton University Press, 1999.

Kaku, Michio, and Jennifer Trainer. *Beyond Einstein: The Cosmic Quest for the Theory of the Universe.* New York: Bantam Books, 1987.

Levy, Ze'ev. *Jewish Aspects of Spinoza's Philosophy.* New York: Peter Lang, 1989.

Mason, Richard. *The God of Spinoza.* Cambridge: Cambridge University Press, 1997.

Schilpp, Paul. *Albert Einstein.* The Library of Living Philosophers. Chicago: Open Court, 1949.

Sears, Francis W., Mark W. Zemansky, and Hugh D. Young. *University Physics.* 7th ed. Reading, Mass., and Menlo Park, Calif.: Addison-Wesley Publishing Co., 1987.

Seeskin, Kenneth. *Searching for a Distant God: The Legacy of Maimonides.* New York/Oxford: Oxford University Press, 2000.

Wetlesen, Jon. *The Sage and the Way: Spinoza's Ethics of Freedom.* Assen, the Netherlands: Von Gorcum, 1979.

Yovel, Yirmiyahu. *Spinoza and Other Heretics.* Princeton, N.J.: Princeton University Press, 1989.

Chapter 4

Faith and Reason

J. Deotis Roberts as Prophet of Reconciliation

Frederick Ferré

I am pleased that reconciliation should have been so natural, even if liberation was consciously being sought.

—J. Deotis Roberts Sr.[1]

I must start with a few personal words about my links to Deotis Roberts. We have not had many direct connections in our careers, except at the annual meetings of the American Theological Society. Still, indirect associations lie deep. My late father, Nels F. S. Ferré, held him in close affection and respect. I believe this regard was fully reciprocated. Both men's faces would brighten when they saw one another. I felt a special bond between them.

Another important link is through the late Howard Thurman, whom we both knew and admired. Roberts cites the great black mystic often in his writings, acknowledging inspiration from Thurman's spiritual wisdom. I too drank thirstily from the same waters at a crucial time in my life when vital decisions needed to be made. Howard Thurman was dean of the chapel at Boston University during my final undergraduate years there. Through hours of private conversation, he taught me to look at ethical dilemmas as opportunities for creative principled inclusiveness, for "taking the moral initiative," as he put it: that is, trying to make every resulting situation better than the sum of the inadequate parts we start with. This was Thurman's interpretation of Jesus' proposal that we "turn the other cheek." Such a counsel does not call for spineless passivity. It is not doctrinaire pacifism. No, it proposes that one should take an active moral initiative, should transform a bad situation by adding a surprise ingredient—a readiness to stay personally and creatively connected even with one who might begin as an enemy. As I meditate on Deotis Roberts's prescriptions for black theology, searching as he does for creative balance between liberation and reconciliation, I feel the spirit of Howard Thurman breathing on us both.

Another link is through Scottish theological education. Roberts completed his Ph.D. at Edinburgh in 1957, during my time also in doctoral study just across the Firth of Forth at St. Andrews. Therefore we share the heritage of the Baillie brothers. John Baillie was at Edinburgh; Donald Baillie, though he died just before my arrival in St. Andrews, was still a strong presence in the Kingdom of Fife. Moreover, Roberts and I both worked at dissertation topics that tried to reconcile through understanding. Mine was engaged in relating the new "language philosophy" then emergent in Britain with the old arguments for God. His was focused on linking seventeenth-century Puritanism with the rise of Cambridge Platonism. We were both wrestling with issues of faith and reason. We both wanted to have it both ways. We still do. How Roberts has worked at this will provide the remaining substance of this chapter.

I

The first two major projects undertaken by Deotis Roberts were explorations of faith and reason as represented by thinkers worth engaging. The first study, Roberts's S.T.M. thesis at Hartford Theological Seminary in 1952, involved the comparison and contrast of Blaise Pascal (1623–1662), Henri Bergson (1859–1941), and William James (1842–1910).[2] All three of these thinkers rejected the adequacy of autonomous theoretical reason (though for characteristically different reasons), and all three offered instead something suprarational (Roberts is willing to call this "faith") as a way of finding fundamental truth or reality. The mystic Pascal, the vitalist Bergson, and the pragmatist James all have much to offer, Roberts argues, but in the end Pascal offers the most. Bergsonian vitalism culminates in mystic union with the *élan vital*, but this vital force, thrusting through and shaping the material universe, is not the equivalent of the Christian God. Further, Bergson's intuition, the ground of his epistemology, "does not harmonize with Christian presuppositions."[3] James's pragmatism offers "courage to risk our lives for the good and the true,"[4] but its weakness is the absence of certainty. For James, "there is only probable belief based on possibility."[5] Therefore, Roberts concludes, the intensity and Christ-centeredness of Pascal make his passionate wager the most adequate way to address the relations of faith and reason. "Joy, peace, certainty are expressed in [Pascal's] affirmation of faith and this is the kind of faith we need."[6]

This early work reveals Roberts's general cast of mind and spirit at this point in his development. It is clearly the product of a man more steeped in theological than philosophical method (as was appropriate to the character of the academic degree being sought). No one with a primary interest in philosophy would rest in the circular argument offered for the superiority of Pascal's position. In his preface, Roberts announces quite openly that "it is my candid opinion that Pascal's is the more reasonable and is supported by Christian thought. The attempt will be made to substantiate this claim by using Pascal as a standard of judgment throughout this study."[7] Correspondingly, from the start, Roberts contrasts the other two subjects of his study, who were searching for answers, with Pascal, who was the recipient of unbidden revelation from God. "Pascal's unique insight is due," Roberts writes, "not to what he found himself as much as to what God reveals to him by the illumination of Grace. . . . For this reason, Pascal has a standard of judgment which the others do not have, namely the fact of the Incarnation."[8] Similarly, Roberts notes approvingly, "Faith differs from proof; it is implanted in the heart and is a gift of God. It is clear that Pascal speaks of revealed knowledge and of the Christian's God. This God is no Idea, First Cause, etc., but the God of Abraham, of Isaac and Jacob, the God Who reveals Himself in Christ."[9] Thus it comes as no surprise that Pascal is favored at the end of Roberts's final chapter on critique and conclusions, since, at the very start of this chapter, he declares: "Pascal expresses in his *Pensées* an immediate knowledge of faith *par excellence*. We shall consider him as the criterion of judgment in this critique. He *lives* his faith, while Bergson and James *study or observe* those who experience faith."[10]

The spiritual incandescence of Pascal remains an important pole of attraction for Roberts, who continues in all his future works to be a theological thinker, to honor Christian revealed imagery, and to breathe prophetic fire. But in the years between his S.T.M. work at Hartford and his Ph.D. dissertation at Edinburgh, Roberts gains maturity and power in philosophical thinking, something that provides him another enduring pole of attraction. Fittingly, the book that came from his doctoral research is itself bipolar, exploring the tension between Puritanism (faith) and Platonism (reason) and how their reconciliation was attempted through the reasonable theology of Benjamin Whichcote, the pioneer and patron of the Cambridge Platonists.[11]

In this first-rate study, Roberts shows new subtlety in his approach to the old tensions. Whichcote was a splendid choice for study, an amiable, wealthy man deeply committed to Christianity, moderation, and balanced thinking in an age of sharp partisanship and often coercive fideism. He was a clergyman and an academic leader, rising, by Puritan appointment, to provost of King's College at Cambridge University, where he served with distinction for many years, shaping his liberal theological views and those of others. From this administrative position he was dramatically ejected by order of the Catholic king Charles II as part of the swirling civil, ecclesiastical, and academic strife that characterized that explosive era. But, recovering from this crisis, he went on to a distinguished preaching career in London, where he was heard and praised by many—among others by John Locke, whose views on the supremacy of reason over revelation were quite probably thereby influenced. Locke's views were to influence many in the Age of Reason to come.

Whichcote's position was more nuanced than that of the rationalist followers of Locke, but it is true that, against Calvinist pressures toward fideism, Whichcote insisted that reason, despite its fallibility, must in the last resort be the interpreter of revelation and distinguish what should count as revelation. The alternative to public reason is "private" interpretation, which can be "wanton" when out of control. As Whichcote put it: "If you give leave, and listen to persons that now pretend to a private spirit of interpreting, and who do not give us assurance that their interpretation is warranted by the context; we set wanton wit at liberty to bring any fancy whatsoever, and lay a foundation for all manner of imaginary conceit; and so frustrate and enervate scripture, as a rule of faith."[12] His more conservative Calvinist Puritan opponent, Anthony Tuckney, condemned this appeal to reason as idolatry and insisted (in tones familiar from mid-twentieth-century neo-orthodox controversies) that human reason itself is utterly "fallen." To this Whichcote replied that it is not reason itself—a good gift of God—that is the problem but, rather, the arrogance of its misuse. "Revelation is only a stumbling-block to that reason which proclaims itself as a final court of appeal even before God. Hence the stumbling-block is not so much to reason itself, as to the arrogance of reason, our self-sufficiency in virtue of reason."[13] Here Whichcote's position is far subtler than that of Locke and his followers. Reason, rightly used, will recognize its limits and acknowledge its subordination before God—while still controlling against "wanton" claims of private revelations. Deotis Roberts comments favorably on this resolution of the ancient struggle. Both faith and reason have appropriate place in a balanced religious life. Whichcote's reaction against Puritan scripturalism and intolerance is salubrious, especially for times like his (and ours) when tolerance and goodwill are in short supply. At the same time, considered historically, Whichcote's appeal to the universals of Platonic reason can get out of hand. "This rationalism which Whichcote attempts to root securely in Scripture and to use as the receiver of revelation, loses its balance and separates itself from the source that gives it life."[14]

In this judgment, Roberts shows his continuing attraction to Pascal's pole, at which life burns with particular intensity beneath and through all of reason's universal pronouncements. Plato without Pascal leads to the arid eighteenth-century Age of Reason; Pascal without Plato leads to the narrowness and violence of seventeenth-century religious warfare. We must not release either pole. We must live in the creative tension between them. Theology and ethical life depend on remaining animated and transformed, sustained between these polarities.

II

Lest we fall into the trap of supposing that the Deotis Roberts we have seen engaged with classical theology and philosophy of religion was a wholly different person from the Deotis Roberts we will see engaged with black theology, it is instructive to notice that Roberts's passion for justice was already plainly manifest in his doctoral critique of Whichcote. Roberts finds two main problems with Whichcote's position. The first problem, already noted, is epistemological: there is a subtle tilt in Cambridge Platonism toward lifeless universals, allowing, if not quite leading to, the desiccated fruits of eighteenth-century rationalism. The second problem, however, is ethical. Whichcote was a wealthy man, and like most of his class, he tended to be insensitive to the anguish of those less fortunate. Whichcote's blind spot is shown in a tension, exposed by Roberts, in his position on the distribution of worldly wealth. Sometimes he argues that distribution of property is not a function of the kingdom of Christ. "Possessions come by inheritance and the like and thus the right of property is based on nature rather than grace."[15] But at other times he asserts "that there is a different 'disposition' of providence as to 'men's state and affairs' which may be explained by God's sovereignty and 'good pleasure.' Further, he suggests that it is commendable to comply with the necessity of one's condition, in other words, to submit to the inevitable with complete resignation."[16] But, Roberts firmly points out, "he cannot have it both ways, either providence is involved in the distribution of wealth or it is not. It appears that in this latter assertion, Whichcote without meaning to do so, gives a religious cloak to the oppressor of the poor and at the same time, deals a deadly blow to the disinherited."[17] It is easy for a rich man to accept his lot and do good works (as Whichcote did) with the means at his disposal. But Roberts notes, with some prophetic indignation, that "it is more difficult with the same natural gifts and convictions to live the good life when one has not the means to procure even the necessities of life to say nothing of helping others. Such a poverty-ridden person is not likely to receive much comfort from Whichcote's assertion that his 'lot' is the will of God."[18]

This same theme, of liberation for the disinherited and poverty-ridden, becomes primary in Roberts's thinking from May 1969, when a conference on "Black Church/Black Theology" held at Georgetown University drew his impassioned engagement. Writing an introductory note about his conference paper, "Black Consciousness in Theological Perspective," Roberts himself acknowledges and correctly predicts the importance of this turning point. He says of his own essay, "It makes a break with my own theological past."[19] And this is clearly true. A shelf of his books dramatically shows the turn in focus to black theology and away from explicit dealing with what I have called classical philosophy of religion. And yet it is not correct to declare a total split. It is demonstrably the same Deotis Roberts who, from the 1970s, began to define black theology on behalf of oppressed and disinherited Christians of his race, who also, in the 1950s and 1960s, wrestled with reconciling Pascal and Plato on behalf of wholeness, balance, and a fuller life.

This discovery of the "continuous" Deotis Roberts, made during my preparations for this volume while reading through all his books in chronological order, explains the title of my chapter. Through this rewarding reading program, I came to see Roberts as exponent of passionate concern for justice and also as leading prophet of reconciliation. His mature passion for reconciliation between groups and individuals, within and between races, and even within and between religious traditions is a continuation of his youthful passion for reconciliation between faith and reason. He does not rest easy in either-or dilemmas. He presses to resolve them into *whole* solutions that offer *balance* and *inclusion*. He reports that even his initial essay at the Georgetown conference, where he was focused on sharp messages of liberation, was seen as offering promises of principled reconciliation—which stimulated from Roberts the epigraph I used at the start of this chapter. He accepts, and is "pleased" by, the fact that reconciliation can be "natural" for him, even as he consciously pursues liberation.

Roberts is right to be pleased. Prophetic calls to conscience are essential in the human situation, the "situation of racism,"[20] the situation of sexism—the situation of oppression, violence, and disrespect for the other through greed, fear, and hatred. These cries are like the urgent utterances of faith, Pascal's cries of "Fire!" without which life itself loses touch with its source. But, just as faith needs reason to articulate, interpret, and knit life's crying urgencies into balanced unities of fulfillment, so prophetic warnings *against* ugliness need direction *toward* something whole, sustainable, and beautiful. For Roberts, it is natural to go on from recognizing problems to suggesting solutions. It is natural to hold reconciliation as the wider goal even while liberation is consciously sought.

This will best be done, Roberts insists, by making use of the human capacity for *thinking*. Even from the pole of intense faith, Roberts reminds us, Pascal himself recognized the exalting role of reason: "as Pascal has so well said, 'man is only a reed, but he is a thinking reed.'"[21] To which Whichcote, agreeing, although from Plato's opposite pole, added that "the 'reason of men is the candle of the Lord; lighted by God and lighting unto God. *Res illuminata illuminans.*'"[22] Thus, from Roberts's initial essay in black theology (and onward throughout his writings), we are not surprised to find an admonition to think as well as to feel. "Our justification for a black theology is based upon the primary need of all enlightened Christians to think theologically about their affirmation of faith. The need 'to love God with all our minds' as well as to *feel* God within our hearts, creates a demand for hard and sound theological thinking for all Christians."[23]

On these terms, appealing to the general standards of good thinking, Roberts makes his critiques of other black theologians such as Joseph Washington, Albert Cleage, and James Cone. Washington is faulted merely for leaving crucial issues undeveloped,[24] but Cleage and Cone are more severely taken to task for epistemological mistakes. Cleage, whose passionate invocation of a black Messiah "makes immediate contact with black consciousness, black pride, and Black Power,"[25] is unfortunately out of touch with the scholarly disciplines for interpreting biblical materials. Cleage "expects us to reject all the intense critical-historical study of the Bible available and accept his restructuring of Bible history without benefit of any references."[26] Substantively, as well, Cleage's message is exclusivistic; it is a gospel meant only for blacks. The redemption offered is too narrow, failing even to envision the possibility of transracial reconciliation. As Roberts gently puts it: "Love is to be operative only between soul brothers and sisters. It is the principle of unity and fellowship within the black nation, but it does not enfold the white person. Thus at the point where theology and ethics meet, Cleage faces a serious problem."[27] Less gently he concludes, "Thus Cleage's chosen people, the black nation, has been launched upon a stormy sea where the ship is at the outset beset by the perils of exclusiveness, and the problems of mutiny upon the ship itself may lead to its utter destruction. The Christian understanding of humanity as sinful is a robust realism. But the Christian faith is optimistic about what God can do in and through our being open to others and to the agency of the divine spirit and grace."[28]

Similar criticisms are made of James Cone's tendency toward exclusivism. Where Cone declares that only the oppressed may write or understand a theology of oppression, Roberts answers with a more inclusive hermeneutic. In contrast, he writes that his studies "of world religions as well as ecumenical theology lead me to hold a broader view. It is possible to study a faith-claim from the inside, but it is also possible to understand a faith-claim from the 'outside.' The inside study is necessary, but it is often too subjective to be sufficiently critical and evaluative. The outside study may be supplementary by being more objective and by bringing careful analysis and critical judgment to bear upon an affirmation of faith."[29] The hermeneutical difference is crucial if there is to be reconciliation between the races. "A Black Theology that takes reconciliation seriously must work at the task of intercommunication between blacks and whites under the assumption that for those who are open to truth, there may be communication from the inside out, but at the same time there may be communication from the outside in. In the latter sense, white Christians may be led to understand and work with blacks for liberation and reconciliation on an interracial basis."[30]

Roberts criticizes James Cone for more than hermeneutical exclusiveness. In addition, he finds Cone's Christology to be excessively influenced by Karl Barth's neo-orthodox mistrust of coherent ties between the Christ of faith and the Jesus of history. For ethics, it is vital that Christians be able to ask, "What would Jesus do?"—but Cone "does not see any relation between the teaching and example of Jesus and his so-called black Christ, who is involved in the black liberation struggle."[31] The black church needs Jesus as ethical guide, particularly first as liberator and then as reconciler. This order is important: "We cannot fully know Jesus in the role of reconciler until we know him in his role of liberator. The way to a knowledge of Christ as reconciler passes through his 'liberator role.'"[32]

Roberts's deepest criticism of James Cone, the one from which the others spring, awaits its forceful expression finally in *Black Theology Today*. "Reason does not have a high place in his theology,"[33] Roberts concludes sadly, after years of wrestling with Cone's thought.

> He has a good grasp of philosophy, but this knowledge he uses mainly to discredit the use of reason in the interpretation of matters of belief. . . . Faith should have first place, . . . but there should also be a quest for understanding concerning what one believes. This means that theological assertions should be carefully and critically examined by means of all our logical and

critical powers. What I observe is that Cone often resorts to the argument from ignorance. It is one thing to accept the finitude of the human intellect in aspects of belief which transcend the reach of the mind. It is quite another matter to buy into a sub-rational stance. In the latter instance we accept beliefs blindly without attempting to think about them. This is inexcusable, the shadow of Kierkegaard notwithstanding. For Cone, admitting that something cannot be subject to thought, provides an escape for a dogmatic assertion that something he affirms should be taken at face value, without question.[34]

In this lament, we are reminded of Whichcote's stand against Calvinist fideism and the "wanton" release of dogma from reasonable control when "private" revelations are claimed. Roberts regrets that "Cone often writes as if God is speaking to him and only to him as a theologian of the black experience. All other theologians, including his brother Cecil, hear a different drummer."[35]

"No theologian, it seems to me," Roberts continues, "is entitled to privileged information from God."[36] And here he states his own faith in the reasoning that rises from open, attentive dialogue within the community of concern. The genuinely liberating theologian must be willing to learn. Likewise, the genuinely reconciling theologian properly eschews either-or patterns of argument in favor of inclusive and creative modes. "There is another model of thinking, the both-and model which mediates between extremes in thought and action. The biblical as well as the African perspectives seem to be wholistic rather than dichotomous."[37]

III

Whether spelled "wholistic" or "holistic," as different editors may demand, holism characterizes any worldview offering the possibility—and the imperative—of deep reconciliation. Only when there are real connections, what metaphysicians call "internal relations," can we hope on firm foundations to nurture societies that are differentiated, self-restrained, and mutually affirming. Roberts's metaphysical vision, as well as his epistemology, is in this sense holistic. Both modes of holism then unite to support his holistic ethics. In this final section, I reflect on these three major topics, both to clarify how I understand his overall thrust and to offer suggestions for continuing development in directions I take it he wants to go.

The best available example of a thoroughgoing holism that can undergird theological and metaphysical efforts to build on the ultimately social character of reality is provided in the writings of Alfred North Whitehead. From the smallest, briefest event of actuality, up to and including the universe as a whole, we find real internal relations in what Whitehead called his "philosophy of organism" (not "process philosophy," a term which came into use later). There are external relations, too, or there would be no freedom. Both freedom and connectedness are given their due—reconciled—in a holistic worldview that extends "all the way down" and "all the way up." Therefore I kept wishing, as I read, that

Roberts would not too quickly reject Whiteheadian thinking as an aid to articulating his own deepest intuitions about the world. In his initial essay in black theology, Roberts recognizes that there is an affinity. But he is focused not on the organismic Whiteheadian framework as a whole but, instead, on neo-Whiteheadian "process *theology*," and in particular on Charles Hartshorne's God of "neoclassical theism," and on these grounds he rejects the whole Whiteheadian perspective as too remote, abstract, and theoretical for use in black theology.

> The Whiteheadian God—"a principle of concreteness"—the God of neo-classical theism (Hartshorne's God) may provide intellectual satisfaction for those preoccupied with the metaphysical problems of the absoluteness and relatedness of God, but black theology must concern itself with more experiential matters. Ours must be a theology of involvement. The biblical paradox of transcendence-immanence sums up for us the nearness and distance of God. It is more important for black theology that God be omnipotent—that is, all-powerful—than it is that we work out an intellectually satisfying metaphysical statement of absoluteness-relatedness in a panentheistic statement in which God is no longer being but becoming.[38]

In other writings Roberts pushes Whitehead away for other reasons. Roberts (rightly, in my opinion) rejects Western substance metaphysics, but even though Whitehead offers a strong alternative, he does not give it much of a chance. "I do not find process thought, with its Whiteheadian metaphysics, to be the proper alternative to the Platonic-Aristotelean tradition. It is not merely because process thought is also Western, it is rather because it does not carry the freight that needs to be carried by the theological mission I have in mind."[39] Likewise, commenting on the work of Eulalio P. Balthazar, who does work with Whiteheadian categories, Roberts writes, "My suspicion is increased when he turns to process theology for a framework. This is a theology from 'above.' Black theology, as all liberation theologies, must seek to be a theology from 'below.'"[40] Still further in criticism, Roberts faults process theology for its relatively light mooring in Scripture, asserting that there is a "deemphasis upon the Bible among process theologians who have pushed the Bible into the background and shoved the metaphysics of Alfred North Whitehead into the foreground."[41]

Suppose that all these charges against process theology are sound. If we postulate that Hartshorne's neoclassical theism is not strong enough for the needs of black theology, that the primary movers of process theology are from the professorate rather than the proletariat, and that being true to the Bible is not as important to process theologians as being true to the demands of "intellectual satisfaction," then what follows? I would argue that none of these defects in process theology, as it has developed, undermine the strengths potentially available from Whitehead's original holism[42] or make this metaphysical holism any less valuable for a dynamic black theology of liberation and reconciliation. I would contend that what is needed is a "black theology of *organism*" to compete with mostly white *process* theology. Do not be put off by inadequate doctrines of God; forge new ones heated in the furnace of black experience! Do not be discouraged by metaphysical abstractions; fill them with content appropriate to the need! This is the proper task of those trained to do the theological labor of thinking at the highest levels of expertise for the faithful community. Do not be offended that the Bible requires a different reading when the images of faith are taken to model new theory; explore the fresh understandings of Scripture that flow within a consistently holistic worldview! Every theoretical substrate adopted by Christianity, whether Plato's or Aristotle's, Hegel's or Heidegger's, has made a difference in what images move to the foreground and what are relegated to the background. "Process theology," as Roberts has seen it, is a highly contingent—and flawed—outgrowth from a potentially much richer foundation in philosophy of organism. Black theology of Roberts's holistic sort, committed to the best use of reason and to the ideals of liberation and reconciliation, can improve on process theology without losing the resources of Whitehead. This is a challenge for the future.

Mention of the "images of faith" is a reminder of Roberts's strong epistemological support for ways of thinking that are richly connected to affect and action. In his listing of norms for theological thinking, he writes that "our theological reflection in context should seek holism. A relationship needs to be established between the secular and the sacred, body and soul, the cognitive, volitional, and affective aspects of the life of faith. The whole person and all of life should inform our theological task."[43] Further, "theology needs to be passionate without being irrational. Our epistemology needs to be carefully thought through. Theology needs intellectual integrity as well as religious fervor. As Afro-American theologians we can no longer denounce the intellectual task. We are entitled to explore other ways of thinking than that which is normative in the West, but we must *think*. Holistic thought is also thought, perhaps at a deeper level than cognition alone."[44] Specifically, Roberts commends African uses of imagery:

> The issue being raised . . . is whether fresh ways of thinking are emerging out of the "African presence" in African and black theologies. For instance, black consciousness has caused Afro-American theologians to mine the rich spiritual heritage of their history for the language of faith. African poets and philosophers have developed the concept of negritude. Furthermore, we are exploiting the use of metaphors, parables, folktales, and stories for a forceful language within which to interpret the gospel.[45]

Here again I suggest that the epistemology of connectedness, of living organic wholeness, that I find in Whiteheadian philosophy[46] could be of huge constructive help. Whitehead's is an epistemology based on reconciliation between direct feeling ("prehensive" connections between organically related entities) and abstract symbolism (one thing standing for, or suggesting, another thing). The vastly important role of metaphor and parable in biblical thought, the immensely promising introduction of folktale and story from African thought, can be affirmed and made sense of in ways entirely compatible with black consciousness (general human consciousness, indeed, freshly approached), if only the resources available for this are given another look, on their own right. In this new program, black theology could unearth exactly the epistemological foundations needed for the "theology of involvement" sought by Roberts. This is a second challenge for the future.

Finally, the ethical "bottom line" for holistic theology of organism lies in the extension and reinforcement of Roberts's strongly bipolar prescriptions for the black church (as for the church in general), for the black family (as for families in general), for black women and men (as for women and men in general), for the Christian faith (as for world religions in general), for the American people (as for peoples in general), and for issues of individualism and collectivism of all sorts, political and economic. Throughout the myriad issues he has analyzed throughout his career, Roberts seeks where there is discord to find a larger context for harmony. The word for this ethical method is not "compromise," nor even Aristotle's "golden mean." Rather, it is creative, principled inclusiveness, where divergent goods are brought into larger unities that reconcile and fulfill them. Put theologically, this involves reconciliation between the prophetic and priestly sides of religion. The prophet points to the jagged edges of things and to the wounds they have caused; the priest, ideally, binds up the wounds and helps the prophet transform things that tear into things that cut a clean path toward additional good for all. Both are needed. Roberts writes of his own aims: "I have been concerned with the protest dimension of black religion, theology, and church. Without downgrading the healing, 'priestly' aspects of black religion, I have rather been seeking a holistic balance."[47]

This holistic balance is exactly the kind of balance that can be sought and sustained within a Whitehead-inspired ethics.[48] These balances may be sought at many levels: small-scale, as within a nuclear family, in which mutually refreshing differentiations may move members beyond egoism versus subordination to loving affirmations of parts by the whole and of the whole by the parts.[49] Or they may be very large-scale, as in world economics, in which forms of capitalism and socialism vie for dominance. Here Roberts is (rightly) satisfied with neither of the presently available alternatives: "What we need to be most concerned about is to what extent any economic order meets human needs. Capitalism may be too tied to selfishness and greed to be acceptable to Christians. Socialism may be so caught up in collective concerns as to overlook the dignity and worth of individuals."[50] But the answer is neither in despair nor in casting a pox on all houses; it is in creative engagement with the imperfect actual on behalf of a sustaining ideal, in which wholes and parts are mutually related and mutually supportive.

In this we have come beyond the black community or even the Christian community and entered the pluralistic, postcolonial thought-world that Roberts, citing Raimundo Panikkar, calls "*ecumenical ecumenism*."[51] Here we care about what is universal, though not forgetting that everything actual appears only in its particularity. As Roberts puts it: "The present writer, as well as many black religious thinkers/leaders, is ultimately a universalist. We must embrace a common humanity, especially for the sake of peace. However, we must not attempt to leap to the universal. Universalism can be a meaningless abstraction. The only concrete way to pursue the universal is though the particular."[52]

And so it must be for every holistic, prehensive ethic recognizing the thoroughly social character of reality "all the way down" and "all the way up." To express this larger point in a meaningful metaphor from race relations, as Roberts puts it—sharply—in his *Liberation and Reconciliation*, "I do not advocate integration as a goal."[53] Integration may contain, hidden in its meaning, the "inferior-superior" mentality. It may also imply loss of particularity. This would destroy the mutuality in holism and turn prehension into bondage or homogenization. But at the same time Roberts also says, "I am equally opposed to separatism as an end in itself. Separatism is at best only a temporary solution."[54] Separatism would indeed sunder prehension and destroy long-term prospects for liberated reconciliation. Something more, wider, principled, inclusive, and creative is needed to hold these poles in harmony. The generation of black and white (and yellow and brown) theologians who follow Roberts's lead will find help in reconciling these ethical polarities by serious dialogue with Whitehead on the many and the one, the one against the many, and the many in the one. Here is a third challenge for the future of a rainbow theology become again universal through the particular.

I believe these challenges can and will be met by good theological thinking. Let Roberts, our deservedly honored prophet of reconciliation, have the last words here:

> What is most important, I believe, is that religion claims the whole person, body and spirit. Thought is lived-thought. It is not a head trip, but neither is it without intellectual reflection. Holistic black worship requires that we bring our heads to church as well as our hearts. . . . This constructive direction of the holism is authentic to the African American religious tradition.[55]

Amen!

Chapter 5

"The Criticism of [Black] Theology Is Transformed into the Criticism of Politics" —Karl Marx

Alistair Kee

The year 1994 saw the second coming, the second coming of Deotis Roberts to the University of Edinburgh. He arrived for the first time in 1953 as a postgraduate student. Always a pioneer, it was still unusual at that time for black Americans to pursue further studies in Europe. His field was philosophy of religion and his Ph.D. dissertation was on the Cambridge Platonists. His return to Edinburgh was in very different circumstances. This time he came as a fellow in the Institute for Advanced Studies in the Humanities. A long and distinguished career stretched out between the two visits, and he returned to us as a scholar of world renown. Deotis Roberts has been one of the founding figures of black theology, but in a world of conflict he has made a distinctive contribution through his work on reconciliation. In a world of religious conflict, he has extended his work into interreligious dialogue. It is a pleasure and privilege to contribute to essays in honor of a scholar of integrity and creativity, a man of great dignity and graciousness. Philosopher, theologian, scholar of religions, Deotis Roberts is a citizen of one country and a welcome visitor to many others. I wish to draw these dimensions together in some observations about black theology.

Alice Walker tells of an incident that took place during a visit to Cuba some years ago. She and her group visited a high school and were greeted with a delightful musical presentation by the pupils. In thanking them, she introduced herself and her group as *black* Americans. She could see the confusion on the young faces. They were of many colors, but they had clearly never thought of themselves as being of different races. Walker regretted introducing what she called a "perverted categorization."[1] To what extent does *black* theology represent a category mistake? I wish to raise this possibility by reference to race in Europe and in South Africa.

Black theology arose in the 1960s, the most radical decade of the twentieth century. In Europe, the rediscovery of the young Marx provided a basis for critical analysis. America turned instead to Freud. Black theology used neither and trusted instead a limited selection of biblical texts and the rhetoric of righteous anger. The most powerful, creative—and underestimated—figure in the early days of black theology was Albert Cleage, who simply claimed that "Marxism does not suit the American condition."[2] Looking back on that period, James Cone observed that "with few exceptions, the chief political concern of black churches has been focused on the problem of racism with almost no reference to Marxist class analysis."[3] In their own ways, both quotations assume that Marx was set aside because he did not deal with race. And what a racist assumption that would be: a "perverted categorization." Race was an issue the young Marx had to face constantly as a practical matter as well as a theoretical issue: race, but not color. We know that he came from a prominent Jewish family that could be traced back on both sides through distinguished rabbis of Krakow and Padua. His father, confronted with the threat of anti-Semitism, "converted" to become a Lutheran. His mother followed only when her devout parents were dead. Although educated in a Christian school, Marx was never alienated from the Jewish community. While living in Cologne he wrote a letter to Arnold Ruge in which he refers to a request made to him: "I have just been visited by the chief of the Jewish community here, who has asked me for a petition for the Jews to the Provincial Assembly, and I am willing to do it."[4] Marx's daughter Eleanor referred to her father as "the Moor," no doubt a reference to that dark skin which is not at all uncommon among Jews from Eastern Europe. Marx certainly experienced racism in Europe: discrimination by race, but not by color. He also reflected on it more theoretically, and it is here that black theology might have gained something from a closer attention to Marx.

In 1844, Ruge and Marx produced the first issue of the *Deutsch-Französische Jahrbücher*. Marx was not the first editor to fill up the initial (and final) volume of a journal with his own articles and letters. The most famous article was his "Contribution to the Critique of Hegel's Philosophy of Law: Introduction." However, he also wrote two articles "On the Jewish Question," both responses to pieces written by Bruno Bauer, *The Jewish Question* and "The Capacity of Present-Day Jews and Christians to Become Free." The "Introduction" is much more famous than the "Jewish Question," and they deal with entirely different material. However, there is one point at which the two come close. In the "Introduction," Marx claims that "the criticism of heaven is transformed into the criticism of earth, the criticism of religion into the criticism of law, and the criticism of theology into the criticism of politics."[5] Today we might ask how the criticism of black religion is transformed into the criticism of law, and how the criticism of black theology is transformed into the criticism of politics. Marx had the capacity to begin with the statement of a contemporary issue and transform it into something altogether more productive. So it is with his treatment of the "Jewish Question," marked by his characteristic dialectical style.

Bruno Bauer addressed the question of Jewish emancipation, a word redolent of racial captivity and constraint. His approach was to discuss the relationship between Judaism and the Christian (Prussian) state. Throughout his early writings, Marx continually identified reversals. Bauer had managed to get the issue entirely the wrong way around. "We do not turn secular questions into theological questions. We turn theological questions into secular ones."[6] Could the emancipation of the Jews from racial discrimination be tackled as a religious project? No, "the criticism of religion must be transformed into the criticism of law." Could it be addressed by comparative theology? No, "the criticism of theology is transformed into the criticism of politics." In the "Jewish Question," Marx proceeds in the opposite direction: "The question of the relation of political emancipation to religion becomes for us the question of the relation of political emancipation to human emancipation."[7] The criticism of theology does not become simply politics but "the criticism of politics." Political emancipation is not the end of the process: that is human emancipation. What is the relationship between the two? There lies before man [sic] a twofold life, what Marx is pleased to call "a heavenly and an earthly life":

> life in the political community, in which he considers himself a communal being, and life in civil society, in which he acts as a private individual, regards men as a means, degrades himself into a means, and becomes the plaything of alien powers. The relation of the political state to civil society is just as spiritual as the relation of heaven to earth.[8]

Marx was a great admirer of the United States, not least during the Civil War, which he regarded (perhaps naively) as a great moral cause, but at this time he was particularly impressed by the constitutional separation of church and state. He was intrigued by the religiosity of a country in which there was no established religion. He was less taken with the so-called rights of man, the rights of "an isolated monad."[9]

> None of the so-called rights of man, therefore, goes beyond egoistic man, beyond man as a member of civil society, that is, an individual withdrawn into himself, into the confines of his private interests and private caprice, and separated from the community. In the rights of man, he is far from being conceived as a species-being: on the contrary, species-life itself, society, appears as a framework external to individuals, as a restriction of their original independence.[10]

By identifying the problem as one of race, black theology conceived of emancipation too narrowly. The aspiration was to gain the rights of man, the liberty of civil society, the freedom to behave as badly as everyone else. Too harsh? Thirty years ago Alice Walker could regret where it had all gone wrong so soon:

> I think Medgar Evers and Martin Luther King Jr. would be dismayed by the lack of radicalism in the new black middle class, and discouraged to know that a majority of the black people helped by the Movement of the sixties has abandoned itself to the pursuit of cars, expensive furniture, large houses, and the finest Scotch.[11]

Political emancipation is not human emancipation. In focusing on race, was the problem too narrowly defined? And was there a "perverted categorization"? Did the term *black* theology further confuse the issue? As we have seen, color is not inherent in racism, but to so identify the matter restricted consideration to the American experience. By focusing on "the American condition," Marx's reflections on religion, race, and emancipation were excluded. For other reasons, which we cannot explore here, female voices (including that of Alice Walker) were not heard. Perhaps more disastrously, the "perverted categorization" meant that voices from South Africa were not heard.

Just as race was too narrowly defined, so Africa has been too selectively imagined. Too often African Americans have in mind village communities of West Africa, an idyllic, romantic view of the life of the ancestors before Sir John Hawkins approached Sierra Leone in 1562 to begin the slave trade with Santo Domingo. We need not rehearse those embarrassing encounters of black Americans and African villagers united by nothing except DNA. Much more valuable would have been a real dialogue with black South Africans. A significant number of urban blacks in South Africa have a level of sophistication and political consciousness seldom recognized by Americans. An attempt at dialogue was indeed made at a conference held at Union Theological Seminary, New York, in 1986, bringing together black South African and American theologians. The intention of this meeting was to demonstrate their essential unity. The papers were published under the title *We Are One Voice*.[12] They were not. In a juxtaposition reminiscent of Marx's derisory representation of Proudhon, we might say that in America the so-called African Americans look very African (especially to those who have never ventured further toward the dark continent than the East River Drive), but in Africa itself, African Americans are always and emphatically Americans.[13] One of the issues that divided them was precisely the narrow concentration on race, and race in the American context. Lebamang Sibidi, writing at the same time, with more honesty than graciousness rejected the race paradigm for black theology as found in America as "inadequate, shallow and misdirected. Talk about something as being only skin-deep! You are talking about the insights of Black Theology."[14] In fact, an alternative path had been set out in 1972, almost at the beginning of the development of black theology, but had never been seriously considered.

The first book on the subject published in South Africa was *Essays in Black Theology*. It was the outcome of the Black Theology Project of the University Christian Movement, headed by Stanley Ntwasa. It was early, indeed too early

for most of the contributors, but there is one essay that stands out. "Black Theology and Authority" was contributed by Mokgethi Motlhabi, originally a candidate for the Catholic priesthood, who became acting director of the Black
Theology Project when Ntwasa was restricted under a government banning
order. His indebtedness to Marxist analysis is clear. During the period of
apartheid all opposition groups agreed that there must be an end to racism, but
Motlhabi claims that this was seldom illuminated by an analysis of racism. "It
should be clear that a frontal attack on racism, even if it were to succeed, would
change society very little."[15] Racism is evil, but it is symptomatic of other evils.
Racism is easily identified, but it is an expression of other factors in society that
are not so obvious. Racism constructs myths, and these myths cannot simply be
scoffed at and set aside. Their appeal and their persistence arise from a deeper,
ideological level: they maintain interests through certain social structures. The
institutions of apartheid were not brought about simply by racism but in order
to further and perpetuate inequalities of power. "This racial prejudice gets blown
up into the huge racism myth in order to internalize the values which place and
keep the whites at the top of the power structure and the blacks at the bottom."[16]
It would be superficial to think that the end of racism would radically alter relations of power and advantage: "no radical social change will be brought about by
attacking the myth without attacking the causes of the myth."[17] Racism is the
narrative that explains why things are "just so." Its removal would not in itself
change the "just so," the status quo. Racism is the legitimation of unequal power
relations, and religion plays its part. "It is not surprising, therefore, that religion
has been one of the major bastions and creators of the race myth of the inferiority and labour—or 'Ham'—quality of the blacks."[18]

Motlhabi's essay stands out from the others in the Ntwasa collection. It provides an analysis of racism and, with its sophisticated consciousness of racism as
an ideology, identifies its true nature and its real roots. It therefore sets a new
agenda for black theology that goes beyond race or color, placing it firmly in the
wider context of liberation theology. Beneath the surface level of racism lies the
privilege of power, the control of the many in the interests of the few. "Racism
as such is not the real poison in inter-personal relations. It is that for which racism
exists, i.e. vast discrepancies in the distribution of power."[19] This has implications
in two directions.

The first is for the churches themselves. They are structured in a patriarchal
and hierarchical way, to ensure that the male prevails over the female and the
clergy over the laity. This is taken to be a matter of religious values and not simply of social management. "It is the social structure in which some people are
regarded as having the right to exercise control over the lives of others by virtue
of the position they hold within the social structure."[20] Below the surface of
racism lies the acceptance of authoritarianism. The ending of racism will not alter
such social relations. The language of religion is inherently authoritarian: the
titles of God are feudal—Lord, King, Master. In this world of social relations,
submission is a religious virtue. (If Motlhabi is correct, then the most revolu-

tionary aspect of the life and teaching of Jesus was to address God as "Daddy.")
Ecclesial structures must liberate rather than control. "We cannot have the
authoritarians who try to tell us what we believe or what to believe and who have
the power to reward or punish us. We need a Church which is authentically a
Church of the people for their liberation."[21] This is a conclusion that Motlhabi
draws concerning the churches, but it is also applicable to society at large:

> To reject racism and leave the authoritarianism basically unchanged may be
> to change the names of the people in "office" but is unlikely to change the
> names or the lot of the people at the bottom of the power pile. And one of
> the main reasons for Black Theology is that black people are the oppressed
> end of society. If all that is achieved is that black rulers replace white rulers
> but those at the "bottom" experience very little change in their freedom and
> recognition, then there will still be a need for a Black Theology, or a theol-
> ogy of the oppressed.[22]

In South Africa, those who identified racism as the enemy find that with the
end of apartheid their work is complete. To criticize the new black leadership
would be politically incorrect, and yet in their liberal souls they are disappointed
that things have changed so slowly, or not at all. Twenty years before the end of
apartheid, Motlhabi offered a more subtle analysis of the roots of oppression. No
one who takes this view could be surprised that the new South Africa is so much
like the old. Indeed, it has followed a pattern in the region. Forty years ago
Malawi became independent, but for the sake of the economy the white tea
planters were allowed to stay on. The race line lost its color. The black elite simply crossed the line to join those who held power and privilege. Twenty years ago
Zimbabwe became independent, but for the sake of the economy the tobacco
farmers and cattle ranchers were allowed to stay on. The land issue was not
addressed at that time. The race line lost its color. The new black elite crossed the
line to join those who held power and privilege. Ten years ago majority rule came
to South Africa. The race line was declared illegal, but the black elite crossed the
line to join those who held power and privilege. The land issue was not addressed.
In a curious but tragic way, liberals who were anti-apartheid were in fundamental agreement with their opponents that race was the problem in South Africa.
Hence their disillusionment with postapartheid South Africa. They have yet to
draw the appropriate conclusion: their analysis was superficial and inadequate. If
racism is the agenda, then black theology becomes redundant with the end of
apartheid. If the roots of oppression are thought to lie deeper, then the end of
apartheid is a welcome development along the way, but black theology as a theology of liberation still has much to do. Indeed, it is unfortunate, though at the
time inevitable, that South Africans ever took over the seductive but destructive
term *black* theology.

Whatever happened to black theology? Why has it stalled? The fact that its
early criticism of racism is still being repeated, together with the usual biblical
texts, does not count as advance. Our conclusions about the situation in South

Africa might suggest an answer. If black theology in the United States is based on a race paradigm, then the successful challenging of racism, personal and institutional, in that society means that its work is largely done. Blacks are now emancipated to engage in "the pursuit of cars, expensive furniture, large houses, and the finest Scotch." But race analysis will not do. We have already quoted Lebamang Sebidi's abrasive criticism of American black theology. He is also critical of the race paradigm, which is unable or unwilling to distinguish between the exploited black worker and the black capitalists who exploit them. It encourages the dangerous fiction that they are part of the same struggle. "Such a movement cannot but be bourgeois—and somehow reactionary."[23] It lacks the analysis that leads to the criticism of politics, which seeks to move from political emancipation to human emancipation.

What is happening to black theology? It is becoming black religious studies.[24] There is a division in Africa between black theology and the study of African religion(s). From an ideological perspective, the latter represents a depoliticizing of the former. The study of African traditional religion has no desire to make value judgments about matters such as power, authority, distribution of wealth, or social control. Accurate description is the goal, and its materials are in common with social history, ethnography, craft work, and social anthropology. Indeed, this is but an instance of the worldwide tension between theology and religious studies.[25] It has even been asserted that religious studies should be merged with cultural studies.[26] As a professor of religious studies, I believe this would be an intellectual (as well as strategic) mistake, but it is indicative of the alienation between the expression of a religious faith and the description of a religious tradition.[27] This division is represented by the diminution of black theology and the growth of studies of the black church and black religion. After the passion and commitment of black theology, they seem anemic. As a retreat into sociology, psychology of religion, and archaeology,[28] they are "somehow reactionary." As Marx might have said, the study of black religion interprets the black world in various ways, but it has lost the will and ambition to change it.[29]

Chapter 6

Martin, Malcolm, and Black Theology

James Cone

All scholars engaged in studies of black theology and black religion are indebted to the major contributions of J. Deotis Roberts. He has been a friend, colleague, and critic of my perspective on black theology. I am delighted to contribute to the *Festschrift* honoring his achievements. In many ways, our relationship to Martin Luther King Jr. and Malcolm X indicate the difference in our perspectives on black theology.

The prophetic and angry voices of Martin Luther King Jr. and Malcolm X together revolutionized theological thinking in the African American community. Before Martin and Malcolm, black ministers and religious thinkers repeated the doctrines and mimicked the theologies they read and heard in white churches and seminaries, grateful to be allowed to worship God in an integrated sanctuary and to study theology with whites in a seminary classroom.

I remember my excitement when I was accepted as a student at Garrett Theological Seminary more than thirty-five years ago. It was my first educational experience in a predominantly white environment. Like most blacks of that time who attended white colleges and graduate schools, I tried hard to be accepted as just another student. But no matter how hard I tried, I was never just another student in the eyes of my white classmates and my professors. I was a *Negro* student—which meant a person of mediocre intelligence (until proven otherwise) and whose history and culture were not worthy of theological reflection.

No longer able to accept black invisibility in theology and getting angrier and angrier at the white brutality meted out against Martin King and other civil rights activists, my southern, Arkansas racial identity began to rise in my theological consciousness. Like a dormant volcano, it soon burst forth in a manner that exceeded my intellectual control.

"You are a racist!" I yelled angrily at my doctoral adviser, who was lecturing to a theology class of about forty students. "You've been talking for weeks now about the wrongdoings of Catholics against Protestants in sixteenth- and seventeenth-century Europe," I continued, raising my voice even higher, "but you've said absolutely nothing about the monstrous acts of violence by *white* Protestants against Negroes in the American South today in 1961!"

Devastated that I—who was a frequent presence in his office and home—would call him a racist, my adviser, a grave and staid English gentleman, had no capacity for understanding black rage. He paced back and forth for nearly a minute before he stopped suddenly and stared directly at me with an aggrieved and perplexed look on his face. Then he shouted, "That's simply not true! Class dismissed."

He stormed out of the classroom to his office. I followed him. "Jim," he turned in protest, "*you* know I'm not a racist!" "I know," I said with an apologetic tone but still laced with anger. "I'm sorry I blurted out my frustrations at you. But I am angry about racism in America and the rest of the world. I find it very difficult to study theology and never talk about it in class." "I'm concerned about racism too," he retorted with emphasis. We then talked guardedly about racism in Britain and the United States.

The more I thought about the incident, then and later, the more I realized that my angry outburst was not about the personal prejudices of my adviser or any other professor at Garrett. It was about how the discipline of theology had been defined so as to exclude any engagement with the African American struggle against racism. I did not have the words to say to my adviser what I deeply felt. I just knew intuitively that something was seriously wrong with studying theology during the peak of the Civil Rights era and never once reading a book about racial justice in America or talking about it in class. It was as if the black struggle for justice had nothing to do with the study of theology—a disturbing assumption, which I gradually became convinced was both anti-Christian and racist. But since I could not engage in a disinterested discussion about race, as if I were analyzing Karl Barth's Christology, I kept my views about racism in theology to myself and discussed them only with the small group of African American students who had similar views.

After I completed the Ph.D. in systematic theology in the fall of 1964, I returned to Arkansas to teach at Philander Smith College in Little Rock. No longer cloistered in a white academic environment and thus free of the need of my professors' approval, I turned my attention to the rage I had repressed during six years of graduate education. Martin Luther King Jr. and the Civil Rights movement helped me take another look at the theological meaning of racism and the black struggle for justice. My seminary education was nearly worthless in this regard, except as a negative stimulant. My mostly neo-orthodox professors talked incessantly about the "mighty acts of God" in biblical history. But they objected to any effort to link God's righteousness with the political struggles of the poor today, especially among the black poor fighting for justice in the United States. God's righteousness, they repeatedly said, can never be identified with any human project. The secular and death-of-God theologians were not much better. They proclaimed God's death with glee and published God's obituary in *Time* magazine. But they ignored the theological significance of Martin King's proclamation of God's righteous presence in the black freedom struggle.

Although latecomers to the Civil Rights movement, a few white theologians in the North supported it and participated in marches led by Martin Luther King Jr. But the African American fight for justice made little or no impact on their intellectual discourse about God, Jesus, and theology. Mainstream religion scholars viewed King as a civil rights activist who happened to be a preacher rather than a creative theologian in his own right.

It is one thing to think of Martin King as a civil rights activist who transformed America's race relations and quite another to regard the struggle for racial justice as having theological significance. Theology as I studied it in the 1960s was narrowly defined to exclude the practical and intellectual dimensions of race. That was why Albert Camus, Jean-Paul Sartre, and Susan Sontag were read in theology courses, but not Richard Wright, Zora Neale Hurston, W. E. B. Du Bois, and James Baldwin. Likewise, Harry Emerson Fosdick and Ralph Sockman figured high on the reading lists in homiletics courses, but not Howard Thurman and Martin King. White theologians reflected on the meaning of God's presence in the world from the time of the exodus of Israelite slaves out of Egypt to the Civil Rights revolution of the 1950s and 1960s and never once made a sustained theological connection between these two liberation events. The black experience was theologically meaningless to them.

Unfortunately, black ministers and theologians were strongly influenced by the white way of thinking about God and theology. When Richard Allen and other black Christians separated from white churches in the late eighteenth and early nineteenth centuries, they did not regard their action as having *theological* meaning. They thought of it as a *social* act, totally unrelated to how blacks and whites think about God. That was why they accepted without alterations the confessions of faith of the white denominations from which they separated. But how is it possible to enslave and segregate people and still have correct thinking about God? That was a question black ministers did not ask.

Even Martin King did not ask that question so as to expose the flawed white liberal thinking about God that he had encountered in graduate school. King thought his theology was derived primarily from his graduate education, and to a large degree it was, especially his ghostwritten books and speeches to white audiences. As a result, he was unaware of the profoundly radical interpretation of Christianity expressed in his civil rights activity and proclaimed in his sermons.

But what King *did* in the South, and later the North, and what he *proclaimed* in sermons and impromptu addresses profoundly influenced our understanding of the Christian faith. King did not do theology in the safe confines of academia—writing books, reading papers to learned societies, and teaching graduate students. He did theology with his life and proclaimed it in his preaching. Through marches, sit-ins, and boycotts, and with the thunder of his voice, King hammered out his theology. He aroused the conscience of white America and made the racist a moral pariah in the church and the society. He also inspired passive blacks to take charge of their lives, to believe in themselves, in God's creation of them as a free people, equally deserving of justice as whites.

King was a public theologian. He turned the nation's television networks into his pulpit and classroom, and he forced white Christians to confront their own beliefs. He challenged all Americans in the church, academy, and every segment of the culture to face head-on the great moral crisis of racism in the United States and the world. It was impossible to ignore King and the claims he made about religion and justice. While he never regarded himself as an academic theologian, he transformed our understanding of the Christian faith by making the practice of justice an essential ingredient of its identity.

It could be argued that Martin King's contribution to the identity of Christianity in America and the world was as far-reaching as Augustine's in the fifth century and Luther's in the sixteenth.[1] Before King, no Christian theologian showed so conclusively in his actions and words the great contradiction between racial segregation and the gospel of Jesus. In fact, racial segregation was so widely accepted in the churches and societies throughout the world that few white theologians in America and Europe regarded the practice as unjust. Those who did see the injustice did not regard the issue as important enough to write or even talk about it. But after King, no theologian or preacher dares to defend racial segregation. He destroyed its moral legitimacy. Even conservative white preachers like Pat Robertson and Jerry Falwell make a point to condemn racial segregation and do not want to be identified with racism. That change is due almost single-handedly to the theological power of King's actions and words.

Martin King was extremely modest about his political achievements and rather naive about the intellectual impact he made on the theological world. Theologians and seminarians have also been slow to recognize the significance of his theological contribution. But I am convinced that Martin Luther King Jr. was the most important and influential Christian theologian in America's history. Some would argue that the honor belongs to Jonathan Edwards or Reinhold Niebuhr or even perhaps Walter Rauschenbusch. Where we come down on this issue largely depends on how we understand the discipline of theology. Those who think that the honor belongs to Edwards or Niebuhr or Rauchenbusch regard intellect as more important than character in the doing of theology and thus do not think that the disparity between morality and intelligence affect theological insight. To place Edwards, Niebuhr, and Rauchenbusch over King means that one cannot possibly regard the achievement of racial justice as a significant theological issue, because none of them made justice for black people a central element of their theological program. Edwards, Rauschenbusch, and Niebuhr were *white* theologians who sought to speak only to their racial community. They did not use their intellectual power to support people of color in their fight for justice. Blacks and the third-world poor were virtually invisible to them.

I am a black liberation theologian. No theologian in America is going to receive high marks from me who ignores race or pushes it to the margin of his or her theological agenda. But my claim about the importance of race for theology in America does not depend on one being a black liberation theologian. *Any* serious observer of America's history can see that it is impossible to understand the political and religious meaning of this nation without dealing with race. Race has mattered as long as there has been an America. How, then, can one be a serious Christian theologian in this land and not deal with race?

Martin King is America's most important Christian theologian because of what he said and did about race from a theological point of view. He was a liberation theologian before the phrase was coined by African American and Latin American religious thinkers in the late sixties and early seventies. King's mature reflections on the gospel of Jesus emerged primarily from his struggle for racial justice in America. His political practice preceded his theological reflections. He was an activist-theologian who showed that one could not be a Christian in any authentic sense without fighting for justice among people.

One can observe the priority of practice, as a hermeneutical principle, in his sermons, essays, and books. *Stride toward Freedom* (1958), *Why We Can't Wait* (1964), and *Where Do We Go from Here?* (1967) were reflections on the political and religious meaning (respectively) of the Montgomery bus boycott (1955–56), the Birmingham movement (1963), and the rise of black power (1966). In these texts, King defined the black freedom movement as seeking to redeem the soul of America and to liberate its political and religious institutions from the cancer of racism. I contend that as a theologian to America he surpassed the others because he addressed our most persistent and urgent sickness.

But two other features of King's work elevate him above Edwards, Rauschenbusch, and Niebuhr. The first is his international stature and influence. I do not mean his Nobel Prize but his contribution beyond the particularity of the black American struggle. He influenced liberation movements in China, Ireland, Germany, India, South Africa, Korea, and the Philippines and throughout Latin America and the Caribbean. Hardly any liberation movements among the poor are untouched by the power of his thought.

Second, King was North America's most courageous theologian. He did not seek the protection of a university appointment and a quiet office. One of his most famous theological statements was written in jail. Other ideas were formed in brief breathing spaces after days of exposure to physical danger in the streets of Birmingham, Selma, and Chicago and the dangerous roads of Mississippi. King did theology in solidarity with the least of these and in the face of death. If physical death, he said, is the price I must pay to free my white brothers and sisters from the permanent death of the spirit, then nothing could be more redemptive. Real theology is risky, as King's courageous life demonstrated.

From King black liberation theology received its Christian identity, which he understood as the practice of justice and love in human relations and the hope that God has not left the least of these alone in their suffering. However, that identity was only one factor that contributed to the creation of black liberation theology. The other was Malcolm X, who identified the struggle as a *black* struggle. As long as black freedom and the Christian way in race relations were identified exclusively with integration and nonviolence, black theology was not possible. Integration and nonviolence required blacks to turn the other cheek to white brutality, join the mainstream of American society, and do theology without anger and without reference to the history and culture of African Americans. It meant seeing Christianity exclusively through the eyes of its white interpreters. Malcolm prevented that from happening.

I remember clearly when Malcolm and black power made a decisive and permanent imprint upon my theological consciousness. I was teaching at Adrian College (a predominantly white United Methodist institution) in Adrian, Michigan, trying to make sense out of my vocation as a theologian. The black rage that ignited the Newark and Detroit riots in July 1967, killing nearly eighty people, revolutionized my theological consciousness. Nothing in seminary prepared me for this historic moment. It forced me to confront the blackness of my identity and to make theological sense of it.

Martin King helped define my *Christian* identity but was silent about the meaning of blackness in a world of white supremacy. His public thinking about the faith was designed to persuade white Christians to take seriously the humanity of Negroes. He challenged whites to be true to what they said in their political and religious documents of freedom and democracy. What King did not initially realize was how deeply flawed white Christian thinking is regarding race and the psychological damage done to the self-image of blacks.

To understand white racism and black rage in America, I turned to Malcolm X and black power. While King accepted white logic, Malcolm rejected it. "When [people] get angry," Malcolm said, "they aren't interested in logic, they aren't interested in odds, they aren't interested in consequences. When they get angry, they realize that the condition that they're in—that their suffering is unjust, immoral, illegal, and that anything they do to correct it or eliminate it, they're justified. When you develop that type of anger and speak in that voice, then we'll get some kind of respect and recognition, and some changes from these people who have been promising us falsely already for far too long."[2]

Malcolm saw more clearly than King the depth and complexity of racism in America, especially in the North. The North was more clever than the South and thus knew how to camouflage its exploitation of black people. White northern liberals represented themselves as the friends of the Negro and deceived King and many other blacks into believing that they really wanted to achieve racial justice in America. But Malcolm knew better, and he exposed their hypocrisy. He called white liberals "foxes" in contrast to southern "wolves." Malcolm saw no difference between the two, except that one smiles and the other growls when it eats you. Northern white liberals hated Malcolm for his uncompromising, brutal honesty. But blacks, especially the young people, loved him for it. He said publicly what most blacks felt but were afraid to say, except privately among themselves.

I first heard Malcolm speak while I was a student at Garrett, but I did not really listen to him. I was committed to Martin King, even hoped that he would accept the invitation offered him to become a professor of theology at Garrett. I regarded Malcolm as a racist and would have nothing to do with him. Malcolm X did not enter my theological consciousness until I left seminary and was challenged by the rise of the black consciousness movement in the middle of the 1960s. Black power, a child of Malcolm, forced me to take a critical look at Martin King and to discover his limits.

It is one thing to recognize that the gospel of Jesus demands justice in race relations and quite another to recognize that it demands that African Americans accept their blackness and reject its white distortions. When I turned to Malcolm, I discovered my blackness and realized that I could never be who I was called to be until I embraced my African heritage—completely and enthusiastically. Malcolm put the word *black* in black theology. He taught black scholars in religion and many preachers that a colorless Christianity is a joke—found only in the imaginary world of white theology. It is not found in the real world of white seminaries and churches. Nor is it found in black churches. That black people hate themselves is no accident of history. As I listened to Malcolm and meditated on his analysis of racism in America and the world, I became convinced by his rhetorical virtuosity. Speaking to blacks, his primary audience, he said:

> Who taught you to hate the color of your skin? Who taught you to hate the texture of your hair? Who taught you to hate the shape of your nose? Who taught you to hate yourself from the top of your head to the sole of your feet? Who taught you to hate your own kind? Who taught you to hate the race you belong to so much that you don't want to be around each other? You should ask yourself, "Who taught you to hate being what God gave you?"[3]

Malcolm challenged black ministers to take a critical look at Christianity, Martin King, and the Civil Rights movement. The challenge was so deep that we found ourselves affirming what many persons regarded as theological opposites: Martin and Malcolm, civil rights and black power, Christianity and blackness.

Just as Martin King may be regarded as America's most influential theologian and preacher, Malcolm X may be regarded as America's most trenchant race critic. As Martin's theological achievement may be compared to Augustine's and Luther's, Malcolm's race critique is as far-reaching as Marx's class critique and the current feminist critique of gender. Malcolm was the great master of suspicion in the area of race. No one before or after him analyzed the role of Christianity in promoting racism and its mental and material consequences upon lives of blacks as Malcolm did. He has no peer.

Even today, whites do not feel comfortable listening to or reading Malcolm. They prefer Martin because he can easily be made more palatable to their way of thinking. That is why we celebrate Martin's birthday as a national holiday, and nearly every city has a street named in his honor. Many seminaries have a chair in his name, even though their curriculums do not take his theology seriously. When alienated blacks turn to Malcolm, whites turn to Martin as if they really care about his ideas, which most do not. Whites care about Martin only as a way of undermining the black allegiance to Malcolm.

When Malcolm X was resurrected in black power in the second half of the 1960s, whites turned to Martin King. White religious leaders tried to force militant black ministers to choose between Martin and Malcolm, integration and separation, Christianity and black power. But we rejected their demand and insisted on the importance of both. The tension between Martin and Malcolm, integration and separation, Christianity and blackness created black theology. It was analogous to the "double-consciousness," the "two unreconciled strivings," that W. E. B. Du Bois wrote about in *The Souls of Black Folk* in 1903.

Martin King taught black ministers that the meaning of Christianity was inextricably linked with the fight for justice in the society. That was his great contribution to black theology. He gave it its Christian identity, putting the achievement of social justice at the heart of what it means to be a Christian. He did not write a great treatise on the theme of Christianity and justice. He organized a movement that transformed Christian thinking about race and the struggles for justice in America and throughout the world.

Malcolm X taught black ministers and scholars that the identity of African American as a people was inextricably linked with blackness. This was his great contribution to black theology. Malcolm gave black theology its *black* identity, putting blackness at the center of who we were created to be. Like Martin, Malcolm did not write a scholarly treatise on the theme of blackness and self. He revolutionized black self-understanding with the power of his speech.

The distinctiveness of black theology is the bringing together of Martin and Malcolm—their ideas about Christianity and justice and blackness and self. Neither Martin nor Malcolm sought to do that. The cultural identity of Christianity was not important to Martin because he understood it in the "universal" categories he was taught in graduate school. His main concern was to link the identity of Christianity with social justice, oriented in love and defined by hope.

The Christian identity of the black self was not important to Malcolm X. For him, Christianity was the white man's religion and thus had to be rejected. Black people, Malcolm contended, needed a black religion, one that would bestow self-respect on them for being black. Malcolm was not interested in remaking Christianity into a black religion.

The creators of black theology disagreed with both Martin and Malcolm and insisted on the importance of bringing blackness and Christianity together. The beginning of black theology may be dated with the publication of the "black power" statement by black religious leaders in the *New York Times*, July 31, 1966, a few weeks after the rise of black power during the James Meredith march in Mississippi. Soon afterward, the National Committee of Negro Churchmen was organized as the organizational embodiment of their religious concerns. It did not take long for the word *black* to replace the word *Negro*, as black ministers struggled with the religious meaning of Martin and Malcolm, Christianity and blackness, nonviolence and self-defense, "freedom now" and "by any means necessary."

I sat down to write *Black Theology and Black Power* in the summer of 1968. Martin and Malcolm challenged me to think deep and long about the meaning of Christianity and blackness. Through them, I found my theological voice to articulate the black rage against racism in the society, in the churches, and in theology. It was a liberating experience. I knew that most of my former professors at Garrett and Northwestern would have trouble with what I was saying about liberation and Christianity, blackness and the gospel. One even told me that all I was doing was seeking justification for blacks on the Southside and Westside of Chicago to come to Evanston and kill him. But I could not let white fear distract me from the intellectual task of exploring the theological meaning of double-consciousness in black people.

Martin and Malcolm symbolize the tension between the African and American heritage of black people. We are still struggling with the tension, and its resolution is nowhere in sight. We can't resolve it because the social, political, and economic conditions that created it are still with us today. In fact, these conditions are worse today for the black poor, the one-third of us who reside primarily in the urban centers such as Chicago and New York.

It is appalling that seminaries and divinity schools continue their business as usual—analyzing so many interesting and irrelevant things—but ignoring the people who could help us to understand the meaning of black exploitation and rage in this society. Why are two of the most prophetic race critics of the church and society marginal in seminary curriculums? If we incorporated Martin's and Malcolm's critiques of race and religion into our way of thinking, it would revolutionize our way of doing theology, just as class and gender critiques have done.

But taking race seriously is not a comfortable task for whites or blacks. It is not easy for whites to listen to a radical analysis of race because blackness is truly *Other* to them—creating a horrible, unspeakable fear. When whites think of evil, they think of black. That is why the word *black* is still the most potent symbol of evil. If whites want to direct attention from an evil that they themselves have committed, they say a black did it. We are the most potent symbols of crime, welfare dependency, sexual harassment, domestic violence, and bad government. Say a black did it, whites will believe you. Some blacks will too.

With black being such a powerful symbol of evil, white theologians avoid writing and talking about black theology. Even though black theologians were among the earliest exponents of liberation theology, we are often excluded when panels and conferences are held on the subject. One could hardly imagine a progressive divinity school without a significant interpreter of feminist and Latin American liberation theology. But the same is not true for black theology. The absence of a serious and sustained engagement of black theology in seminaries and divinity schools is not an accident. It happens because black is the Other—strange, evil, and terrifying.

But theology can never be true to itself in America without engaging blackness, encountering its complex, multilayered meaning. Theology, as with American society as a whole, can never be true to itself unless it comes to terms with Martin and Malcolm together. They spoke two different but complementary truths about blackness that white theologians do not want to hear, but must hear if we are to create theologies that are liberating and a society that is humane and just for all its citizens. Only then can we sing, without hypocrisy, with Martin King, along with Malcolm X, the black spiritual: "Free at last, free at last, thank God almighty, we are free at last."

Chapter 7

Black Theology

The Notion of Culture Revisited

Dwight Hopkins

The notion of culture has been and remains one of the prominent emphases in black theology as it has emerged and continues to develop in South Africa, in the United States, and in its various forms in different regions of the world. A basic claim of black theology historically and today is that there is a positive and affirming relationship between, on the one hand, people of African descent or the darker peoples of the world and, on the other hand, the liberating message of Jesus Christ as a manifestation of God's justice and attention to the "little ones" of society. In other words, the divine presence amid the brokenness of injustice reveals itself in the particularity of oppressed peoples' cultures. Thus, though there are varieties of black theology, they all presuppose the reality of culture, the centrality of culture, and the necessity of culture as a location for revelation. One only has to have a cursory acquaintance with the emergence of black theology in South Africa, the United States, Zimbabwe, Ghana, England, Cuba, Brazil, Jamaica, India, and other global regions to see the taken-for-grantedness of the notion of culture.

In these theological movements (which are basically attempts to discern the role of culture in developing a theological anthropology), we can notice profound grappling with how God relates to or encounters locked-out voices in their Christian and indigenous faith claims. Debates unfold around the nature of black culture, black Christian culture, African indigenous culture, and the mixture or intertwining of different cultures. Questions arise such as: How does God liberate in the midst of contemporary postmodern culture? In the struggle to become full human beings, who can live out the authenticity of cultural identities as black people or people of African descent? What is the relationship between politics and culture or economics and culture? There are even concerns relative to the culture of globalization and its impact on the movement of black theology as a global phenomenon. And, furthermore, the question arises: What are the spiritual dimensions of culture?

Again, what is presupposed in the complex nuances of these investigations and queries is a preunderstood notion of culture in black theology. What I suggest in this presentation is that the notion of culture needs to be revisited. We need to deepen the conversation around its definition in order to bring clarity to that which is so easily assumed.

Moreover, the idea of culture, I would argue, is central to any conversation about Christianity. One looks at the Christian religion and discovers an additional warrant for investigating culture. The Christian religion logically presupposes the Divine descending vertically into the horizontal cultural plane. Even without biblical "evidence" or textual verification, we can deduce the following. If an ultimate power greater than oneself exists, the human person has knowledge of or encounters such an entity only in culture. We become aware of this ultimate spirit, hope, vision, faith, or presence by this revelation revealing itself. If we could discern the ultimate without the ultimate coming into the penultimate, then the penultimate would have the potentiality and actuality of initiating (and thereby in a sense controlling) the divine–human encounter. With that power, why would the human person need an ultimate? Obviously, the range of the different positions is vast: from a Christian humanist position that God created humans with free will and God removed Godself from human affairs in order to allow humans to arbitrate the will in human culture, to a more fundamentalist Christian stance of an absolutist, all-controlling deity.

Finally, biblical instructions call for a clarification of the notion of culture. Philippians 2:5–8 reads: "Let the same mind be in you that was in Christ Jesus, who, though he was in the form of God, did not regard equality with God as something to be exploited, but emptied himself, taking the form of a slave, being born in human likeness. And being found in human form, he humbled himself and became obedient to the point of death—even death on a cross." Here the ultimate reality or sacred being decides to relate to the penultimate by emptying itself into the cultural clothing of the human realm. God pours out Godself into human culture. Similarly, the birth narratives indicate the conscious decision of Divinity to reveal itself into human culture, this time underscoring marginalized human culture. An unwed mother engaged to be married gives birth to an "illegitimate" son in a barn with livestock, straw, dirt, and cow dung because there were no accommodations in an inn; and one could speculate that the family did not have any wealth to use to bribe any innkeepers for lodging. And the political and military authorities (i.e., the apparatus of the state and those who control the state) search for this child in order to destroy it. Again, in Jesus' inaugural remarks about his purpose on earth, as announced in Luke 4:18ff., we find his accenting the fact that God consciously chose to enter human affairs for those in systems of exploitation—such as the materially poor, those in jail cells, the broken-hearted, and the oppressed in society. The Bible offers various narratives. Yet a central thread is the incarnation of a divinity into the dire predicament of people far from the centers of power and wealth. In a word, Christian revelation is a cultural dynamic colored by the social conditions and collective experiences of peripheral communities in the biblical witness.

If we accept the dynamic of doing theology as a cultural process, in the sense of an ultimate intermingling with the penultimate (that is, the God–human connection is profoundly situated in culture), and that culture is a foundational cornerstone in black theology, then it follows that more fully to comprehend this intermingling or connection, one is encouraged to unpack the notion of culture.

What I have found helpful, particularly as it relates to black theology, is to begin to examine critically some conceptual sources from various writers throughout Africa. They have proven insightful for different reasons. They represent engagements with culture from different African perspectives. First, culture is approached from the vantage of African ethnicities. Second, culture is engaged from the viewpoint of what it means to be black. Third, culture is approached from the position of marginalized voices. And fourth, culture is attended to from an interdisciplinary orientation. So let us turn to the constituent dimensions of culture.

THE NOTION OF CULTURE

Culture, as defined by Randwedzi Nengwekhulu, has three intertwined aspects. It is (1) "the totality of the results of human labour, i.e. the results of material and spiritual wealth created by human labour, culture is 'the development of human productive forces.'" Human labor is complemented by what Nengwekhulu calls (2) "spiritual culture. This includes philosophy, science, ideology, art, literature, religion, education, etc.," "expressed in and through concepts of spirit and spirituality." And these two (i.e., human labor and the spiritual) are closely tied to (3) "'artistic culture' which is in reality the figurative objectification of artistic creativity." Culture, defined in its three manifestations of human labor, the spiritual, and the artistic, operates in an interpenetrating activity as it experiences the interplay between the material and the spiritual. Nengwekhulu underscores the relative autonomy of the spiritual aspect from the material. That is, the spiritual aspect of culture is not a passive reflection of the material/economic. Spirituality is relatively autonomous. It, too, can take the lead in the human labor–spiritual–artistic relations. Nonetheless, though relatively autonomous, Nengwekhulu states that the spiritual is rooted in the material aspects of social life. Hence changes in the economics of production are accompanied by changes in the other definitions of culture.[1]

At this stage of the discussion, a three-part definition of culture helps underscore the interconnections between material and spiritual realities in such a way that all of humanity's activities include the realm of culture. In addition, we see a clear distinction between the material and the spiritual. The separation (obviously for intellectual purposes, for, in the real world of human activity, they occur together, simultaneously) fosters a further look at each component part.

The human labor aspect of culture surfaces issues of political economy. However, it does not pertain to a vulgar Marxist concept whereby the economic base gives rise to a superstructure that, in turn, is merely a passive, noneffecting reflection of the material base. Stuart Hall, drawing on Raymond Williams's *Long Revolution*, lays to rest this theoretically polarized flaw when he argues "against the literal operations of the base-superstructure metaphor, which in classical Marxism ascribed the domain of ideas and of meanings to the 'superstructure,' themselves conceived as merely reflective of and determined in some simple fashion by 'the base,' without a social effectivity of their own." In this clarification, one avoids a vulgar materialism and a unilateral economic determinism, where the superstructure's role acts as an epiphenomenon.[2] Such a conceptual failure obscures the full liberating creativity and potential of the spiritual and artistic parts of culture.

Moreover, Stuart Hall discerns this understanding of culture not only in opposition to the mistaken, crass epiphenomenon move but also in contrast to highbrow cultural definitions. Incorrectly, the latter stance portrays and privileges a notion of real culture emanating from the realm of ideas. In the skewed lens of this highbrow culture, culture becomes one of perfection, or "the sum of the 'best that has been thought and said,' regarded as the summits of an achieved civilization." Such elite or bourgeois culture excludes vibrant possibilities from the remainder of society (indeed, the majority of the citizenry) and therefore, for Hall, requires a democratization and socialization. To combat this deviation, he suggests that culture really consists of disparate forms of a social process—"the giving and taking of meanings, and the slow development of 'common' meanings—a common culture." Hence he takes on the "idealist" and "civilized" notions of culture by substituting a sense of culture as "ordinary."[3]

Again drawing on Raymond Williams, Hall further clarifies culture as referring to and disclosed in social practices. By social practices, he underscores the interrelations among "elements or social practices normally separated out," so that culture as a whole way of life does not simply represent practices (i.e., in some sociological works) or mere ethnographic accounts (i.e., in some anthropological renderings) but an organized intertwining of human efforts. Culture is indeed, for Hall, "threaded through all social practices, and is the sum of their interrelationship." Culture underlies all social practices as patterns of organization or forms of human energy. The theoretician's task is to unravel the layered dimensions of these relationships as they are organized throughout society. Hall terms this reconfigured definition of culture (that is, reconfigured over against the idealist, civilized, and vulgar Marxist approaches) as "radical interactionism"; a nonprivileging of any one practice as the sole initiating agent in causality.[4]

Similarly, W. Emmanuel Abraham adheres to a more comprehensive notion of culture. Though not employing the suggestive phrase "whole way of life," Abraham's sense of culture verifies this definition. For him, culture encompasses not only the spiritual and material; it denotes, in addition, emotional, intellectual, and ethical features "which characterize the heritage of a society or social group."[5] With additional nuance, he expands the elements of culture with politics, economics, education, art, literature, and religion. In a certain interpretation, Abraham mirrors Stuart Hall and Hall's appropriation of Raymond Williams. Abraham appreciates the complexity and challenge of deciphering an investigation of culture that yields no simple description. Thus he opposes a static locking of culture into a metaphysical idealism or a false civilized elitism. And, in symmetry with Williams, he shuns a mechanical effectivity of economic base producing the superstructure.

What is interesting about Abraham's take on culture is his inclusion of such phenomena as the emotional, intellectual, and religious, without obscuring concepts of politics, economics, and more. In this fashion, he broadens the notion of culture beyond, perhaps, a commonsensical intuitive posture that portrays culture as primarily constrained within the boundaries of art and a narrow understanding of the aesthetic; and he launches the conversation beyond the arguments sometimes captured in reaction to the base–superstructure program already established by crude Marxism. Abraham unlocks the broader and more creative potentiality of perceiving culture pervading the too often underrecognized vectors of human energy or practices (in Stuart Hall's and Raymond Williams's signification). That is to say, the very texture of human being (i.e., to feel, emote, and think) exists as a cultural moment. For my purpose, as I develop further my own stance below, Abraham establishes a threshold for viewing the sacred seeping into more obvious traits of the human person that separate us from the nonhuman world.[6]

In addition, Emmanuel Abraham, drawing on his own heritage, cites the African as a complex cultural being—"an accumulation of a variety of cultural fragments. He [or she] is endowed with a base of . . . traditional culture, which is by now irreversibly impregnated at various levels by elements of other cultures, some of which were imposed and others sought and acquired."[7] In this regard, culture denotes a syncretism, a core intermixed with various and sundry cultural strands combined to yield the culture of a people. Because he utilizes the African (more pointedly, his Ghanaian lineage) to substantiate his claim, I find it highly instructive in forging clarity on the definitional dimensions of the notion of culture. For instance, I am currently working on a project that is developing a theological anthropology using as primary sources African American folktales, which are the offspring of an African matrix. These black folktales also result from a cultural hybridity or cultural syncretism. Clearly, one does not have to submerge oneself in the vibrant and intricate controversy between Melville J. Herskovits and E. Franklin Frazier (the first an anthropologist, the second a sociologist) or the similar debate between William A. Bascom and Richard M. Dorson (both anthropologists).[8] And neither does one have to be an Afrocentrist theoretician (such as

Molefe Asante) to accept some impact of African culture on those Africans enslaved in the so-called New World and on their descendants today.[9] Likewise, at some historical juncture in the North American context, some creative and vital interface occurred between Native Americans/American Indians and black Americans.[10] And Frazier and Dorson both claim a heavy dosage of European and European American substance in black culture.[11] Indeed, culture exists as a variety of cultural fragments, with some more prominent than others.

Returning to Emmanuel Abraham's stance on culture, he concludes his theoretical remarks by suggesting a three-part typology for culture in general:

> The culture of a people has many dimensions. They include a pedagogical one, teaching the common wisdom to succeeding generations and yielding the symbols and means for communicating that wisdom; an ethical one, declaring principles of sensibility and action, and sketching out the basis and limits of tolerance and cooperation; a prophetic one, bearing on the norms and future history of its people.[12]

The importance of culture, for him, does not lie in an abstract descriptive mode. Nor is it just an interesting cerebral exercise. Culture matters for the well-being, survival, freedom, and future of a people. Therefore, it brings with it hortatory import that teaches intergenerationally, provides boundaries for right and wrong action in community, and declares normativities as internal, self-critical mechanisms in order for a people to keep renewing, renourishing, and thereby growing. Such a cultural frame is heuristic for advancing a theological anthropology, since theological anthropology surfaces out of and spreads throughout culture. In other words, a goal of theological anthropology (itself wrestling with what have human beings been created and called to be, believe, say, and do regarding matters of ultimate concern), assuming Abraham's schema, is to participate in these instructive aspects of culture. What is intimated is that culture and theological anthropology take stands (obviously within the human predicament) on perceived rights for definite communities.

To further the conversation around culture revisited, the remainder of my presentation uses the three categories from Nengwekhulu's definition of culture to frame our examination—the categories of human labor, the artistic, and the spiritual.

HUMAN LABOR

Amilcar Cabral's insights build on Abraham's position linking culture with pedagogy, ethics, and the prophetic; that is to say, culture is contextual and impacted by social location. Moreover, we move to Cabral's stance because he takes up the debate (mentioned previously) about the human labor or political-economic trajectory in the notion of culture advanced by Nengwekhulu. Within black theology, this sector of the African or black peoples finds itself located in a definite political economy. Hence, revisiting economics vis-à-vis culture is warranted at this point.

Cabral offers the following broad materialist-related definition of culture: There are

> strong, dependent and reciprocal relationships existing between the *cultural situation* and the *economic* (and political) *situation* in the behavior of human societies. In fact, culture is always in the life of a society (open or closed), the more or less conscious result of the economic and political activities of that society, the more or less dynamic expression of the kinds of relationships which prevail in that society, on the one hand between [the human person] (considered individually or collectively) and nature and, on the other hand, among individuals, groups of individuals or classes.[13]

Culture emerges out of the human energy, creativity, and struggle exerted by the human person (i.e., individual self or communal selves) in relation to nature (i.e., technological and natural) and in relation to various human beings occupying definite societal positions. The idea of culture, then, operates not in and of itself, as a conceptualization isolated from the material formations of how people organize both their micro-everyday living and their macro-systemic arrangements. Human beings are conscious of their cultural choices and intended creations. Culture, furthermore, has definite links to political and economic activities prevailing in a period and ties to specific traditions again influenced by culture's relation to the historical development of humanly created economic and political setups. Cabral's accent on the dependent and reciprocal connections of the cultural and the political-economic allows for more interplay among these human factors. Not a unidirectional dynamic but an effecting and receiving movement obtains here.

Cabral also adds a view of history and the mode of production as they play a part in cultural development. Whatever culture's traits, culture acts as an essential part of a people's history; and, for Cabral, history and culture both have the mode of production for their concrete basis. His definition of the mode of production fosters an understanding of the culture–history–mode of production overlapping. He comments:

> Now, in any given society, the level of development of the productive forces and the system for social utilization of these forces (the ownership system) determine the *mode of production*. In our opinion, the mode of production, whose contradictions are manifested with more or less intensity through the class struggle, is the principal factor in the history of any human group, the level of the productive forces being the true and permanent driving power of history.[14]

Culture is greatly determined by the economic interactions and positioning among people. More specifically, one's ownership of, power of distribution of, and relationship to material wealth (i.e., nature, technology, machinery, and people) can impact on one's cultural creativity and perception of culture. Likewise, class relations (that is, who owns wealth rather than only income, and who owns, controls, and distributes the materials used for economic production in a society) express the dynamics and traditions of human interactions—hence the mode of production powers human history. Because class connections are dynamic, are expressions of the mode of production, and provide the engine for history, and because culture has both the materialist base of the mode of production and is an element of human history, then when one speaks of culture, one simultaneously speaks about history and the mode of production. Therefore, however one defines culture, if culture is somehow wrapped up in the mode of production (i.e., issues of ownership of wealth), then culture touches on classes and their social, economic, and political differentiations.

Cabral, no crass economic determinist, states that culture is constituted by oral and written traditions, works of art, dance, cosmological ideas, music, religious beliefs, social structures, politics, and economics. Yet his underscoring the culture–history–political economy dimension facilitates a perspective of culture as a mode of historical and dynamic resistance. Because culture has a materialist relationship, the advancement of progressive culture (i.e., one against the monopolization of power over others) can, in its reciprocal relationship to its materialist connection, both reflect the level of wealth ownership and distribution and spur on opposition to nondemocratic social relations in the areas of material life. Culture can assume an agential role in the resistance to and possible transformation of how people operate in the structures of a society's economics and politics. Indeed, cultural resistance, Cabral submits, generally precedes comparable resistance in the domains of economics and politics.

Again exemplifying the reciprocal nature of culture, Cabral claims that those who intentionally participate in "liberation" movements signify "the organized political expression of the culture of the people who are undertaking" the effort for the democratization of ownership of wealth, environment, and social activities. Not only can culture influence certain parts of the mode of the production, but politics can also impact on certain dimensions of culture; thus politics, by way of culture, can act on the mode of production as well.[15] As with Emmanuel Abraham's above-mentioned argument, Cabral subscribes to the traits of culture being, among other things, pedagogical, ethical, and prophetic.

Yet Cabral brings additional conceptual categories into the notion of culture. He clearly opts for a popular culture, that which emanates more or less from social sectors lacking ownership and control over wealth. While embracing the creativity from all civic strata, including the privileged, Cabral emphasizes "people's culture." In his summation, he offers these final cultural goals: the development, first, of popular culture, or people's culture, based on positive values indigenous to this grouping; development of a national culture based on the history of struggle for justice; promotion of political and moral awareness along with patriotism (of course, a patriotism circumscribed by the democratization of the mode of production and all that relates to it—i.e., history and culture); development of scientific culture to foster material progress; the advancement of a universal culture inclusive of art, science, literature, and so forth; and the assertion of humanistic practices such as solidarity with, devotion to, and respect for other people.[16] I agree with Cabral's method of focusing on the initial dynamic of people's culture;

for me in my social location, this indicates black folktales—a unique tradition of those North Americans of African descent occupying structures of poverty and extreme locations away from ownership of wealth and distribution of wealth (that is to say, peripheralized citizens within the mode of production). And I concur with his emphasis on moving from this particularity out into the universal implications of people's culture as they contribute to the general human storehouse of experiences while, concomitantly, learning from and appreciating what overall human creativity and energies offer all specific cultures.

If the sacred-human connection unfolds within culture, if political economy pertains to a part of cultural definitions, and if class differentiations express the mode of production within political economy, then Lucius T. Outlaw adds a further nuance to the interplay among economics, politics, and ideology as living phenomena in culture. Lucius Outlaw argues that classes result from, as previously detailed, their connection to the mode of production. Outlaw, however, wants to delve into the mixture of political and ideological causality (linked to class, of course). That is to say, how is it possible actually to foreground the effectivity of class relations while accounting for the agential and proactive role of politics and ideology as parts of culture? For Outlaw, "classes . . . are effects of 'an ensemble of the structures of a mode of production and social formation . . . and of their relations, first at the economic level, second, at the political level, and third, at the ideological level.'"[17] Classes, therefore, come about not exclusively from economic factors or motivations. Classes arise from the determinations by the mode of production as well as social-political and ideological relations.

Outlaw then clarifies more specifically how classes are constituted by both structures and relationships. Structure signifies one's position in the ownership and distribution of the economic production process, while relationships underscore one's political and ideological realities, linked to the economic but in a non-hermetic fashion. The structural location, moreover, simply denotes that objectively everyone has class location vis-à-vis the mode of production. In fact, some people own wealth and others merely work to receive income. Appeal to a unifying and positive cultural goal of *e pluribus unum* does not obscure this objective fact. Social agents, therefore, occupy a given social location independent of their will. Outlaw terms this the "structural determination" of classes.

Next, he moves to the distinction between, on the one hand, "objective" or "structural" and, on the other hand, one's class "position" in the social relations of production—that is, how one relates to reality through the media of the political and the ideological. At these junctures, social agency can decide to act to maintain the economic status quo or seek transformation. The rise of the economic productive forces (i.e, wealth, technology, and utilization of nature) includes a rise of political and ideological relations among citizens. In general terms, those who disproportionately own, have access to, and exert decision-making power over a country's productive forces develop certain political modalities and ideological justifications to maintain their objective ties to the mode of production. Because the political and ideological aspects provide more autonomous activity than one's link to the economic, there exists a fluidity in the choices that different classes make and even the choices acted on intraclass.

This inter- and intraclass maneuverability in the political and ideological domains, for Outlaw, is further brought to light in his notion of "subgroupings." Classes are constituted by subgroupings. These conceptual additions provide the conditions for the possibility for people to use their human wills to carry out choices and actions. He states:

> However, classes can be further distinguished by subgroupings. There can be "fractions" and "strata" that have their bases in differentiations within the relations of production and in differing political and ideological commitments/ relations of various groupings of people. And there are "social categories," i.e., groupings of agents defined principally by their place in political and ideo-logical relations such as intellectuals or a state bureaucracy.[18]

Though they might have objective structural economic positioning in society, disparate subgroupings can, in fact, act contrary to their class/structural location. Consequently, working-class people can act politically and ideologically against their own position in favor of the owners of wealth. So, too, members of the own-ing class can act politically and ideologically against their own economic status and in favor of working people. Therefore, ideological and political intricacies sometimes supersede and condition one's perception of the economic. Culture, as a total way of life inclusive of dynamic and living class and subgrouping real-ities, means the possibility of ever-changing micro-everyday activities and macro-structural configurations. In other words, class and subgroupings can transform cultures because cultures are, in large part, the creations of proactive human indi-vidual and collective human beings.

THE ARTISTIC

Culture, drawing on Randwedzi Nengwekhulu's previously cited definition, con-sists of the totality of human labor, spiritual culture, and artistic culture. Our extended conversation regarding the political economy of culture attempts to broaden Nengwekhulu's dimension of human labor. Now we view what he terms "artistic culture"; specifically, what I'd like to talk about is culture's aesthetic tra-jectories. For this part of the discussion, we draw on Barry Hallen's interesting suggestions in his work on Nigerian culture since the 1970s.

Hallen's scholarly work (that of a formerly trained philosopher) approaches indigenous worldviews of the aesthetic by conversing with the elders of a local community. In his case, he argues that the systematic comprehension of the aes-thetic aspects of culture are disclosed in the intellect of the *onisegun*. The latter, roughly translated as the masters of medicine, herbalists, or alternative medical doctors, are the repositories of the collective wisdom, experience, and traditions of the Yoruba.[19] After decades of interrogation of and being, in turn, interrogated by the *onisegun*, Hallen discovered that cultural aesthetics pertained not so much to arts or crafts, though these were not lacking in his investigation, but to the relevance of "beauty" as a manifestation of the aesthetic. Here, too, beauty was deployed not primarily regarding arts and crafts but as beauty related to people or human beings.

The aesthetic or beauty of a person referenced the body and the type of clothing worn by an individual. For instance, one is liked, in the sense of being beautiful, due to the color and fitting of clothing; hence beauty of the physical is enhanced by the type of outerwear or exterior trappings displayed in bodily appearance. Yet even this perspective of beauty is consistently coupled with ethical traits of the human being's personality. Hallen comments: "In virtually every account of the term, . . . beauty as a physical attribute was rated superficial and unimportant by comparison with good moral character as a . . . form of 'inner' beauty."[20] One recognizes beauty manifested in the corporeal, highlighted by clothing or other outer adornments. Still, deeper beauty, which supersedes even the initial perception of the eye, must be detected by righteous ethics in conduct. The absence of a good moral character defiled perceived beauty, making the latter rather superficial. In contrast, individuals can lack in good looks, rhetorical eloquence, and social adeptness but embody a good person's personality. Therefore, beauty and character accompany one another. The *onisegun* claimed consistently: "If the person . . . is good looking . . . , but his or her innermost self . . . is bad, they will still call him or her an immoral person. . . . Whenever anybody does bad things, it means his or her inside self may be bad." The inside of an individual controlled the community's determination of the individual's beauty. When a physically attractive individual actually turns out to possess bad moral character, this signifies that the innermost self of the individual is bad or immoral.[21] The verbal and nonverbal behaviors become decisive in adjudicating the presence of beauty in character. The aesthetic or beauty in culture coexists and accompanies moral attributes, and thus the community (i.e., the collective selves) offers a norm to ferret out beautiful and nonbeautiful human character in the human being (i.e., the individual self).

The aesthetic of the person is accompanied by the aesthetic of the natural. "By natural," Hallen purports, "is meant the 'world of' nature, of all those things that are neither human nor (hu)man-made. In a sense, 'human' being also is a part of nature, of course, but what sets it apart from all other things in the world is the kind of self."[22] The distinguishing marks between human self and nature denote the former's intelligence, ability to speak, and possession of moral character. With this differentiation in genus, the aesthetic of the natural consists of the human self admiring or valuing an object of nature simply for its external, physical beauty. For instance, the coloration of the natural or the fullness of its bodily dimensions can point to beauty in and of itself. Such an aesthetic passes the consensual judgment understood or enunciated by a communal perspective. Still, in the same cultural context the aesthetic of the natural can result from its utility, somewhat like that criterion elaborated about the aesthetic of the person whereby, though one acknowledges the potentiality of beauty of the human self for its own sake, the moral character provides a more genuine sense of an individual's beauty. In this context, one labels the "character" of the natural based on situating the natural object within human groups and adjudicating beauty relative to the natural object's utilitarian functions for that community.[23]

Finally, Hallen offers the aesthetic of the "(hu)man made," the consequence of human creation and energy to manufacture that which is neither strictly the natural or inherently already given in the definition of the person. Common characteristics of such beauty include color, newness, the finishing process, or the shininess of human-manufactured objects. Hallen, moreover, concedes that these aesthetic traits are found in descriptions of art. What he hopes to add to this commonly accepted portrayal is the aesthetic aspects of and, usually, disregarded beauty of "plebeian objects" such as a person's farm, thereby aiding in righting "the aesthetic imbalance" resulting "from collectors' and art historians' disproportionate concerns with figurative carvings and sculpture." Again, like the aesthetics of the person and of the natural, the aesthetic of the human-made draws its character (that is, a community's hierarchy of values regarding better and lesser quality) from the usefulness and durability of the human-manufactured object.[24]

J. P. Odoch Pido, from his extensive knowledge of the Acoli community (in northern Uganda), cites a similar interweaving of behavioral and physical qualities relative to the idea of aesthetics. Within this framework, aesthetics, for him defined as good appearance, is constituted by avoidance of too many extremes in the material makeup or natural attributes of the object of beauty. For example, one can be tall but not too tall, and neither too fat nor too thin. Furthermore, "in addition to [this] inherited proportion and complexion," one appreciates beauty due to the nature of the "characteristic makeup, hair, and clothing . . . styles."[25] Pido goes on to deploy the concept of "classic beauty" when the beauty of an individual self merits the approval of the norms of community. Though such beauty initially appears to suggest approbation, it also intimates a negative dimension, for two reasons. First, classic beauty has a tendency to attract an "evil eye," one who has no righteous intention. Second, in a more theological vein, such a beauty could rival absolute beauty inherent only to God. Thus, in his further refinement of the beautiful trajectory in the aesthetic, Pido presents "good" beauty in contrast to classic beauty. Good beauty is that which has or evokes unambiguous approval on the part of one's community. He argues:

> The socially approved appearance is human, not overly extreme, and is what I refer to as "good," as opposed to classic, appearance. Good appearance is attractive, likeable, and beautiful; it influences in a positive fashion the relationships among the individual who bears this appearance and the people around him [or her]; consequently, it makes the person comfortable and secure, especially around people he or she is well acquainted with.[26]

At first glance, one perceives a potential contradiction in this depiction of beauty. Beauty is welcomed and affirmed in community; still beauty has to not be automatically accepted but interrogated for its potential underlying negativities. Pido resolves the apparent dilemma by drawing in the idea of "fame" and its attendant problematic. Fame, exemplary of the complexities of beauty, carries with it a certain degree of uncomfortableness and insecurity for individuals representative of the attribute—"often a source of focused public gaze, obsession, and even envy and hate toward those who have it." Concomitantly, it suggests for the community that shortcomings accompany beauty, such as lack of industriousness or other imperfections. Hence, the human self does not participate in any abstract portrayal of pure beauty, for that would defy normative communal claims and, perhaps even more important, challenge the status of God's unblemished aesthetic.

Lastly, Pido pushes his position to further broaden his understanding of beauty or an aesthetic of the body. Specifically, good behavior becomes an integral component of desired beauty within the communal context. Good behavior, akin to good beauty (in contrast to classic beauty), avoids extremes. And sought-after behavior does not evince a natural state. On the contrary, how one acts in an acceptable manner derives from a combination of training and experience. In general, "a person is said to behave well when he or she is humble, tolerant, kind, considerate, and morally right." Hence the truly beautiful, for Pido, embodies the marriage of good appearance and good behavior.[27] In this regard, beauty is a dynamic or process of acquiring attributes through socialization as part of social interaction, sometimes by instructions and at other times by trial and error. One attains beauty when one's physical characteristics are amplified by the repeated grooming of doing in accord with those who surround the physically beautiful individual. In this more precise way, the group fosters and forges an aesthetic of the body and an aesthetic of behavior into the truly beautiful.

Innocent C. Onyewuenyi sums up the idea of the aesthetic (or artistic culture), as the second subset of the larger notion of culture, in three frames. Art, for him, is constituted by the functional, the depersonalized, and the community-oriented. The arts (i.e., the visual, kinetic, poetic, and musical) participate in functionality when they "are designed to serve practical, meaningful purposes, and that beauty of appearance is secondary. All the same, functional beauty can also be regarded as beauty."[28] A mask or other form of art exhibits beauty not because it might seem "ugly" in appearance but due to its role in the ritual of dance or the practice of religions or its otherwise serving the vivification of a local context. In a word, it facilitates life-giving or community-building energy. Again we encounter the viewpoint of not art for art's sake but a measure of determining the configurations of beauty or the artistic by way of contextualized lenses and norms of socialized and traditioned warrants.

Regarding the attribute of the depersonalized, Onyewuenyi asserts, as a combination, artistic individuality and social functionality. Drawing on disparate exemplars of African art, he declares:

> When we say that African art is depersonalized we mean that the artist's concern is not to express his/her own individual ideas and feelings. The African

artist works from a background diametrically opposed to the Nietzschean expressionist influence. . . . He/she performs rather in such a way as to fulfill the ritual and social purposes of a community for whom the arts are meant to regulate the spiritual, political, and social forces within the community.[29]

In a sense, beauty, aesthetics, or artistic sensibilities of individual creativity harmonize with the other people around the particular artist. Such an aesthetic venture suggests great art as that which forges and engenders positive community interaction. It adumbrates the possibility of gifted artists embodying, and being embedded by, the well-being of one's social location. Furthermore, art links to the spiritual, political, and social forces in which a community is engaged. In this sense, art and the artist perform a function amid the power dynamics deployed by different selves or groups of individuals. The product and the producer of aesthetics do not transcend politics; both operate within social specificity. And concluding his three facets of the aesthetic or artistic, Onyewuenyi adds the element of the community-oriented. The practices of functionality and the depersonalized orient themselves toward serving the health, needs, and desires of community. Clearly the aesthetic discloses itself as an interrelational dynamic or breathing phenomenon. Yet the individual adheres to professional freedom and individual creativity while she or he remains cognizant of the community's accepted and established forms of beauty. Within the parameters of responsibility to society, she or he can add nuance and the particularity of his or her genius.

THE SPIRITUAL

In the beginning of this conversation on the notion of culture and theological anthropology, Randwedzi Nengwekhulu elaborated three aspects to the definition of culture. So far, there has been an engagement with two of those postulations: *human labor* (or political economy) and the *artistic* (or the aesthetic). We turn now to his final category regarding the *spirit* in culture. Kwame Gyekye helps in this manner when he offers an understanding of "spirit" as inherent to culture: "I use the term 'culture' in a comprehensive sense, to encompass the entire life of a people: their morals, religious beliefs, social structures, political and educational systems, forms of music and dance, and all other products of their creative spirit."[30] Consequently, discussion about spirit denotes the creativity that unfolds in culture, a creativity that animates both human labor and the artistic. Beneath or powering all that human beings concoct (i.e., both the means of production and the relations of production) and each realization of art (i.e., as the aesthetic of the classical and the good works; as functional, depersonalized, and community-oriented) resides the spirit that weaves throughout the entire life of a community of common discourse and historical memory. Hence, when one speaks of the creative genius of that which results from human effort, either by the work of human labor or artistic labor, one speaks about a spirit often termed a special gift to create.

Again, aiding us in summing up our overarching approach to the spirit–culture interchange, Gyekye submits that one would be remiss to separate absolutely or draw too strong a divide between the religious and the nonreligious, the sacred and the secular, or the spiritual and the material. For my purposes, it is the last pairing that corroborates my claim of the spirit inherently dwelling as a dimension of culture. One cannot detach oneself from the ever-presence of something or someone or some being or some force greater than the human self or collective selves.[31] For Christians of all stripes, God fulfills this definition. God is the source of the creative energy of the human psyche, soul, and body—an originative force that allows the human self or the human selves to produce, by way of innovation, products that humans, on first take, would seem unable to produce. This is precisely what one often calls genius, or in more Christian language, a miracle. True acts of labor (as labor interacts with nature, other humans, and technology) and exceptional products of art (in the modes of the classical, good, functional, depersonalized, and community-oriented) are acclaimed by most communities as work far beyond the ordinary human feat. Indeed, it is often hailed as an *extra*ordinary accomplishment especially because it surpasses the expectations of the everyday, the mundane, or the usual.

If one still assumes that spirit is meshed in culture, then the former's positionality serves as foundation and scaffolding for culture's configuration. Patrick A. Kalilombe universalizes spirituality in the following assertion:

> Spirituality has been described generally as "those attitudes, beliefs and practices which animate people's lives and help them to reach out toward the super-sensible realities. . . ." It is the relationship between human beings and the invisible, inasmuch as such a relationship derives from a particular vision of the world, and in its turn affects the way of relating to self, to other people, and to the universe as a whole. In this sense, spirituality is not restricted to any one religion, but can be found variously in all religions and cultures. It is determined in the first place by the basic worldview of the persons or people concerned. It is also shaped by their life context, their history, and the various influences that enter a people's life.[32]

The outlook, practices, values, beliefs, and attitudes that underlie and animate religion and culture define spirituality. Deepening the question of animation, Kalilombe discerns two sources in the dynamic of spirituality engaging culture. In a word, from whence does spirituality originate? Two primary sources, among others, are the past and the present. One cannot track spirit in culture without historical genealogy commingled with contemporary investigation; for culture, which encompasses spirit, mutates and develops. The history of all cultures seems to suggest the prior existence of what one might call indigenous culture. As regional and global interactions process in human history, indigenous cultures become modified, either by absorbing foreign cultures or by suffering from the dominating presence of foreign culture. The original precontact culture does not become entirely obliterated when aggressive alien forces become present. Nor does indigenous culture absorb outside influence without the former undergoing disparate degrees of transformation. Therefore, uniformity and alteration occur in culture and spirituality. Extrapolating from his own native culture of Malawi (Central Africa), Kalilombe claims that culture and spirituality change due to the interaction with foreign pressure (i.e, the external encounter) and the natural unraveling within indigenous culture (i.e., the internal exigences). Thus, on the one hand, people never emerge as a *tabula rasa*; history matters. On the other hand, to avoid a romantic conception of traditional culture, one has to take very seriously contemporary impact and gifts that arrive from whatever point of origin. The past worldview serves as a lens for interpreting the new contact; and the new contact, in turn, interweaves with the traditional to forge something novel that allows for the remainder of some core planks from indigenous spirituality or culture, yet synthesizes them with the modern.[33]

For Malawian traditional spirituality, humanity "(individuals and community) is at the center of consideration. . . . African spirituality is based on this centrality of human beings presently living in the concrete circumstances of life this side of the grave. It consists of their attitudes, beliefs, and practices as they strive to reach out toward the super-sensible realities: God, the spirits, and the invisible forces in the universe."[34] The first mark of indigenous spirituality, then, is its anthropocentric nature, human beings' reception of and vivification by divine spirit, or supersensible reality. Such a spirit allows human self and selves to make sense of the cosmic and quotidian struggle between the forces of life and the threat of death. Ultimately it concerns the pursuit of life worth living as good, harmonious, and meaningful. Given the consistent corporate theme adhered to so far in our conversation, traditional culture underscores humanity as primarily the community. Kalilombe, to highlight this point, offers the following aphorism: "It has often been said that where Descartes said, 'I think, therefore, I am' (*cogito ergo sum*), the African would rather say, 'I am related, therefore, we are' (*cognatus ergo sum*)."[35] The second mark of traditional spirituality, consequently, is its profound emphasis on "the value of interdependence through relationships" in contradistinction to individualism and personal independence in-and-of-itself. A submark of this community solidarity is hospitality, wherein family members and nonthreatening strangers are not allowed to suffer, be alone, or go hungry.

A third spirituality mark, flowing from community solidarity, is the outlook, value, and practice of "sharing and redistribution of resources so that no individual accumulates and hoards resources that become unavailable to others when they need them."[36] The individual self and collective selves are obligated by this requirement. The corollary of negative spirituality follows: the nonsanction of those who oppose the obligations and rights of solidarity and the more likely concomitant spirit of unkindness, unforgivingness, egotism, cruelty, and quarrelsomeness. Fourth, communal solidarity extends outward toward nature and the rest of the nonhuman created universe. Traditional culture and spirituality therefore shun the perception of and active struggle with the universe as an oppositional adversary that one seeks to conquer, destroy, and divide up for utilitarian human purposes. Rather, an indigenous spirituality conceives of partaking in common dependence and shared heritage with all of existing ecology and the cosmos broadly construed.[37]

Not only does spirituality originate from the *past* (that is, indigenous, traditional, or precontact spirituality) but also from the *present*, circumstances noted both for traditions offered by foreign or external spiritual developments and the contemporary maturations rendered by the natural dynamics internal to the growth of traditional culture. Hence, the legacy of history and the occurrences of more recent adaptations amalgamate into existing spiritual realities. For instance, the present forced arrival of foreign culture carried with it a debilitating spirituality that challenged traditional spirituality in Africa. Specifically, new values and priorities undergirded a different worldview governing human labor, artistic efforts, and the foundational core sense of a communal priority. The contemporary new spiritual thrust

> promises attractive, immediate, and palpable results and has the capacity to validate these promises by offering samples of success that are hard to ignore or pass by. Central to this spirituality is the supremacy of the value of acquiring, possession, multiplying, and enjoying material goods by individuals. This value precedes all others and should not be unnecessarily restricted by other values, such as the consideration of other people's needs and feelings.[38]

Basically, the distortions of the foreign acting on the indigenous signify two different viewpoints on human beings' relationship to the ultimate or God. One encounters two distinct theological anthropologies resulting from two contrasting notions of the spirit. Clearly, at least in this instance, the spiritual aspect of culture undergoes a warring of its two sources of the past and the present, while, simultaneously, it adapts from each of the two to formulate something new: spirit as animating force toward the supersensible.

Mercy Amba Oduyoye reminds us that spirituality as the third and animating trajectory in culture does not remain neutral. It brings normative claims that judge, critique, and correct the traumatic ramifications in the sources of both the past and the present. "Spirituality is a holistic and continuous process of becoming," she asserts. "It enables me to look at others with mutual respect. Spirituality is always coupled with justice. The more I grow spiritually, the more I am concerned with justice and taking action for justice."[39] Through this normative value and worldview, Oduyoye sifts through both the past and the present and discerns the harmful effects of both cultures on the status and role of women. As typical examples, she references women's negative part in childbearing, marriage, nurturing, and segregated decision making by sex. Her reasoning points to the disempowerment themes in modern and indigenous spiritualities. Moreover, traditional proverbs and modern Christian dogma, each containing and teaching definite values and sensibilities about women, are spiritually flawed. "The Hausa [of Nigeria] have a proverb that many African women need to hear. It goes like this: 'They pat the cow before they milk her.' So beware of adulation. For Christian women it is the theology of the cross that they have to suspect. A spirituality of the cross without resurrection is promoted among women."[40] Thus all spiritualities exist as sites of contention between salutary qualities and incapacitating effects.[41]

CONCLUSION

In this presentation, looking at the framework of human labor, the artistic, and spirituality, we have advanced the position that the notion of culture must be taken seriously due to its fundamental presuppositional status in the varieties of black theology in South Africa and the United States, as well as in other global regions. For my purpose, J. N. Mugambi's schema of culture clarifies, in summary fashion, what culture is. He establishes what he terms seven pillars of God's house constituting culture: politics (i.e., deciding the process of sharing and distributing); economics (i.e., sharing and distributing resources); aesthetics (i.e., dealing with proportions and forms of beauty); kinship (i.e., the basic primary relations in society—the family); recreation (i.e., relaxation and renewal of self and selves); religion (i.e., worldviews and interhuman relations around ultimate concerns); and ethics (i.e., values of right and wrong).[42] All seven are sacred or relate to an ultimate vision or concern upon which matters of life and death are decided. A qualitative vision or concern transcends the individual self or communal selves; consequently the spiritual trait appears. And culture is not pristine, neutral, romantic, or statically given. It operates in a flow that is animated by the spirit (for Christians, God's Spirit) in contention with adverse spirits (i.e., that which harms life and systematizes a monopolization of God's creation by one group).

Culture is where the sacred reveals itself. As a result, one knows only what she or he is created to be and called to do through the human created realm of culture. On our own, we are limited to this realm. If we could enter the divine realm by using human efforts, there would be no need for the Divine; indeed, such a human capability would restrict divine power to ultimately determine the definition of what it means to be a full human being. Because humans cannot create the divine realm, the ultimate vision or the divine spirit must impinge upon and enter the human condition.

Not only does the divine spirit or ultimate vision enter the human sphere, but the human being has the presence of the divine spirit or ultimate vision within the human being itself, no matter how smothered or covered over this sacred dimension may appear. Therefore, culture is sacred insofar as the ways of being human in the world entail some yearning for, belief in, and ritualization around that which is ultimate vision—that which is both part of and greater than the self. Culture is sacred because the ultimate vision is both present in the material (the tangible manifestation inspires humans to keep moving forward) and in the transcendent (the imagination of the ultimate is not limited to the self).

However, though all of culture contains the sacred, the ultimate goal or vision (i.e., divine spirit) of what it means to be human in community is continuously challenged by evil or that which prevents individual full humanity in relation to healthy community. Culture is contested terrain between marks of life and death.

And finally, the norm is liberation, that is, whatever fosters the freedom of the individual self and the interests of those structurally occupying the bottom of community (i.e., in particular citizens dwelling in systemic poverty as well as working-class people) is good culture because the movement toward practicing freedom for the poor marks the revelation of God. Basically, as one attends to black theology in the twenty-first century, it is important to maintain its focus on those who still suffer. Furthermore, we need further conceptional clarity around the notion of culture, which is central to the everyday lives of those with whom and for whom we say we speak a word of justice.

Chapter 8

J. Deotis Roberts and the Roman Catholic Tradition

Charles Curran

To my knowledge, no real dialogue of Catholics with J. Deotis Roberts's theological writings has taken place, and that is unfortunate. Catholic theology and ethics, to its shame, has not in the past been in great dialogue with black theology in this country. Recently, however, some dialogue has taken place especially with the work of James Cone. Cone himself has explicitly addressed the Catholic Church and the Catholic theological tradition.[1] Black Catholic theologians in response have engaged in important dialogue with Cone.[2] The thesis of this essay maintains that strong affinities exist between the theology of J. Deotis Roberts and theology in the Roman Catholic tradition. Consequently, dialogue between the two will be helpful and constructive, and the Catholic tradition itself can learn significant insights from Roberts's work.

Although Roberts has not addressed the Catholic tradition and community as explicitly and directly as has James Cone, he is quite familiar with the Catholic approach. I first had contact with J. Deotis Roberts in the middle and late 1960s, when he was teaching at Howard University and I was a young assistant professor of theology at the Catholic University of America. In fact, we invited him to teach at Catholic University in the 1968–69 school year. Later I recall recommending that a white religious woman student who had worked in the inner city visit Professor Roberts at Howard to see if she could take courses with him. I believe she took two courses with him and frequently talked with him about her own ministry. She has often told me that she remains ever grateful for the help and the knowledge that Professor Roberts so graciously gave her. In the 1970s I assigned his book *Liberation and Reconciliation* as required reading for my course in social ethics at Catholic University, which was directed primarily, but not exclusively, to Catholic seminarians.

Deotis Roberts's first venture into black theology came at a conference on "Black Church/Black Theology," sponsored jointly by the Graymoor Ecumenical Institute and the Georgetown University Department of Theology in 1969. The coordinator of the conference was a young white Graymoor priest, Father James Gardiner, who had been a student of Deotis Roberts at Catholic University.[3] From that beginning thirty-five years ago, Deotis Roberts has gone on to develop his understanding of African American theology and ethics in many significant publications and books. In the process, he read and appreciated the work of Catholic liberation theologians in South America. He also dialogued with a few other Catholic theologians such as Avery Dulles.[4]

Professor Roberts has only occasionally commented on the Roman Catholic Church, but his comments have been both strong and perceptive. He has pointed out and forthrightly criticized the racism in the Catholic Church. Black Catholics have experienced powerlessness in a powerful church. The move by Father George Stallings to launch his Imani Temple for disenchanted black Catholics in 1989 was both logical and inevitable.[5] No honest Catholic can deny that charge. We white Catholic theologians have also contributed to the problem. I personally have never written anything substantial on racism despite the oppression and injustice suffered by African Americans in my church and in our society.

Roberts has been both appreciative and supportive of black Catholics. Despite his recognition of the inevitability of the new Stallings church, Roberts affirms a black Catholic layperson friend of his who appreciated the African American culture of the Imani Temple but elected to stay in the Catholic Church despite its racism.[6] Professor Roberts has often been called on to be a retreat leader among black Catholics and was pleasantly surprised to find them seeking to recover their African roots.[7] He realistically recognizes the need for black Catholic leadership. Unfortunately, clerical celibacy together with racism discourages many blacks from becoming priests. Some black bishops have been appointed, but Roberts points out with wry wisdom that bishops of whatever race or denomination are cautious and conservative. The Catholic Church desperately needs to develop good black theologians. He was disappointed that a black Catholic theologian, Father Edward K. Braxton, was more interested in metaphysics as a basis for black theology than in black history and culture. Roberts also perceptively recognizes that some of the best minds among black Catholics today are black Catholic women scholars.[8]

AFFINITIES BETWEEN ROBERTS
AND ROMAN CATHOLIC THEOLOGY

But I want to move beyond Roberts's familiarity with Catholic theology and his sharp and perceptive comments on racism in the Catholic Church and the plight of black Catholics. The bulk of this essay will demonstrate strong and significant affinities between Roberts's theology and the Roman Catholic theological tradition.

Ironically, one can apparently cite J. Deotis Roberts as disagreeing with my thesis. Roberts has recognized that much of Latin American liberation theology comes out of the Roman Catholic theological tradition. He also points to a developing black Catholic theology in Francophone Africa. But he explains "the similarity of Roman Catholic and Protestant Afro-American theology more on cultural grounds than on theological foundations."[9] In one sense I agree with Roberts. The commonality of Catholic liberation theology and Afro-American theology stems directly from the analogous situation of oppressed people who are victims of injustice and sinful social structures. But at a deeper level strong affinities exist between Roberts's own theology and theology in the Roman Catholic tradition. I now want to prove this point.

The Roman Catholic Theological Method

Roman Catholic is also catholic with a small "c." Catholic is universal, all-embracing, and all-inclusive. The theological thesis for this universality and inclusivity comes from the belief that God is creator and redeemer and thus all reality is related to God.

Two significant theological methodological approaches follow from this all-inclusive catholicity. First, the Catholic approach has insisted on a "both-and" approach. Karl Barth has said his greatest problem with Roman Catholicism was its "and." At the very minimum, Barth has put his finger on what is characteristic of the Catholic theological approach. This "catholic and" figured prominently in the classical Protestant and Catholic polemics that in the last decades have happily been transformed. Protestants emphasized the Scripture alone; Catholics insisted on Scripture and tradition. Protestants stressed faith alone; Catholics, faith and reason. Protestants insisted on grace alone; Catholics, on grace and works. Protestants emphasized Jesus alone; Catholics insisted on Jesus and Mary and the saints.[10] In my judgment at times, the Catholic tradition put the two aspects together rather poorly. In the above both-and approaches, the first aspect is the more significant and the second is the junior partner and in some way dependent on the first. But for some Catholics, tradition became more important than sacred Scripture, reason more important than faith, works more significant than grace, and Mary more important than Jesus. But properly understood, the both-and approach, in my judgment, makes great theological sense.

A second characteristic of Catholic theological method, following from the all-inclusive attitude and the recognition of both creation and redemption, is analogical thinking based especially on the analogy of being.[11] The shadow of the Creator is found in all of creation. From what we see in creation, we can learn something about God. The danger in the Catholic tradition was to forget that an analogy is partly the same and partly different. Too often the Catholic tradition has known too much about God. Contemporary Catholic theology uses different words and concepts here but still frequently insists on an analogical approach by which we can go from the human to the Divine even though we must be careful in the process. Here again, Karl Barth explicitly opposes the analogy of being. One cannot go from the human to the Divine. One must always start with God and God's revelation in Jesus Christ.[12]

I believe the Christian tradition from its very beginning has used such an analogical approach. For example, why do we celebrate Christmas on December 25? We have no idea what day or even what year Jesus was born. December 25 falls during the darkest part of the year. It seems most fitting (this is the word the Catholic tradition uses in developing analogy—the Latin word is *conveniens*) to celebrate the coming of salvation and light into the world at this time. In addition, there were pagan feasts at the same time that Christians took over and transformed in the light of their own faith. Yes, it is most fitting that we celebrate Christmas at that time of year, but it also reveals a problem that is inherent in analogical thinking. This makes great sense from the perspective of one in the Northern Hemisphere. But what about one in the Southern Hemisphere? Here, too, there is a danger of the Northern Hemisphere imposing its own views and perspective on the Southern Hemisphere. We must constantly be conscious of the danger of making God into our image and likeness, but still, analogical thinking about God is most helpful if one is conscious of the dangers.

Roberts's Theological Methodology

J. Deotis Roberts frequently describes his own methodology as both-and and as holistic. "[I]t is important to remind ourselves that the black perspective is 'holistic.' Even our way of thinking is 'both-and.'"[13] No reader of Roberts can deny his insistence on a holistic and both-and approach.

In the course of all his writings, going back over a period of almost fifty years, Roberts consistently and often disagreed with the neo-orthodox theology of Karl Barth. There is no doubt that he disagrees with Barth more than with any other white theologian he has discussed. Roberts's first two books were in the area of philosophical theology, and he returned to this topic in his 1991 *A Philosophical Introduction to Theology*. "In Protestant theology we find a powerful challenge to the philosophical approach to theology in neo-orthodoxy under the leadership of Karl Barth. Theology turned anti-intellectual and advocated biblical revelation as the sole source of religious knowledge."[14] He wrote the 1991 book because his holistic understanding of religion requires and deserves the best that our intellects have to offer in the service of faith. Philosophy has been an instrument for theological interpretation throughout Christian history. Today, faith continues to seek understanding in philosophy. Faith has priority, but "reason is the means by which we enrich and enhance our understanding of faith. We love God from the top of our minds as well as from the bottom of our hearts."[15]

In addition, Roberts's corpus on black and African American theology and ethics frequently disagrees with Karl Barth. Very often this disagreement comes out in his early criticism of the influence of Barth on the liberation theology of James Cone.

The beginning of the very first chapter of *A Black Political Theology* deals with foundations and method. For Roberts, "James Cone will need to break with Barthianism if he is to enter into meaningful dialogue with African theologians who are taking seriously their pre-colonial religious traditions." A narrow christological view of revelation based on Karl Barth is inadequate. "Black theology requires an understanding of revelation sufficiently comprehensive to deal with the pan-African context of the black religious experience. . . . What would be helpful is an understanding of the revelation of God as manifest in all creation and all history as measured by the supreme revelation of God in the incarnation."[16] Roberts frequently criticizes Barth and his influence on Cone while recognizing some movement of Cone away from a Barthian approach.[17] Our author also criticizes Jürgen Moltmann's approach to human rights as being too Barthian. Such a narrow and exclusive christological approach cannot guarantee human rights for all human beings, the vast majority of whom are not Christian.[18]

Perhaps the most central aspect in the Catholic theological and ethical methodology concerns the insistence on faith and reason. This Catholic approach is well illustrated in the work of Thomas Aquinas (d. 1274), the foremost figure in the Catholic historical tradition. Contemporary Catholic theologians still continue to follow his insistence on faith and reason. In his 1991 book, Roberts is quite sympathetic to the Thomistic harmony of revelation and reason. According to Aquinas, faith and reason grow into an organic unity because they both spring from the same source. Roberts's description of Aquinas also describes himself—"He was a person of faith before he became a philosopher."[19] His own position is similar to Aquinas's—"I assume that faith has priority and reason is a means by which we enrich and enhance our understanding of faith."[20]

Thus, there can be no doubt of the similarity between the Roman Catholic theological method and that followed by Deotis Roberts.[21] Roberts insists on a method that is inclusive, both-and, analogical, and based on the primacy of faith but the harmony between faith and reason. The basis for this approach in Roberts is not cultural but theological.

In my judgment, this method is behind the two most significant contributions made by J. Deotis Roberts to black and African American theology and ethics—his holistic understanding of black theology and his ethical approach to the situation of African Americans in the United States.

First, his approach to black and African American theology. Our author has always insisted on the primacy of Christian faith and the Bible in his approach to black theology and has also given great importance to the experience of blacks in the United States in the light of slavery and the later white racism that created such sinful social structures. But from the very beginning, he has also insisted on the need to root black theology in the African cultural and religious traditions. One cannot understand the African American experience without knowing the roots of the black experience in Africa, even though this experience is quite different from that of an enslaved people in the United States. Roberts has also learned much from other liberation theologies, especially the liberation theology coming from Latin America. Our author has brought to his understanding of African American theology his study of world religions. And, as mentioned above, he also continues to use his philosophical knowledge to understand better and explain more adequately the meaning of African American theology. He frequently calls for an interdisciplinary approach. *A Black Political Theology* already insists on such an approach in its very first chapter on foundations, and subsequent writings have continued to use this holistic methodology to develop Roberts's African American theology.

Black Theology in Dialogue by its very title recognizes such a holistic method. The first chapter insists on an interdisciplinary, ecumenical, contextual, and historical approach, with the Bible at the center of theological reflection. Subsequent chapters put special emphasis on the African roots of black theology and an Afro-American–African theological dialogue. Later in the book, Roberts also dialogues with Minjung theology, which was then just developing in South Korea, and with the Palestinian liberation theology proposed in the United States by Jewish scholar Marc Ellis. Roberts's latest book, *Africentric Christianity*, continues and deepens this dialogue with African roots. He believes African American theology can learn much from Africentrism, but the Christian faith for him must always be the primary and deciding criterion. This broad, holistic, and interdisciplinary approach to black theology, with a special emphasis on its African roots, is a most significant and lasting contribution of Professor Roberts.

An equally important and lasting contribution concerns his insistence on both liberation and reconciliation in describing the struggle of African Americans in the United States. The 1960s were tumultuous times. Black power replaced the integrationist approach of Martin Luther King Jr. A great number of blacks abandoned the Christian church, accusing it of failing to support true black liberation. Roberts, the Christian theologian, called upon the church to play a central role but insisted on both liberation and reconciliation. Some black communities insisted on liberation alone and called for a separate black nationalism. Whites in general, including liberal whites, wanted reconciliation without liberation. In their perspective, reconciliation and integration were based on the existing white power structure. Our author insisted that the Christian understanding definitely calls for reconciliation, but reconciliation can truly occur only in the light of a full liberation of blacks, so that blacks and whites could come together as equals, and not with dependent and inferior blacks being integrated into the already existing white structures. Looking back from the vantage point of the present, one can appreciate both the wisdom and the courage behind Roberts's insistence on both liberation and reconciliation.[22] Unfortunately, his agenda has not yet been accomplished and still faces us. Without doubt, his both-and rather than an either-or approach was the most adequate one in the 1970s and remains the most proper answer to our problems today.

Agreement on Substance and Content

Anthropology constitutes a fundamental concept for Christian ethics and social ethics. Here again, Professor Roberts and the Catholic tradition share the same basic understanding. Catholic tradition has built on the biblical, Aristotelian, and Thomistic approaches to insist that the human person is social and political by nature. This tradition has recognized and strongly opposed the tendency to individualism and materialism that is so prevalent in the United States. On the basis of such an anthropology, the Catholic tradition has developed its understanding of the state as being natural, necessary, and good but limited. The state has as its function securing the common good that involves many aspects, such as justice and human rights. This tradition, precisely because of its both-and approach to anthropology (personal and social), constitutes a middle position avoiding the two extremes of individualism and collectivism. Individualism is interested only in individual goods and does not give enough importance to the community. Collectivism emphasizes the collectivity but fails to give enough importance to the individual person. The common good ultimately redounds to the good of the individual persons living in that society.[23]

Roberts's concern has been with the real issues facing African Americans, and so he has not developed in a systematic way a social, political, and economic ethics. However, what he has said on these issues basically agrees with the Catholic tradition because he starts with the same fundamental anthropology. According to Roberts, the human person is social because God made us for fellowship. No person is an island. We are all persons in community. Our well-being as persons depends on a healthy group life in families, communities, and nations. Social consciousness is built into the very nature of Christian anthropology.[24] In his writings, Roberts frequently refers to the East African concept of *ujamaa*, or family-hood and the extended family, and also to the Swahili concept of *harambee*, or social solidarity.[25] Our author favorably cites Aristotle in describing humans as "political animals" and in calling for government to promote justice and equity.[26]

Roberts insists that the state is the broadest expression of full community life apart from humanity itself, and in this respect it is necessary for a complete satisfaction of human sociability. The state or government has its chief roots in the need of citizens for justice, and it is for that reason that the state has its power.[27] In his realism, our author also recognizes that the state is subject to human sinfulness and can readily support an unjust status quo or wishes of the majority. But the state also has the constructive role of promoting justice and the common good. Here, too, Professor Roberts, like Catholic social teaching, sees capitalism and socialism as direct opposites. Capitalism is too tied to individual selfishness and greed. Socialism is too concerned with the collectivity and downplays the dignity and worth of persons. Like Catholic social teaching, he recognizes what he calls "an acceptable 'communalism' inherent in the Christian ethic that is authentically human."[28]

Roberts recognizes a role for the church as "servant critic of the state." Such a role requires both critical and supportive functions. At times the church must protest the injustice of the state and work to overcome sinful structures such as racism, but at other times it supports the public structures in the struggle for justice, human rights, and the common good. Roberts also recognizes the complexity of political problems with the realization that no agreement will often exist among good Christians about what should be done.[29] Catholic theology agrees with such approaches.

The Catholic social tradition has consistently recognized the family as the basic, fundamental unit of society. However, I doubt if there is a general theologian discussing primarily other matters who has paid as much attention to the family as Professor Roberts. He recognizes problems stemming from what slavery, discrimination, and white racism have done to the black family in this country. In his analysis of the family, Roberts emphasizes the African roots of the family and its importance. Special attention is paid to the extended family. He also develops the important role of the church with regard to the family, which again combines a both-and aspect—a priestly and prophetic ministry of the black church to the family.[30]

Another strong affinity between Professor Roberts and the Roman Catholic tradition concerns the importance and general understanding of the church. Roberts primarily does his theology for the church. He is a theologian in the service of the black church but also recognizes the broader church universal. At first glance, it would seem that a black Baptist theologian and the Roman Catholic tradition would have very diverse views of church. But such is not the case. Professor Roberts correctly recognizes that the Catholic Church has always given special attention to the institutional aspect of the church.[31] I think he would have been justified in pointing out that at times Roman Catholic theology has given such great importance to the institutional aspect of the church that it has failed to see the institution as a means for carrying out the transformative ministry of the church. But Roberts's basic understanding of the church, including some institutional aspects, shares much with the contemporary Catholic understanding.

Our author sees the church as connected with his own both-and approach. One of his chapters is titled "Jesus and the Church"[32] and another, "Jesus, the Church, and Ministry."[33] In practically every one of his books he addresses the role of the church, and some of them concentrate almost exclusively on the role and ministry of the church.[34] Jesus established the Christian church as an extension of the incarnation to be a community that carries on his saving mission in the world. The metaphors that Roberts uses to understand the church are very similar to those in contemporary Catholicism. He develops at some length the metaphors of the church as the family of God, the communion of saints, the body of Christ, and the people of God.[35] Professor Roberts and the Roman Catholic tradition share a primary concern for the church and its transformative life and ministry as a corporate and communitarian assembly of the people of God.

LESSONS THE ROMAN CATHOLIC TRADITION CAN LEARN FROM ROBERTS

The affinities and similarities between Professor Roberts and the Roman Catholic tradition are more significant and central than most people would realize. As a result, fruitful dialogue can and should take place between these two theologies. Above all, from Roberts and others, the Catholic Church must learn to confront its own racism. In addition, I will conclude this essay by pointing out two important aspects that the Catholic tradition can learn from Professor Roberts. Obviously, Deotis Roberts is not the only one saying these things, and even some Catholics themselves are already moving in this direction, but in the context of a dialogue between Roberts and the Catholic tradition, the Catholic tradition can and should incorporate these two emphases.

First is a greater emphasis on the particular. Roberts emphasizes the particular but also holds on to the importance of the universal aspect. Roman Catholicism has often so emphasized the universal that it has failed to give enough significance to the particular. Roberts insists that Christians must do their own theological reflection based on their understanding of the Bible, Jesus Christ, and their own histories and experiences. Such a theology should be contextual and particular but not provincial. Theology needs to combine a concrete contextual orientation with a universal vision that takes biblical revelation and authority seriously.[36]

In his own work, Roberts emphasizes the importance of the particular and the contextual without denying the universal. His great contribution in insisting on both liberation and reconciliation well illustrates an insistence on the particular while still holding on to the universal. The liberation aspect for blacks is obvious. But reconciliation is an integral part of the gospel, the very essence of the good news. Reconciliation involves a cross both for racist whites and for oppressed blacks. The cross for whites is repentance; the cross for blacks is forgiveness. There is no cheap grace. But reconciliation cannot take place without liberation. Reconciliation must involve equals.[37] Roberts approaches the concept of the black Messiah in a similar way. The universal Christ is particularized for the black Christian in the black Messiah; but the black Messiah is at the same time universalized in the Christ of the Gospels, who meets all believers in their particular situations.[38]

Just as Jesus Christ is lord and redeemer of each people and of all people, so too Jesus Christ is judge of each and of all. He judges in history and beyond history. He stands outside and above black culture as well as in it.[39] No culture, however oppressed and sinned against, is itself completely without sin.

While holding on to the need for a universal vision, Professor Roberts also recognizes the dangers of a false universalism in which a particular perspective has claimed to be universal. There is no completely universal perspective. Too often white Western Christian theologians have been guilty of a theological neo-colonialism. The cosmic Christ must always stretch the limited boundaries of every particular Christian perspective.[40] The Catholic tradition can and should learn from Roberts and others to give more emphasis to the particular and the contextual while holding on to a proper universalism.

Second, the Roman Catholic tradition can learn from Roberts's understanding of the importance and role of power in social life and ethics. Liberation theologies in the Roman Catholic tradition often refer to power, but the papal and hierarchical teaching known as Catholic social teaching fails to recognize the importance of power and conflict in social ethics and life.[41]

Catholic social teaching refers to the official documents, beginning with Pope Leo XIII and continuing to the present, that address social issues facing the church and the world. (One must also note the abject failure to address racism in these documents.) A number of factors contribute to the failure of Catholic social teaching to discuss power. The approach heavily depends on an organic understanding of society based on the organism of the human body. Each part has its own role to play for the good of the whole. Later documents in the tradition recognize sinful social structures, but Catholic theology and ethics have not given enough recognition to the power of sin and the conflicts brought about by it in social life. The Catholic tradition has emphasized human reason and appeals to all people of goodwill, but unfortunately evil and evil people exist in our world. Even the Catholic emphasis on both-and often tends to bring the two different elements together into a harmonious whole.

Professor Roberts has dealt with power in all his writings. Black power came to the fore in the 1960s. Roberts recognized the importance and need for black power from a Christian understanding. No change could be brought about without it. However, together with Vincent Harding and others he opposed "the religion of Black Power." Such an understanding tended to substitute this religion for Christianity, emphasized total black separatism, and accepted and even promoted violence.[42] *A Black Political Theology* devotes a chapter to "The Gospel of Power," which insists on the radical change needed in our society that can come about only through power, confrontation, and conflict. But still all this is a means to reconciliation.[43]

Roberts's most extensive treatment of black power comes in three chapters in *Black Theology in Dialogue* that were originally three lectures delivered at Brite Divinity School. Here he uses Paul Tillich in developing separate chapters on love, justice, and power. Power is deeply rooted in the Judeo-Christian understanding of God—almighty and all-powerful God. But with Tillich, Reinhold Niebuhr, and Martin Luther King Jr., Roberts insists that power is neutral and must always be used in the service of love and justice. Power is not an end in itself. Power is to be used to realize the highest human values: personal, social, and institutional.[44]

Catholic social teaching can learn much from Roberts about power. Power is absolutely necessary in social life and social ethics, but it must always be in the service of love and justice. Conflict and confrontation are legitimate means against the forces of evil, but they are strategies that must serve Christian values and always aim at ultimate reconciliation.

This essay has studied the writings of Professor Roberts from the perspective of the Roman Catholic theological tradition. Our author has worked with Roman Catholics over the years and has been familiar with the Catholic tradition. But more important, significant similarities and affinities exist between his theology and Roman Catholic theology. In the context of this dialogue, the Catholic Church must confront its own racism, and the Catholic tradition can learn significant lessons from the writings of J. Deotis Roberts.

Chapter 9

African Contributions and Challenges to the Ecumenical Movement

Peter J. Paris

INTRODUCTION

It is a great privilege to contribute this essay to a volume honoring the academic career of Professor J. Deotis Roberts, whom I first met over three decades ago when I joined the faculty of what was then called the School of Religion at Howard University. Dr. Roberts was a distinguished member of that faculty and soon became an excellent mentor to me in those early days of my teaching career. One of the most memorable events of those years was attending an autograph party celebrating the publication of his first book, *Liberation and Reconciliation: A Black Theology*, which was a significant response to James Cone's first book, *Black Theology and Black Power*, which launched the black theology movement. Thereafter, however, Roberts has always been viewed as one of the founders of that movement.

Roberts's works cover a great breadth of issues and concerns in theological scholarship, not the least of which are his many initiatives in promoting various types of ecumenical and interreligious dialogue. Hence, I dedicate this essay to him with the hope that it will serve as a reminder of his contributions to and participation in the ecumenical movement as evidenced in the World Council of Churches and its constituent bodies.

Let me at this point locate myself in the ecumenical movement. When I was an undergraduate student at Acadia University in my native Nova Scotia, I joined the local branch of the Student Christian Movement (SCM) of Canada. After graduation from seminary, I spent a total of seven years working for that organization: three years as general secretary at the University of Alberta; three years as the national traveling secretary for the Student Christian Movement of Nigeria; one year as special traveling secretary to all the universities in Canada. The purpose of the last position (1964–65) was to introduce university students to the moral and religious issues emerging from the new nations in Africa and, most important, the continuing scandal of constitutional racial apartheid in South Africa. My work in Nigeria had been sponsored by the Ecumenical Assistance Program of the World Student Christian Federation, which enabled a partnership among the World Student Christian Federation (WSCF) and the SCMs of both Nigeria and Canada, all three of which shared financial responsibility for the project.[1]

Those were invaluable years of exposure to the ecumenical movement and its many and varied global concerns. I felt privileged to be involved in the student wing of that movement because so many of its prominent leaders had been members of the World Student Christian Federation in their youth. Further, I was impressed both then and now with the global dimensions of the ecumenical movement because it had helped me transcend the confines of my own Baptist denomination by introducing me to the wider Christian world.

Through the World Student Christian Federation, many learned theologians visited my alma mater, Acadia University, to lecture, lead Bible studies, and discuss momentous contemporary issues in light of the Christian faith. Prior to meeting people such as Elizabeth Adler from East Germany, D. T. Niles and M. M. Thomas from South India, Bola Ige from Nigeria, Arthuro Chacun from Chile, Ralph Potter from Jamaica, and Martin Luther King Jr., I had been totally ignorant of the so-called Christian–Marxist dialogue, the work of the Iona Community in Scotland, the East Harlem Protestant Parish, the Taize Community in France, the Worker Priest Movement in England, the life and mission of the churches in Africa, and a host of other Christian endeavors.

I first met some of Africa's leading theologians and laypersons in the Student Christian Movement. For example, Professor E. Bolaji Idowu,[2] who wrote the first book correlating traditional African religions with Christianity, was the president of the Nigerian Student Christian Movement, for whom I worked for three years in the early 1960s. Also, Dr. Francis Ibiam, Idowu's predecessor with the SCM, had studied medicine in Scotland with a scholarship from the Presbyterian Missionary Society and returned to his native Nigeria as the first native Nigerian medical missionary. Later he was knighted by the queen of England, appointed governor of the Eastern Region of Nigeria, and, as a trusted statesperson, played a key role in effecting an end to the so-called Biafran War in Nigeria. Both men had served as presidents of the National Board of the Student Christian Movement of Nigeria.

LIBERATING AFRICAN VOICES
IN THE UNITED STATES AND AFRICA

In this essay the term *African* designates all peoples of African descent both on the continent of Africa and throughout the diaspora. Further, the purpose of this essay is to discuss the impact of African peoples on the ecumenical movement as evidenced in the World Council of Churches.

From the late 1950s onward, the ecumenical movement experienced a steady growth in racial diversity. In large part, that growth was due to the progressive achievements of the Civil Rights movement in the United States, which eventually culminated in the Civil Rights Act of 1964 and the Voting Rights Act of 1965. One of the sources of inspiration for the Civil Rights movement in America was the independence of Ghana from colonial rule in 1957, which was followed by the rapid emergence of numerous new black sovereign nations throughout the continent of Africa. The spirit that had inspired freedom movements on both sides of the Atlantic also inspired the rise of similar black consciousness movements within the so-called mainstream white churches and the missionary societies in the United States and Europe.

In the late 1960s, the rise of a new genre of theology in the United States called "black theology" sent shock waves throughout white liberal Protestantism. The audacious call for "black power" issued by young militants in the left wing of the Civil Rights movement provided the impetus for this nascent theological focus. It originated with a full-page piece in the *New York Times* (July 31, 1966) wherein a group of influential black clergy provided a theological rationale in support of the contentious slogan "black power." That constituted the first document in which black clergy publicly responded to the problem of racism by using categories of thought that were quite different from those employed by liberal white Protestant clergy. Most important, that statement became the basis for the formation of a new organization, the National Committee of Negro Churchmen (NCNC; later changed to the National Committee of Black Churchmen).

The National Committee of Black Churchmen and the theological movement it spawned continued to affirm much of Martin Luther King's thought and action while criticizing his views of racial assimilation and especially his reluctance to thematize the issue of power in the struggle against racism. Many of the black clergy in the NCNC were members in predominantly white denominations. Moreover, these had begun to embarrass their white colleagues by forming black caucuses within those denominations for the purpose of developing strategies and goals for black empowerment. Undoubtedly, in the context of the newly developing black consciousness, those caucuses helped legitimate the continued presence of blacks in those predominantly white denominations. Suffice it to say, one of the primary focuses of the black theology movement was the empowerment of blacks who had been excluded from all spheres of power in both the secular and religious spheres of white America.[3]

In Africa, the various national achievements of independence from European colonialism provided the basic condition by which the African churches, founded and controlled by missionaries, began the process of liberating themselves from the continuing hegemonies of the overseas missionary societies. At the time, however, none could have imagined that such a process would have been as long and arduous as it was. Yet that process coupled with various incremental achievements comprises one of most important contributions that Africans have made to the ecumenical movement.

Contrary to the thought of many, however, that process of liberating themselves from the domination of others has had a corresponding effect on their former ecclesiastical rulers. That is to say, the experience of African liberation also freed unjust overseers from their sinful arrogance of viewing Africans as genetically inferior to Europeans in all matters pertaining to societal organization, morality, and religion.

In the 1960s, the ubiquitous spirit of hopefulness and enthusiasm that pervaded the citizenry of these newly emergent sovereign nations in Africa produced what many have called a *kairotic* moment, that is, a time when conditions are ripe for radical social change. During those happy years, the churches in Africa participated with their respective nations in celebrating the end of colonialism and in laying the groundwork for developing the necessary conditions for their peoples to flourish in the postcolonial era.

In 1963, during the first decade of independence, Africans established two significant international organizations: the Organization for African Unity (OAU) and the All Africa Council of Churches (AACC). Those organizations reflected the traditional values of community and solidarity that Africans have always held in the highest esteem. Most important, the purpose of those organizations was to achieve political and religious unity among African nations. The OAU represented the dream of many of the political progenitors of independence, and the AACC represented a similar hope among Africa's church leaders.

In the late nineteenth century, the various missionary societies agreed to concentrate their missionary activities in separate, relatively homogenous ethnic areas in order to minimize competition among them in their respective evangelistic endeavors. Not surprisingly, those divisions followed on the heels of the horrific European division of the African continent at the 1884 Berlin Conference, when the present-day national borders of the continent were arbitrarily drawn through the territories of various ethnic groups.

One of the greatest scandals of Western Christianity occurred immediately after the Berlin Conference when the Christian missionary enterprises began their work of evangelism under the protection of their respective colonial governments. Effiong Utuk claims:

> Before the Berlin Conference, the Christian missionary enterprise seemed
> to be committed to the principle of establishing African Christian commu-
> nities that would be self-governing, self-supporting, and self-propagating.
> After the partition of Africa, missionary societies became tied to the policies
> of the metropolitan governments which offered them protection in the
> colonies.[4]

Similarly, the theologian Eboussi Boulaga has written that "one of the reasons for
the loss of credibility of African Christianity has been its dangerous alliance with
might and force."[5]

The dawn of African independence enabled both the Organization of African
Unity—now the African Union (AU)—and the All Africa Council of Churches
to assume the mission of correcting the abuses of their colonial past by striving
to rebuild their beloved nations on African models of participation, community,
mutual respect, ancestral devotion, social justice, and fidelity. In the ecclesial
realm, the conditions seemed ripe for launching a series of novel processes to give
institutional form to the long-hoped-for dream of independent African churches
owned and controlled by African peoples. It was hoped that the realization of
such a goal would help reestablish the dignity of African peoples both on the continent and beyond.

Yet it is important not to lose sight of the fact that neither political nor ecclesial independence in Africa resulted in any absolute separation of these newly
independent nations from their former colonial powers. Rather, most African
nations have continued to remain heavily dependent on economic assistance and
educational curricula from their former rulers. Similarly, African churches have
relied on the largesse of their former parent churches in Europe and America.

The favorable disposition of the African churches toward church union is
unmistakable. Clearly, the many and varied denominational divisions within Western Christianity have resulted from various theological and ecclesiastical disputes.
They were Western, not African, disputes. Consequently, African theologians,
clergy, and laity have never identified very deeply with those inherited denominational divisions. Thus they have been able to feel at home in virtually any denominational context, whether Protestant, Roman Catholic, or Orthodox. Ironically,
however, several subsequent attempts to establish church union in Africa have
failed, demonstrating the power of colonial and missionary structures to endure.

The collective spirit of toleration and respect for others that underlies the
comfort with differences seen among African Christians is grounded in the traditional experience of most Africans of rarely having lived farther than a few kilometers from a different language group or clan. Every open marketplace in Africa
is composed of a variety of peoples speaking different languages. In short, most
Africans have well-developed capacities for tolerating and respecting differences
both within and outside their communities, including their churches. Although
most individuals speak several African languages, most African churches in urban
areas translate their services into one to three different languages as a concrete

way of demonstrating their respect for the ethnic diversity within their congregations. Clearly, the spirit of religious toleration is another of Africa's great contributions to the ecumenical movement.

Even a casual observer of Christianity in Africa will notice the high status that the ecumenical movement enjoys throughout the continent. In virtually every country its institutionalization assumes the form of national councils of churches comprising Anglicans, Presbyterians, Methodists, Baptists, and a small number of African-initiated churches.

The initial impetus for the twentieth-century ecumenical movement arose from the theology of European and Euro-American men. More often than not, their theologies had been filtered through the thought-forms inherited from ancient Jewish, Greek, and Roman sources. Similarly, their anthropologies (doctrines of humanity) were almost wholly Cartesian inheritances from the Enlightenment that produced the autonomous individual isolated from community: thought abstracted from practice, subjects divided from objects, and facts separated from values. In fact, the German sociologist Max Weber gained enduring significance in academe by arguing that the spirit of Protestantism greatly facilitated the rise of capitalism. That thesis is presupposed by the francophone African theologian Eboussi Boulaga, who calls the Christianity that was transported to Africa "middle-class Christianity":

> At bottom, the middle-class Christian is a creature free of all natural ties, one who has broken with the tribe—the great family—and is before all else an individual, a closed subjectivity, finished and perfect in itself, maintaining no purely extrinsic relationships with society. Such, at any rate, is the goal and representation that bourgeois Christianity conceive for and of themselves. The first and last reality is individuals. They preexist and survive all else. Society is the result, at times even the voluntary result, of the interaction of individuals in the pursuit of their self-realization. Institutions, then, are but means that are exterior to each individual. The expansion of the individual comes before all else. This is the absolute value. All other things shall pass—individuals alone shall abide, in immortal individuality, in their souls. The aim of faith is save those souls, to immortalize that individuality.[6]

Boulaga goes on to say that this constitutes the crux of Christianity's attack on African worldviews. Individualism constituted an essential mark of Christian authenticity. Such an alien philosophy implied a profound disassociation from the communalism of tribal community in which the identity of the traditional human as person was formed: "a being-one-self-with-the-others."[7] Clearly, the radical isolation of the individual from community has had a profound impact on all Western theology, including the doctrines of God, humanity, creation, law and gospel, nature and grace, faith, and the sacraments. Conversely, the primacy of community has had a corresponding impact on the nascent rise of African theology.

Though the process of inculturating Christianity into African spirituality began several decades ago, it was greatly hindered by the fact that so many African theologians were locked into Western theological thought-forms, which in turn prevented the emergence of authentic African spirituality. Yet in the midst of such political crises as the anti-apartheid struggle that eventually gained the moral, economic, and political support of Western Christians, a dimension of African spirituality became evident in the willing sacrifice of many lives for the good of the larger community. Such sacrifices were seen in the suffering of countless numbers of men and women who courageously faced exile, imprisonment, homelessness, unemployment, denial of education, torture, terrorization, and death for their just cause.

Nelson Mandela was imprisoned for twenty-seven years for refusing to comply with the evils of the apartheid system. The quality of his resistance gradually catapulted him into a global icon of respect and praise. His suffering and perseverance became universal symbols of justice not only for thirty-five million black Africans but for countless peoples around the world. Christian prophetic spokespersons such as Nobel laureate Desmond Tutu, Frank Chikane, Alan Boesak, Winnie Mandela, Abertina Sisulu, and Russell Botman became significant intermediaries in interpreting that struggle to the Western world as they sought moral support for their struggle. Let me hasten to add, however, that a small group of white South Africans were consistent allies and interpreters both within and outside the South African situation. They included such persons as Bishops Alan Paton and Trevor Huddleston as well as John DeGrucy, Charles Villa-Vicencio, Byers Naude, Margaret Nash, Joe Slovo, and Helen Suzman.

Suffering in the battle for social justice is what Martin Luther King Jr. called "unmerited suffering." Most important, he viewed such suffering as redemptive because it occurs in the service of striving to establish what he called the "beloved community," which is the historical representation of the "sovereign reign of God." The theology and ethics of Martin Luther King Jr. and of Archbishop Desmond Tutu (both Nobel Peace laureates) have made enduring contributions to the strivings of the ecumenical movement.

A BRIEF OVERVIEW OF THE WORLD COUNCIL OF CHURCHES' EARLY RESPONSES TO RACISM

It is important to note that all assemblies of the World Council of Churches (WCC) from its first meeting in Amsterdam in 1948 have issued lengthy statements on racism. In fact, long before the WCC's first official meeting statements opposing racism had been issued: as early as 1925, at the Stockholm Conference on Life and Work, and in 1928, when the International Missionary Conference in Jerusalem adopted a statement calling for "world-wide interracial unity."[8]

In 1926 one of the major pioneers of the ecumenical movement, J. H. Oldham, wrote a prophetic book titled "Christianity and the Race Problem," "stressing the fundamental unity of human nature, the white race's responsibility and the Church's obligation to be in the mid-stream of the world's life."[9] Also, the

Secretariat on Racial and Ethnic Relations of the Department of Church and Society issued a series of similar statements between 1937 and 1964.

Thus the ecumenical movement recognized racism as a significant problem from the beginning of its history onward. In the movement's early decades, ecumenical attention centered on the persecution of the Jews. Yet, in spite of its admonishments to the churches to cleanse themselves of racist practices, it was not until 1959 that the WCC provided a full-time secretary to help its member churches deal with "interracial relations." Up to that time its opposition to racism had been solely rhetorical.

THE PROGRAM TO COMBAT RACISM:
A MEDIATING CENTER FOR AFRICAN
AND AFRICAN AMERICAN CHURCH LEADERS

The World Council of Churches' Program to Combat Racism, established in 1969, cannot be understood apart from the struggle of African Americans to give theological justification to the concept of black power and to demand the repentance of the white churches for their racism through a program of reparational empowerment for black people. As mentioned above, the first official justification of black power was issued by the National Conference of Black Churchmen in June 1969.[10] That statement was destined to have widespread national and international implications. The responses of the white churches to these black proponents of black power soon evidenced considerable estrangement between them.

James Forman, who will always be known as the one who rudely interrupted the congregational worship at the prestigious Riverside Church in New York to read his audacious "Black Manifesto," had been the chair of the radical Black Economic Development Conference with which the NCBC was allied. In June 1969 the NCBC issued its strongest pronouncement to both white and black Christians, titled "The Message to the Churches from Oakland, California." That message called upon both the white and black churches to make sizable amounts of money available to powerless peoples in Africa, Asia, Latin America, and the United States. For the first time, African American Christians were acknowledging the international dimensions of white racism.[11]

After the demands of the NCBC were heard at the 1969 Nottingham Consultation of the World Council of Churches, the first general secretary, Dr. W. A. Visser't Hooft, lowered the gauntlet by declaring the following:

> (a) We have believed too much in persuasion by declarations and have not been sufficiently aware of the irrational factors of the situation; (b) We have not given adequate attention to the economic factors making for racial injustice; (c) We have insisted too little on the very considerable sacrifices which have to be made if racial justice is to prevail; (d) We have not yet found common answers to the problem of violence and nonviolence as methods of transforming present patterns and present structures.[12]

Some months later the Central Committee at Canterbury recommended the establishment of an Ecumenical Program to Combat Racism and outlined a five-year program that was destined to encounter many bitter battles in its various endeavors to engage the churches in the mission of combating racism. Numerous regional ecumenical conferences were held in Africa, Asia, Latin America, North America, and Europe. One of the principal consequences of those meetings was the gradual emergence of a global forum for numerous voices from the Southern Hemisphere that had not hitherto been heard in ecumenical circles. Those voices were strong, articulate, and courageous. Most of them were deeply enmeshed in the struggles for racial justice in their own particular regions.

Many lives were lost in those righteous struggles for justice. For example, African Americans had buried some of their greatest leaders and allies: the Nobel laureate Martin Luther King Jr., Robert Kennedy, Malcolm X, Medgar Evers, and President John F. Kennedy. South Africans had been greatly reinvigorated in their struggle by Chief Albert Luthuli's receipt of the Nobel Peace Prize, the horror of 1961 Sharpeville massacre, and the steady rise of imprisonments, brutalities, and killings by the South African police and military forces.

The 1969 Notting Hill Consultation on Racism called upon the WCC and its member churches to apply economic sanctions against all corporations that practice racism and to divest church funds from all corporations that engage in business dealings with South Africa. For the first time, the WCC found itself engaged in direct action against racism, a battle that would intensify as time went on. In fact, after much rigorous debate, the Notting Hill Consultation issued one of the most radical statements that has ever been released by an ecumenical meeting:

> The Notting Hill Consultation advocated for the first time the controversial statement referred to above: "that all else failing, the Church and churches support resistance movements, including revolutions, which are aimed at the elimination of political or economic tyranny which makes racism possible."[13]

In short, these radical actions of the WCC were greatly influenced by the strong, persuasive appeals of the African American representatives at the meeting. Most important, the WCC Central Committee decided to set up a fund of $200,000 to be distributed to "organizations of oppressed racial groups whose purposes are not inconsonant with the general purposes of the WCC."[14]

> In 1970, financial allocations from the Special Fund to Combat Racism were made to a number of regional liberation movements in Australia, the United Kingdom, the Netherlands, Japan, Colombia, Zambia, Southern Africa, South Africa, Mozambique, Angola, Guinea-Bissau, Namibia, and Rhodesia.[15]

In 1971 the Central Committee of the WCC requested a study be undertaken on violent and nonviolent methods of social change, as well as a study on investment policies of countries where racism is entrenched. That action was prompted by criticisms associated with alleged funds having been distributed to groups in South Africa that supported the armed struggle. Others were seriously interested in exploring the relationship of traditional "just war" theory to the use of violence in certain liberation struggles.

In 1972 the WCC began the process of divesting its funds from corporations that were doing business with South Africa. It also increased to $1 million the special fund of the Program to Combat Racism. Thenceforth, both the Central Committee and the Executive Committee of the WCC gave higher priority to the agenda of the Program to Combat Racism, its special fund, and the issue of divestment from South Africa. These committees continued to praise the work of the Program to Combat Racism while urging it to give priority to the claims of indigenous peoples for land rights, to racism in Asia, and to racism in children's textbooks in their schools as well as in Christian educational materials.

This increasing moral and financial investment of the World Council of Churches in the Program to Combat Racism was painstakingly wrought through much arduous activity on the part of African voices both from the diaspora and the continent. Special recognition, however, is due those from the U.S. diaspora who represented black caucuses within such predominantly white denominations as the United Methodist Church and the Presbyterian Church, U.S.A. These denominations exercised considerable power in the WCC. The black minority caucuses within them represented prophetic voices demanding the reallocation of their funds for racial justice through the economic empowerment of racially oppressed peoples.

Thus, those prophetic voices signified another major contribution that African peoples have made to the ecumenical movement. As Gayraud Wilmore attests, that contribution "was the conceptualization of a theological basis for breaking the suffocating embrace of White liberalism and exposing the racism that continued, under siege and by no means vanquished, in the institutions that presumed to be the conscience of the nation."[16] That contribution in the American context greatly influenced the World Council of Churches, and it also helped Africans on the continent, and especially in South Africa, to project their voices onto the world stage of the ecumenical movement.

In the 1970s the World Council of Churches underwent considerable financial loss in a backlash response to its support for the South African anti-apartheid struggle. Many denominations accused it of supporting the African National Congress commitment to "armed rebellion" by sending financial gifts directly to the liberation movement in South Africa or supporting the establishment of ANC offices for the work of exiles in Europe and America.

Much of the WCC's financial support for the liberation movement in South Africa came out of a special fund set up in 1968 when it first launched its Program to Combat Racism. That fund, intended to support liberation movements, had always been under fire by the conservative constituencies within WCC's member churches. The decision to give financial support to the liberation struggle in South Africa added fuel to a smoldering fire, and the WCC would later feel the consequences in its revenues. Yet, in return for its moral and financial support, the WCC maintained good faith with its African constituents both on the continent and abroad. In fact, in his address to the Eighth Assembly of the World Council of Churches in Harare, Nelson Mandela offered the following apt assessment of black Africa's appreciation for the WCC:

> As part of an international effort to ensure that never again should such things happen, the WCC helped voice the international community's insistence that human rights are the rights of all people everywhere. In doing so you helped vindicate the struggles of the oppressed for their freedom.
>
> To us in South Africa and Southern Africa, and indeed the entire continent, the WCC has always been known as a champion of the oppressed and the exploited.
>
> On the other hand, the name of the WCC struck fear in the hearts of those who ruled our country and destabilized our region during the inhuman days of apartheid. To mention your name was to incur the wrath of the authorities. To indicate support for your views was to be labeled an enemy of the state.
>
> Precisely for that reason, the vast majority of our people heard the name of the WCC with joy. It encouraged and inspired us. . . .
>
> Above all you respected the judgment of the oppressed as to what were the most appropriate means for attaining their freedom. For that true solidarity, the people of South and Southern Africa will always remember the WCC with gratitude.[17]

During the anti-apartheid struggle in South Africa, the South African Council of Churches (SACC), the primary ecumenical institution in the country, virtually served as a government as it distributed monies and social services throughout the country. With substantial financial help from abroad, the SACC provided financial assistance to those families whose wage earners had been imprisoned, maimed, or killed in the struggle. They also provided the spiritual and educational dimension for the movement itself through conferences, retreats, workshops, publications, alliances, rallies, protest marches, and the like.

Thus it is important to note that black theology's identification of the Christian gospel with God's solidarity with the oppressed in their struggle for justice constituted then and now a significant contribution to ecumenical Christianity's spiritual conscience. Further, from the beginning black theology demonstrated its concern for developing alliances with African and Caribbean theologians. To that end, African Americans held consultations in Abidjan, Cote d'Ivoire (1971); with the AACC and the Society for the Study of Black Religion at Union Theological Seminary in New York (1973); in Jamaica (1976); and in Ghana (1977 and 1996) at the Pan African Conference of Third World Theologians.

AFRICAN "VISIONS OF AUTHENTICITY"

Black theology, African theology, and Caribbean theology grew out of the rise of a new consciousness of racial, cultural, and national identities that had been severely hindered by the practices of slavery, racism, and colonialism. This new consciousness implied a radical break with all European values of conquest and domination that have permeated all dimensions of Western culture. Most important, this new black consciousness would enable African peoples to establish what the first assembly of the All Africa Conference of Churches called "authentic Christianity" based on "faithfulness to Christ's prophetic ministry."

From the time of its inaugural meeting, in Ibadan in 1958, up to the present day, the AACC has challenged the African churches to seek the meaning of authentic Christianity and establish it in Africa. The Africanization of the gospel constituted one major implication of that concern. It remained for the churches to determine the substantive meaning of the concept "Africanization." The inaugural processional of the AACC began with a distinctive African beat. For the first time, African Christians heard the sound of the drums in a Christian procession. The use of the drums had long been proscribed during the missionary colonial period. This audacious act signaled a break from foreign control and the blessing of a traditional African musical instrument fully integrated into Christian worship. Both the rhythm and the beat signaled the rejection of inauthentic Christianity as delivered to Africans by the missionary movement.

The first and second assemblies of the AACC, in Kampala (1963) and in Abidjan (1969), struggled to give meaning to the concept of "authentic Christianity" by discussing the need for independence from all vestiges of colonialism. Those early years of independence were times of widespread euphoria in Africa and an altogether wonderful time to be there. In fact, a Nigerian scholar, Effiong Utuk, captures that spirit in his own commentary about the first assembly of the AACC in Kampala in 1963. He wrote, "For good or ill, Kampala was to the founding churches what Pentecost was to the apostolic band."[18] It declared legitimacy for Christianity in Africa at a time when everything foreign was being discarded. But the rhetoric failed to translate itself into programs, and it avoided any strategic budgetary discussion.

The third assembly of the AACC at Lusaka in 1974 brought matters to a head program-wise by shocking the ecumenical world when it boldly called for a moratorium on missionaries and monies from abroad. The AACC's young, dynamic general secretary, Canon Burgess Carr, described authentic African Christianity as "the struggle to recover the stolen dignity of our black personhood; the struggle to seize our history in our own hands and to reshape it according to our own designs; the struggle against drought, poverty, alienation, and exploitation."[19]

Luksaka's moratorium on foreign missionaries was viewed as a necessary condition for the Africanization of the gospel.[20] Needless to say, perhaps, Africa's European and Euro-American ecumenical partners were not very sanguine about the moratorium. In light of the budgetary crisis that the AACC suffered as a result, the Nairobi assembly (1976) modified it so as to affirm a mixed modality of authenticity by allowing for a mixture of African and non-African heritages. Undoubtedly, the moratorium had two effects. First, it sensitized many Western churches to the problem of economic dependency. Second, its modification of the policy opened the floodgates for conservative evangelicals to provide monies for church development and to develop aggressive programs of evangelism throughout the continent. The implications of the latter practices have not yet been fully determined.

The fifth assembly of the AACC met in Lome, Togo, in 1987. Archbishop Desmond Tutu's unanimous election to the presidency enabled him to bring his persuasive skills and global prestige to bear on the task of strengthening the AACC's mission. When Tutu came to the podium to give his address at Lome, the assembly broke into extended applause. Utuk vividly describes the dramatic aspects of the scene, which united the struggles of Africans and African Americans for freedom:

> First, Tutu invited all the South Africans at the meeting to the rostrum. As they came, one by one, he reminded the entire gathering of apartheid's numerous victims, naming some who were detained, jailed, or harassed. Finally, they all joined in singing a common liberation song: "What have we done? Our sin is that we are black. . . ." As soon as the song was over, the Assembly unanimously and instinctively "broke into a vibrant rendition of 'We Shall Overcome,' immediately followed by "nkosi sikele Africa" (God Bless Africa). The day witnessed a piece of Africana previously unseen in this kind of ecumenical setting.[21]

In his address, Tutu discussed African partnerships with the churches in the West in such a way as to affirm the process of Africanization as a godsend. In fact, he "tied authentic spirituality to incarnation in the world without being polluted by it."[22] Most important, he said:

> We must be authentically African. We must be who we are. You know God did not make a mistake in creating us Black. We are not carbon copies of any one else. We are glorious originals. We are unique. We are not meant to apologize for our existence; we have to have a most worthy "Africanness" about us.[23]

Bishop Tutu then went on to discuss at length the African value of community, and on the basis of that value he argued for the interdependence of all humanity. "My humanity is totally incomplete without yours. My humanity is bound up with yours."[24] As a result of his leadership, the AACC's deficit was eliminated under his watch. But that elimination did not imply financial self-sufficiency for the AACC. The sad fact remains that the overwhelming majority of African delegates to the seventh assembly of the AACC at Addis Ababa in 1997[25] were dependent on monies from abroad to cover their transportation and assembly costs. Thus the heavy economic dependence of the churches in Africa on those in the West portends continuing problems with the development of authentic partnerships between the two.

Finally, let me say a brief word about my native African Canadian Christians.[26] They have not enjoyed much direct participation in this ecumenical Christianity, since their history has been largely one of exclusion from and dependency on the largesse of the mainstream white churches. Yet one cannot discuss this subject without invoking the memory of the Reverend Dr. William P. Oliver, longtime pastor of the Cornwallis Street Baptist Church in Halifax. Inspired by the black consciousness movement in the United States and the liberation movements in Africa, Dr. Oliver persuaded sizable numbers of blacks to initiate a novel event that was destined to have widespread impact on the consciousness of the African churches in Canada and on the consciences of white Canadians. By utilizing the insights and strategies of the black consciousness movements for racial self-determination, and by developing nascent alliances with the Canadian government, he and others were effective in establishing institutions that have had a profound impact on the black communities in the province of Nova Scotia and elsewhere. Various local incentive programs, community recreational centers, the Human Rights Commission, the Black Cultural Center for Nova Scotia, and various black professional associations constitute part of that legacy—a legacy greatly inspired by wider Pan-African struggles for freedom, equality, and self-determination. Like their Pan-African brothers and sisters elsewhere in the world, and despite their lack of direct experience in the ecumenical movement, African Canadians have bequeathed similar gifts to the larger world—gifts of struggle for survival and for racial justice; gifts of community, religious toleration, respect for racial differences, and the quest for self-determination. In their quest for human dignity, they have given their former oppressors the seeds for their own redemption through the expansion of democracy in both the secular and religious worlds of all peoples.

PART 2
FAITH IN DIALOGUE

Chapter 10

Centrality of Periphery

Geography of Ecumenical Relations

Kosuke Koyama

Biblical faith is time-oriented. Rabbi Abraham Heschel writes:

> We expend time to gain space. To enhance our power in the world of space is our main objective. Yet to have more does not mean to be more. The power we attain in the world of space terminates abruptly at the borderline of time. But time is the heart of existence.[1]

"To have more does not mean to be more" is a principle for healthy community. Valuing time means valuing community. It is justice that binds time and community. Time is indeed the heart of existence as it struggles for justice in community. Without justice, time will lose the quality of community: "therefore because you trample on the poor and take from them levies of grain, you have built houses of hewn stone, but you shall not live in them" (Amos 5:11). Likewise Jesus: "If one of you has a child or an ox that has fallen into a well, will you not immediately pull it out on a sabbath day?" (Luke 14:5).

The prayer of Jesus, that "they may be one, as we are one" (John 17:22), has nurtured our image of ecumenical blessing. That "they may be one" implies the creation of a wholesome (*shalom*) human community in which "trampling on the poor" has no place and "the sabbath was made for humankind, and not humankind for the sabbath" (Mark 2:27) is affirmed. Ecumenical unity without justice would be a demonic human environment, an imperial globalism in contradistinction to ecumenical relations with justice.

The word *ecumenical* implies the faithfulness of God to embrace the whole, inhabited world with the blessing of abundant life. Upon this divine faithfulness are built webbed, interdependent human relations, personal and communal, even international (2 Cor. 9:8). Ecumenism, from the word *oikos*, meaning "house," means "good housekeeping" for all the inhabited world. The *oikos* theology listens to the catholicity of mercy: "God has imprisoned all in disobedience so that he may be merciful to all" (Rom. 11:32). That "God may be merciful to all" is at the heart of the *shekinah/emmanuel* (divine presence/"God is with us") message. This God of the catholicity of mercy is "an impassioned God" (Ex. 20:5 *Tanakh*). The *pathos* of God rejects our self-serving image of status quo, God of "law and order."

In 1963, in his Letter from Birmingham Jail, the Baptist minister Martin Luther King Jr. wrote with the mind of the impassioned God:

> Frankly, I have never yet engaged in a direct-action movement that was "well-timed," according to the timetable of those who have not suffered unduly from the disease of segregation. For years now I have heard the word "Wait!" It rings in the ear of every Negro with a piercing familiarity. This "wait" has almost always meant "never." . . . We have waited for more than three hundred and forty years for our constitutional and God given rights.

These words bind time with justice in the concrete context of human community. Here the warning of the biblical tradition, that time is miscarried when justice is not established, has been articulated. Authentic Christian eschatology, the destruction of the *never*-god idol, was proclaimed from a jail in the American South. Racism makes the *never*-god out of the eternal God by equating the divine eternity with the status quo. In his speech "I Have a Dream," Martin Luther King envisions that someday humanity will walk away from the status quo God to the passionate God of just community. In this vision that "time is the heart of existence" is demonstrated.

That the quality of time is decided by the degree it creates a just community is called eschatology. There is no eschatology apart from this striving toward a just community. This eschatology is discerned in "the midnight tears," as James Baldwin writes:

> Only the Lord saw the midnight tears, only He was present when one of His children, moaning and wringing hands, paced up and down the room. When one slapped one's child in anger the recoil in the heart reverberated through heaven and became part of the pain of the universe. . . . It was the Lord who knew of the impossibility every parent in that room faced: how to prepare the child for the day when the child would be despised and how to *create* in the child—by what means?—a stronger antidote to this poison than one had found for oneself.[2]

Full of *pathos*! There is no easy escape! The status quo is experienced as tyranny. Our concept of the *oikumene* ("family room") is shaken by the knowledge that some of our brothers and sisters are "pacing up and down the room" shedding "midnight tears." These words of inner struggle express the authentic yearning for the unity of time, community, and justice. The question remains: How is ecumenical space related to "the impossibility every parent in that room faced"?

On a similar note, Deotis Roberts has written:

> Oppression that leads to ethnic suffering casts the God question in a different context. One has to search for the meaning of life and historical existence while facing the negativities of life. We must ask often if God cares. Does God really bear our griefs and carry our sorrows? The questions Why? And how long are often on the hearts and minds of blacks.[3]

"In that room" the question "Does God care?" is raised. The question echoes the cry of Jesus on the cross: "My God, my God, why have you forsaken me?" (Mark 15:34). "Does God care?" is asked by those who experience that "only the Lord saw the midnight tears." Only faith can ask the question: "Does God care?" The *pathos* hidden in this question takes me to the Reformer Martin Luther's "To flee to God against God."[4] The astounding paradox of the Christian faith is that the new time and space came to the world through one who was *nailed down* on the cross, losing all mobility in space. This is the essence of the theology of the cross (*theologia crucis*). "A revelation is final if it has the power of negating itself without losing itself."[5]

Time connotes space. I understand God is eternally spacious, and spaciously eternal. Justice brings time/space and community together. I pay attention to the space of that room in which the question "Does God care?' is asked. Every space must symbolize justice. This is the God-given mission of space, since God is eternally spacious and spaciously eternal. Tragically, however, history is replete with violent misappropriation of space: the tragic story of the Native American "Trail of Tears" demonstrates that the American continental spaciousness occasioned the violent human greed that expelled native peoples from their home community space. Hitler's campaign for *Lebensraum* for the German race devastated both time and space for all of Europe. Japanese imperialism, the same greed for space, is disguised under the name of "The Great East Asia Co-Prosperity Sphere."

I suggest a theological concept of the spacious God who creates spaciousness in the very room in which a man or woman paces up and down in the midnight. The suggestion is absurd. Yet, paradoxically, the people who ask the question "Does God care?" create meaningful human space for all people. For the question is devastatingly valid (John 8:32). Truth is "scandalous" (1 Cor. 1:23) because it is about the theology of the cross: in the crucified God authentic human dignity and freedom are demonstrated. How thoroughly absurd! This absurdity is not a work of the status quo god but the God of the *creatio ex nihilo*.

"The scandal of the cross" is accompanied by a firm law: "It is a terrible, an inexorable, law that one cannot deny the humanity of another without diminishing one's own. In the face of one's victim, one sees oneself."[6] In a different historical context John Donne, the seventeenth-century Anglican divine, famously wrote: "any man's death diminishes me, because I am involved in mankind, and therefore never seem to know for whom the bell tolls: it tolls for thee."[7] What is at stake here is what John Mbiti says of the African culture of social belongingness: "I am because we are, and since we are, therefore I am."[8] The paradox of the scandalous cross comes to us together with the "terrible law." Christ's scandal is not a groundless absurdity. Ecumenical speech must not be ignorant of this "terrible law." The christological paradox invited ethical command.

Derrick Bell laments "the permanence of racism" in his book *Faces at the Bottom of the Well*.[9] Since the questions "Why?" and "How long?" will not disappear from the face of the *oikumene*, Baldwin's law will remain valid as long as history continues. This is the material content of Christian eschatology. This eschatology must not become an eschatology of hatred: "Hatred destroys finally the core of the life of the hater."[10] If this happens, it will go against the *shalom* of the human community. This eschatology, experienced by the people who ask the question "Does God care?" guides us into the true eschatology, that is, the true understanding of the nature of time and space in which all of us in the whole inhabited world live.

My life in the city of New York brought me, an Asian theologian, for the first time, to an empirical proximity with black people. As time passed, I learned to see them as a people of the "sign" (*semeion*) for all humanity. Lani Guinier, using a practical image, says that "race functions in American society much like a canary in a coal mine."[11] In my private meditation, black people are like giraffes that can see the approach of lions before the zebras of the lower vista notice. Robert M. Franklin writes: "[Black congregations] also made claims upon the nation's identity, conscience, and moral obligation to practice fairness and mercy toward its most disfranchised citizens."[12] The *semeion* must point to both transcendental and practical safety. If it signals only the transcendental beyond, it may eventually become lifeless. Mysticism must be practical. "But you have kept the good wine until now" (John 2:10).

The biblical "sign" fosters the quality of community. The sign Jesus gave at the wedding of Cana enhanced the quality of life of that community. It reinforces the dictum of John Mbiti. In my life in the confusing and dynamic city of New York, I came to notice an alliance between transcendence and hierarchy ideologies. I recognize that transcendence ("that side") must be communicated to us who are on "this side" of transcendence. The methodology of this communication must be guided by the desire to enhance the health of community. My nervous cautiousness about the scheme of hierarchy ("command from the above") derives from my own personal pilgrimage. As a person who lived through the destructive fanaticism of the Japanese imperial cult and of the American application of the cosmic heat to the two populated cities of Japan during World War II, I learned, unfortunately, to distrust the words of the dominant group of society. I became aware that a vertically imposed fanaticism is far more toxic to human welfare than one horizontally generated. Hierarchy is a power system. Power is always misused. There is no hierarchy, religious or secular, that is never misused. I believe that the distance between God and an archbishop is equal to the distance between God and a peasant.

American racial hierarchy is brutally obvious. Whites (male) are in the top and blacks (female) in the bottom, and other kinds are placed somewhere in between. The racial hierarchy "persists in income levels, residential patterns, incarceration rates, life expectancy, and a variety of other empirical measures."[13] Racial hierarchy derives from "the conscious or unconscious belief in the inherent superiority of persons of European ancestry which entitles all white peoples to a position of dominance and privilege."[14] James Cone writes: "The essence of the gospel of Christ stands or falls on the question of black humanity."[15]

The categorization of "above" (the hierarchically higher) and "below" (the hierarchically lower) is one of the fundamental symbols of religious, cultural, and social discourse in general. In religious speech this becomes prominent. The above is the abode of the holy God, *gloria in excelsis Deo.* God is in the hierarchical apex. The above is thought to be truthful and authentic while the below is wanting in these. Granting the hierarchical prestige of God to itself, white Christendom of the West has employed hierarchical ideology to engage in wide-ranging acts of colonial domination, as K. M. Panikkar's *Asia and Western Dominance* (1953) articulates. But this transference is problematic. In the light of the biblical truth of the divine *shekinah,* the church is possessed by, not possessing, the truth of salvation. The Pentecost created the church, not the other way around. Theology of hierarchy tends to become an ideology of the hierarchical distribution of power and prestige.

The ecumenical presence of God must not be imprisoned in our authority structure of social hierarchy. The *shekinah* gospel declares: "You know that the rulers of the Gentiles lord it over them, and their great ones are tyrants over them. It will not be so among you; but whoever wishes to be great among you must be your servant" (Matt. 20:25–26). This politically revolutionary suggestion is made by the one who said "the Son of Man has nowhere to lay his head" (Luke 9:58). The healing truth of human community in the *oikumene* is found in the figure of the servant. Grace does not "lord it over" the community. There is an important contrast between the two origins and forms of power, one symbolized by Bethlehem and the other by Rome. The gospel rejects a facile identity between "the higher" and "the truer."

I propose an image of "center and periphery" instead of the hierarchical "above and below." This suggests a horizontal rather than a vertical movement. I cherish the transcendence hidden in horizontality more than the more apparent transcendence concomitant with verticality. I notice a different tone and message coming from the periphery from the one imposed from above. The dynamism of my suggestion springs from the theology of the cross; that is, in it the center person has gone to the periphery, and hence the periphery has now become the center. Howard Thurman speaks of this new center: "When I love someone I seem to be at the center of all meanings and values."[16] A new orientation in the experience of history is here suggested. "He has sent me to proclaim release to the captives and recovery of sight to the blind" (Luke 4:18). This is the theme of *Jesus and the Disinherited* (Howard Thurman, 1949), *The Letter from the Birmingham City Jail* (Martin Luther King Jr., 1963), *A Black Theology of Liberation* (James Cone, 1970), *Black Theology in Dialogue* (J. Deotis Roberts, 1987), *Faces at the Bottom of the Well* (Derrick Bell, 1992), and *Sisters in the Wilderness* (Delores S. Williams, 1993) and other prophetic words from the periphery.

The universal *shekinah* embraces humanity from the periphery. Its prophetic quality is realized in history by the successive apostolic acts that make the periphery central. The rule of God is being effected upon the earth by the disinherited who speak from the jail and from the bottom of the well. This dialectic is apostolic. The words of Delores Williams, "To be a Christian in North America is to wage war against the white cultural, social and religious values that make the genocide of black people possible,"[17] come from the bottom of the well. The voice from the periphery, rather than from the height of the hierarchy, would more adequately describe the four essential marks of the church: one, holy, catholic, and apostolic. The marks of the church are intrinsic and extrinsic. They speak of the essential character of the church *and* of the church's relationship to the world. The church would lose her marks if her relationship with the periphery were *not* one, holy, catholic, and apostolic. Thus the periphery becomes a clue to ecclesiology.

The church is *one* when it is one for all people of all races. Racial hierarchy is inconsistent with this vision. The church is *holy* when the peoples of periphery are sanctified. Holiness must demonstrate the "boundary breaking God."[18] The church is *catholic* when its center is located at the periphery. The catholicity of the church is biased; it is not an ordinary universality. And the church is *apostolic* when it imitates the Head of the church who has gone to the utter periphery. The apostolicity is defined by the theology of the cross.

The theology of the cross is community-centered. The spirit of this theology may be expressed most concisely in one line of the Lord's Prayer: "Give us this day our daily bread." When "Give *us*" is recited, the integrity of the whole human community is intended. This petition summarizes the nature of ecumenical relations. All of us, but particularly those who are afflicted by poverty, need food. Ecumenical concerns are concrete and direct. They are about our basic daily needs (James 2:16).

The pluralism of our time calls into question, in philosophical as well as practical terms, the concentration of power and prestige. It has a goal, *telos*, to achieve: the *shalom* of the human community. Baldwin writes: "Being black affected one's life span, insurance rates, blood pressure, lovers, children, every dangerous hour of every dangerous day. There was absolutely no way *not* to be black without ceasing to exist. But it frequently seemed that there was no way to be black, either, without ceasing to exist."[19] To set the right *telos*, our pluralism must learn of this "no exit" (no plural choices) human situation; otherwise we would fall into an irresponsible "anything goes" pluralism.

Steve Biko, victim of South African apartheid (martyred on September 12, 1977), wrote: "We did not believe that religion could be featured as a separate

part of our existence on earth. . . . We believed that God was always in communication with us and therefore merited attention everywhere and anywhere."[20]
In the "Letter from Birmingham Jail," Martin Luther King, in line with Steve
Biko, wrote: "Injustice anywhere is a threat to justice everywhere." The theological basis of pluralism is the possibility of communication between God and our
souls "everywhere and anywhere." The spacious God is the God of "everywhere
and anywhere" of whom Biko and King, two martyrs, spoke so passionately.

Christian eschatology must share in this passionate sense of "everywhere and
anywhere." The confession "from there he shall come to judge the living and the
dead" is an expression of the *shekinah* God "everywhere and anywhere." This is
the geography of ecumenical relations. In it the periphery is constantly made center. This is where theology and ethics intersect. That God's presence among us
does not come to an end is the promise of the doctrine of *eschaton* ("end"). The
struggle for social justice, "combat against racism,"[21] is the eschatological engagement that makes time the heart of existence.

Chapter 11

African Christianity as African Religion

Beyond the Contextualization Paradigm

Tinyiko Samuel Maluleke

INTRODUCTION

We are honoring Deotis Roberts at a time when all radical theologies are facing great challenges. In Africa, no sooner had black and African theologies found their voice than they have been swept aside by other developments in the world. Chief among these developments has been the end of the cold war and all its ramifications, as well as the seemingly unbridled growth of the phenomenon of globalization. In this atmosphere, notions of blackness and liberation have come under attack from many different quarters. There is, for my purposes, no better way of honoring so distinguished a black scholar as Deotis Roberts as offering an essay that grapples, methodologically, with some of the challenges facing black and African theologies today. In this essay I argue that African Christianity is and has become an African religion and that we ought to adjust our theological methodologies and analytical tools to reflect this reality.

THE LEGACY OF METHODOLOGICAL RESTLESSNESS

Elsewhere, I have suggested (Maluleke 1997a) that the ultimate contribution of South African black theology to African Christian theology lies not merely in foregrounding race as an analytical tool but in the areas of sociotheological hermeneutics and methodology. Few theologies (in Africa, at least) make a bigger fuss on issues of method, hermeneutics, ideology, assumptions, and orientation. Whereas many African theologies have tended to choose and be satisfied with a specific methodology and proceeded to get on with the task at hand, South African black theology has been methodologically restless and theoretically ill at ease—deliberately so. So important have issues of methodology and ideology become that South African black theology has often seemed "bogged down" with these kinds of issues, so that some have seen this as a handicap rather than a strength.

Critics have often called for a halt to the seeming "obsession" with ideological and methodological debates in favor of the commencement of "real" theology. Others have seen black theology's often complex concern with issues of method, theory, and ideology as a sign of elitism and distance from ordinary people. Hence some have been calling for a "simpler" black theology that can be easily digested by the masses. The alleged obsession with theory and method sometimes has been used to explain why black theology has allegedly not managed to grab the imagination of the masses. In contrast, black theologians—notably I. J. Mosala (1989)—have often argued that it is not the abundance but the lack of theoretically astute methodologies that have hindered black theology. For this reason, in black theology writings much space is yielded to and much energy is spent on a relentless search and exploration for finer method and more astute theory.

The subject of such exploration has been marked by concerns about definitions and roles of interlocutors, the question and place of blackness, blackness in relation to gender, Marxist tools of analysis, the ideological weight of the Bible, and so forth. The late but forceful emergence (Maluleke 1997b) of the category of gender in the mix of method and interlocutor discussions in black theology has served to intensify the debate and the contestations—even to effect a paradigm shift. Today the issues of poverty, identity, culture, the devastation of HIV-AIDS, as well as post–cold war racism have been added to the mix. All these matters are fertile ground for vigorous contestations and lively debate. But it is in such contestations and such debate that black theology has thrived over the years. From a black theology point of view, therefore, it has not been considered good enough to have a moral stand on which to build a theological project—however sound and well-intentioned such a moral stand might be.

Therefore theological premises such as those that operate from (moralistic) notions such as "the Bible is the Word of God," "God is on the side of the poor," and "God is black" are considered at best discussion starters, at worst potentially unhelpful, if not misleading, methodological pointers—and not ever as useful as accomplished methodological starting points, let alone blueprints. This is especially true if the ultimate goal of our theological project is comprehensive liberation. For poor and oppressed people, comprehensive liberation is nonnegotiable. Methodologically, therefore, it is not enough to (think we) know who we are, who and what we are against, and what we wish to achieve. South African black theology has taught us that to achieve our goal of total liberation precisely and comprehensively, we need to think precisely and astutely about method, ideology, and theory. Such has been the commitment to fine-tuning issues of method that often black theologians have appeared to be at great and unnecessary loggerheads, one with the other. It is all part and parcel of the quest of steering away from ideologically naive and theoretically bankrupt theological projects, however well-meaning and well-intentioned such projects might be. Such projects will—willy-nilly—serve to prolong, intensify, and entrench the misery of the oppressed, which is the majority of people on the African continent, the black peoples. This is particularly deadly and unacceptable when it is ignorantly done in the name of liberation.

In light of the great many challenges facing black and poor people in Africa today—racism, sexism, HIV-AIDS, and globalization—the temptation is there to call for a halt in methodological exploration. Old critical voices that poured scorn over what they saw as obsession with theory and method may speak with renewed energy against lengthy methodological debates. After all, we are faced with matters of life and death. We are faced with the scourge of HIV-AIDS. The death statistics tell us that we are living through a catastrophe of major proportions. As if this were not enough, we have the challenge of globalization, which divides in the name of uniting, impoverishing even as it promises wealth for all, strengthening the strong at the expense of the weak even as the world is said to become a global village. Surely, with all these challenges and more before us, we should spend less time on theory and more on practice. On the contrary, I suggest that because of the complex challenges we face, we need to keep vigilant theoretical focus.

METHODOLOGICAL "OIL CHECK"

Car owners do not have to check the oil levels of their cars in the same way they do their fuel levels. Lack of fuel can bring the car to a sudden halt, whereas the effect of a drop in oil level and pressure will take longer to manifest—only with more deadly and long-term consequences. It is therefore crucial for car owners to have the occasional oil check, or else they risk extensive damage to the engine. I want to suggest that in keeping with black theology's traditional quest for a theological project based on and constantly guided by an astute theoretical framework, we (need to) do a methodological "oil check" on the major theoretical framework or paradigm within which several theologies of liberation have operated and continue to operate. If the project of liberation remains important for African Christian theology—even if the word itself may have gone out of fashion—then it is important that we undertake the exercise that I am proposing. What we need to ask ourselves is whether the assumptions, premises, and theological methodologies we have been using are sufficient.

Signs of Change

Admittedly, the end of the cold war and apartheid eras have prompted many to propose theologies that go beyond the traditional liberation theology. Within African theology such proposals would include those of Charles Villa-Vicencio (1992), Jesse Mugambi (1995), and Kä Mana for a theology of reconstruction in the pace of conventional theologies of liberation. Kwame Bediako's (1995) "African identity" theology, as well as Lamin Sanneh's (1988) "translation theology," contains specific suggestions for change of emphases and starting points in the conceptualization of theological projects on the continent. The work of African women theologians in challenging patriarchy in African culture (Oduyoye 1995), as well as the deployment of such new methods of theologizing as storytelling and divinization (Dube 2001), *Bosadi* (Masenya) has also pushed the boundaries of African theologizing in significant ways. Within and outside South African black theology have been several proposals for change. Some of these have been too rushed and gloomy—proclaiming the sudden death and necessary burial of black theology. Others have suggested that now more than ever before black theology ought to identify with or as an genre of African theology (cf. Motlhabi 1995). What is noteworthy is that, in the process, black theology has recently tackled issues that would not have been on its agenda a few years back. One is thinking here of such issues as globalization, the HIV-AIDS pandemic, reconciliation, and the African independent churches. These are indications of a significant expansion and adaptability of the black theology agenda. Already in these works one gets a sense of methodological restlessness, a sense that what has been inherited may not address what is emerging. Indeed, what I suggest is that most of the proposals for "new" methods and "new" names for black and African theologies testify to the limits of what is theologically achievable through the tool of the contextual theology paradigm, as well as its basic premises. Not taking full cognizance of the limits of the contextual theology paradigm, some of the "new" proposals have effectively called for what amount to half-measures and mere name changes. Others have called for changes in the goals of the theological project but have nevertheless continued to use the very methodologies that produce the outcomes they deplore.

AFRICANITY AND CHRISTIANITY:
TOWARD A DIFFERENT VIEW

Almost all innovative theological projects in Africa regard as one of their key subject matters something called "African Christianity," "Christianity in Africa," "black Christianity," "church in Africa," or some other linguistic estimation of the same. The basic quest in much of the theological output of black and African theology has been to discover, articulate, and give shape to this reality of African or black Christianity. Basic to the quest is the suggestion that peculiarly and manifestly African and black ways of being Christian are desirable, possible, and have already been accomplished if they were not in existence already. This premise—itself seldom probed—is basic to almost all hues of black and African theologies.

The Comparative Roots of the Premise

The other side of the premise is the implied suggestion that Christianity is itself not of Africa but that Africans *should, can,* and indeed *have* put their stamp on it. It is a comparativist concept—born out of a comparison between Christianity and African religiosity. The very formulations "black Christianity" and "African Christianity" denote the coming together of two realities, Africanity on the one hand and Christianity on the other. This comparative formulation has formed the basic framework and premise upon which countless black and African theologies have been constructed. This path was established from the time when pioneer missionaries and evangelists went about looking for cultural equivalences (and, by implication, differences) between Christianity and African religiosity.

A classic example of this comparative approach is to be found in some of the criteria that pioneer missionaries are said to have used to determine and establish religiosity among Africans. Such criteria included the search for evidence of belief in gods and or monotheistic ideals. We are often told that pioneer missionaries would regularly choose a name for God that was already in usage. Clearly, in societies where different names were used for either the same god or different gods, there was much confusion. Here the adoption of one name above others might have seemed tantamount to the introduction of a new deity altogether. Furthermore, in societies where God cannot be "counted" as "one god" or "two gods" but is seen as uncountable and innumerable, the idea that one God only ought to be worshiped must have sounded rather peculiar, if not altogether suspicious. As for pioneer missionaries' search for evidence of religiosity, this was—as suggested by Chidester (1996)—regrettably often a function of the colonial politics of conquest and subjugation. People not yet conquered would be invariably be declared nonreligious, if not irreligious. This was often a moral pretext for engaging in wars of conquest against people of lower status—those without religion and without souls. But soon after conquest, the very same people of no religion would be discovered to have a religious system—a system that would be described as elementary and needing to be overhauled or fulfilled by the new Christian message. But once religion was "discovered," the route of comparison was established. If Africans were, religiously speaking, no clean slates upon which a fresh and new religion was written, then it stands to reason that such comparative issues as continuity and discontinuity, syncretism and conversion, innovation, adaptation, and conformity would become part of the theological grammar.

There were particularly theological elements in the comparison. Hence the search was not merely for God equivalence but for monotheism, and also for Christ and church equivalents. The theological output in response to questions such as those resulted in treatises in which Christ was described as an ancestor, the elder brother, the chief, and the crucified among crossbearers (cf. Mofokeng 1988). Inevitably, some gods of Africa were christened as the Christian God, while others were seen as forebears of one and the same God (cf. p'Bitek 1970). The adoption of African names of God long used was both a stroke of genius and a confusing act. It underlined continuity but was also confusing since the "new" god was not simply the same as the old one, even though the same name was used.

In other words, the comparison of which I speak was not necessarily a fair and even-handed one. In many ways it was an attempt at a violent rewriting of a people's religious consciousness. This is especially true when seen against the backdrop of colonial conquest. But precisely because of the many admittedly feeble attempts to defer to local religious sensitivities (such as the use of familiar names), and because of the resilience of local people and their religions, pioneer missionaries did not have total control even as local people lost total control over their own religious and political milieu.

CHRISTIANITY AS AFRICAN RELIGION

Breaking Out of the Kraal

The basic methodological problem that has faced black and African theologians over the years has been the inability to go beyond the binary and dualistic analyses informed by a presumed black or African reality versus a Christian reality. Almost all the theological output on the continent has been built on this premise—in both black and African theologies. Even the latter-day attempts to bring African independent churches into the fold have not escaped but intensified the dual freeway of Christianity versus Africanity. Book after book, article after article, thesis after thesis has been produced only to add color and detail to the presumed clash and need for better cooperation between Africanity and Christianity. Even our most radical theologies, such as black theology and the theologies of African women, have not wandered far from the kraal of the Christianity-versus-Africanity conundrum. Both black theology and African women's theology have, admittedly, stated most articulately and very starkly the problem at which I am hinting. Black theology has done this by pointing to the paradox of being black and Christian—oppressed by the very "thing" that has stolen one's heart. No one stated this dilemma more starkly than Gabriel Setiloane, who, upon being challenged by a young student as to why he stays a Christian pastor and in that way continues to seek Christian converts even though he asserts that African religion is just as good, replied thus: "For myself, first I am like someone who has been bewitched, and I find it difficult to shake off the Christian witchcraft with which I have been captivated" (Setiloane 1979:63). Clearly, being Christian and being African is here presented as a vexing and problematic state to be in. Black theologians have stated the same dilemma. Today, African women theologians are making the same point about the painful paradoxes of being African, woman, and Christian at the same time—a kind of triple jeopardy. For this reason African women have become critical of patriarchy in African culture, sexism in contemporary culture, patriarchy within Christianity. But neither black theology nor African women's theology has been able to make a break with the Africanity-versus-Christianity conundrum. It seems therefore that even the most radical African theologies launch themselves from the premise of Africanity versus Christianity, however differently stated. African women theologians present the problem in terms of the challenge of staying African, Christian and woman in light of patriarchy both within Africanity and Christianity. Black theologians present the dilemma in terms of the challenge of being black, poor, oppressed, and Christian in situations where Christian teaching and people are the agents of oppression and where blackness is justification for discrimination.

Part of the reason that the methodological problem we have highlighted recurs is the use made of the contextualization method, wherein text and context are the pillars. This approach tends to strengthen the Africanity-versus-Christianity problem, since Africanity is often seen as the context and Christianity as the text. Needless to say, such a view is simplistic in the extreme. The other problem is simply that debates in other social sciences seem to have moved beyond the binaries of text and context. It has been suggested by some, for example, that both text and context are texts, and that there is no text without context. This has led to a situation where, for example, African women theologians have been radically critical of the inability of renowned contextual and liberation theologies to speak for women, and yet women theologians persist in using these very methods, whose bankruptcy they themselves have demonstrated.

Beyond Du Boisian Twoness

I am not an ordinary Christian and have never been. I am not an African Christian in the sense of being half-African and half-Christian. In matters religious, I have never really suffered from the psychological condition of African Americans that W. E. B. Du Bois (in Montmarquet and Hardy 2000:10) has described in term of "twoness, an American, a Negro; two souls, two thoughts, two unreconciled strivings; two warring ideals in one dark body." In other words, I have never naturally, voluntarily, and intensely felt two disparate strivings, an African, a Christian. Many have imposed a kind of Du Boisian "twoness" analytical category as a basic hermeneutic into understanding African Christianity and Christianity in Africa, suggesting that these two realities jostle for supremacy inside the souls of African Christians. I want to suggest that scenario is largely a product of artificial manufacture and perhaps pedagogic and theoretical sensibilities and necessities. It is seldom part of the real and lived experience of many Africans. African Christianity is unorthodox, rich, varied, and untidy—borrowing, taming, radicalizing, bending, deflecting, and reflecting thoughts and experiences from many traditions. But there is a coherent conspiracy that has produced and continues to sustain African Christianity. In this sense, African Christianity is a new but coherent African religion, not merely a battleground for Africanity and Christianity. It is new in relation to both conventional Christianity and conventional African religiosity, but it is no mere re-formation of these two. We make a mistake, therefore, when we constantly seek to understand and evaluate African Christianity against the framework of either conventional Christianity (often theologically) or conventional African religion (often phenomenologically). Therefore, while I think that Du Boisian–type twoness is often forced and strained, what may be applicable is his idea of "double consciousness, this sense of always looking at one's self through the eyes, of measuring one's soul by the tape of a world that looks on in amused contempt and pity" (in Montmarquet and Hardy 2000:10). Here Du Bois speaks of a slightly different problem—the problem of self-perception and the foreign lenses used in the actual perceiving. I suggest that this has, in fact, been one of the problems in the interpretation of African Christianity: namely, that until fairly recently it has almost always been measured by the "tape of a world that looks on in amused contempt and pity." In positing African Christianity as African religion, we are proposing a way of relieving African Christianity from a form of debilitating double consciousness.

Biographical Illustration: Toward a Conclusion

I will now proceed to demonstrate how African Christianity is an African religion by referring to my own biography. The rural home in which I grew up at the northern part of South Africa, toward the Zimbabwean border, was an African Christian home. In the middle of the homestead was a Morula tree—an important symbol of African religion, a tree whose fruit produced an lovely drink, called *vukanyi*, which, when appropriately fermented, became alcoholic. This drink was also pleasing to the ancestors, so it could also be used for libations. The Morula tree at the center of the homestead had other uses. It was a shrine. I remember how the men would squat around the tree while women knelt down around the tree during libation and ancestral prayer sessions. At those occasions, we would be required to chant certain words in a call-response structure of homage and intercession while a senior aunt or uncle would take the lead. And yet every evening we would first listen to Grandma's great storytelling. After that we would read the Bible together, and we children would take turns to read the text aloud, and passionate nightly prayers would be offered to Jesus. On Sundays we all walked to church at the mission station chapel, ten kilometers away. There we would sing glorious songs from the hymnbook that the missionaries from Switzerland had given us. As children we would first go to Sunday school early in the morning, then we would hang around until the adult service commenced later in the day.

At the beginning of spring, for a few Saturdays there would be celebrations in the village as the graduates from the traditional circumcision school would return home triumphantly with new names and new identities. The initiates go into circumcision school as boys and come out as men. There would be wild jubilation in the village as the graduates filed in, led by their captains. From then on, all in the village would call them by their new names, acquired at the school, and only pronouns of respect would henceforth be used to refer to them. Many of the initiates were also members of the mission station church congregation, who would soon resume normal church attendance even as their chests swelled with pride for having survived the tough trials of circumcision school.

Ghosts, snakes, and witches roamed the maize fields, the streams, and the forests at night. Occasionally some of us children would get strangely and inexplicably ill—developing strange and huge boils at awkward bodily places or coughing incessantly for months. At those times we would be taken to the local clinic, the local herbalist, or the African independent churches, which had no chapels but met in people's houses. At these churches there was much noise, loud singing, and dancing. What captivated me at these African independent church services was the sight of grown people bobbing around to the tune and rhythm of African gospel singing, adults crying out loud in orderly liturgical disorder. There, it seems to me, everyone was free to speak to his or her God or gods in a language and manner they saw fit. I remember vigorous and never-ending circle dances, in the middle of which would be the sick and the afflicted. A few times I have stood with other sick people in the middle of that swirling circle, my ears bursting from the singing, smelling the sweat of the worshipers, feeling their heat protecting me. Such circle dances were interrupted only by the occasional collapse of an old man or woman who could take it no more. Then would follow the prayer rituals of reviving the fainted; if all else failed, some libations would be poured on the ground to invoke ancestral intervention. As youngsters, we also assisted the traditional doctors in their training of new traditional doctors. Our role was to hide the pig gallbladder, the unassisted finding of which is the ultimate examination in one's training as a traditional doctor. We would all stare in amazement as the trainee doctors would retrace our steps until they reached the place where the gallbladder was hidden. Yet on Sundays almost all the village, the traditional doctors included, would go to the mission station chapel for worship.

With this brief biographical illustration, I am suggesting that many African Christians do not experience their religion in terms of conflict between Africanity and Christianity. Admittedly, African Christianity is not textbook Christianity. It is not the same as conventional Protestant or Catholic Christianity. Nor is it a rehash of traditional religion. I am suggesting that in African Christianity we have a new religion—new in relation to precolonial African religion and new in relation to colonial Christianity. What we need to do is to begin looking at this new religion in its own terms, and not constantly judge it against either conventional Christian doctrine or conventional African religion. African Christianity is a dynamic young religion that we have not yet begun to appreciate. But first things first. We must first acknowledge it as a largely coherent religion that borrows from, negotiates with, and interprets various religious traditions. Before we rush to evaluate and judge this religion, we must acknowledge its reality. This means rethinking many of our inherited analytical categories, whether they be phenomenological or theological. An appreciation of African Christianity as African religion is the challenge facing radical black and African theologies today. We can meet this challenge only if we are prepared to relinquish some of our long-held methodological starting points.

References

Bediako, Kwame. 1995. *Christianity in Africa: The Renewal of a Non-Western Religion.* Edinburgh: Edinburgh University Press; Maryknoll, N.Y.: Orbis Books.

p'Bitek, Okot. 1970. *African Traditional Religions in Western Scholarship.* Kampala: East African Literature Bureau.

Chidester, David. 1996. *Savage Systems: Colonialism and Comparative Religion in Southern Africa.* Charlottesville: University Press of Virginia.

Dube, Musa. 2001. *Other Ways of Reading: African Women and the Bible.* Geneva: WCC Publications.

Maluleke, Tinyiko Sam. 1997a. "Half a Century of Christian Theologies of Africa: Elements of the Emerging Agenda for the 21st Century." *Journal of Theology for Southern Africa*, no. 99 (November): 4–23.

———. 1997b. "The 'Smoke-Screens' Called Black and African Theologies: The Challenge of African Women Theology." *Journal of Constructive Theology* 3:2 (December): 39–63.

Mana, Kä. 1992. *Foi chréttienne, crise africaine et reconstruction de l'Afrique. Sense et enjeux des théologies africaines contemporaines.* Nairobi: CETA/AACC.

———. 1993. *Theologie africaine pour temps de crise. Christianisme et reconstruction de l'Afrique.* Paris: Karthala.

———. 2000. *La nouvelle évangélisation en Afrique.* Paris: Karthala; Yaoundé: Clé.

Masenya, M. J. 2004. *How Worthy Is the Woman of Worth? Rereading Proverbs 31:10–31 in African-South Africa.* Bible and Theology in Africa 4. New York: Peter Lang.

Mofokeng, Takatso Alfred. 1988. *The Crucified among the Crossbearers: Towards a Black Christology.* Kampen: Uitgevermaatschappij J. H. Kok.

Montmarquet, James A., and Willima H. Hardy, eds. 2000. *Reflections: An Anthology of African American Philosophy.* Belmont: Wadsworth.

Mosala, I. J. 1989. *Black Theology and Biblical Hermenuetics in South Africa.* Grand Rapids: Wm. B. Eerdmans Publishing Co.

Motlhabi, Mokgethi G. 1994. "Black or African Theology? Toward an Integral African Theology." *Journal of Black Theology in South Africa* 8:2 (November): 113–41.

Mugambi, J. N. K. 1995. *From Liberation to Reconstruction: African Christian Theology after the Cold War.* Nairobi: East African Educational Publishers.

Oduyoye, Merci Amba. 1995. *Daughters of Anowa: African Women and Patriarchy.* Maryknoll, N.Y.: Orbis Books.

Sanneh, Lamin. 1989. *Translating the Message: The Missionary Impact on Culture*. Maryknoll, N.Y.: Orbis Books.

Setiloane, G. 1979. "Where Are We in African Theology?" In Kofi Appiah-Kubi and Sergio Torres, eds., *African Theology en Route*. Maryknoll, N.Y.: Orbis Books.

Villa-Vicencio, Charles. 1992. *A Theology of Reconstruction: Nation-Building and Human Rights*. Cape Town: David Philip Publishers; Cambridge: Cambridge University Press.

PART 3
SHAPING THE PRACTICE
OF MINISTRY

FAMILY LIFE STUDIES

Chapter 12

The Ministry of the African American Church as Liberator of Families

Janice E. Hale

Religious historian Albert Raboteau (1995) has pointed out that the church has served both as a source of stability and as a vehicle of change in the African American community. The church has supported African Americans through large-scale social change associated with migration and urbanization. Also, in the arena of civil rights, the churches not only reacted to social and political change, they were in the forefront of bringing it about. In addition to these external frontiers, Raboteau traces the internal theological, liturgical, and institutional developments that have shaped African American religious life over the past five decades.

Sociologist Andrew Billingsley (1992) maintains that in addition to what it does for its members, the black church has always served important functions for the black community as a whole.

> It is in this respect both a preserver of the African-American heritage and an agent for reform. Indeed no successful movement for improving the conditions of life for the African-American people has been mounted without the support of the church. (p. 350)

The Reverend Cecil Murray (in Schneider 1992) stated, "The coming-to-church-for-personal salvation days are over. Now we are looking not only for personal salvation but for social salvation" (p. E–1).

Billingsley maintains that it is a mistake to think of the black church in America as being primarily a religious institution in the same way as a white church is thought of. He points out that community service was an important element of the black religious expression from the beginning. When Absalom Jones, Richard Allen, and others walked out of the white Methodist church in Philadelphia over two hundred years ago, they did not form a new church. They formed the Free African Society, with forty-two members:

> The society fostered socioeconomic cooperation in the form of savings, mutual aid, education to children and charity to indigent, widowed, and orphaned members. Only three years later did Richard Allen form Mother Bethel, the first African-Methodist-Episcopal Church in America. (p. 352)

Billingsley affirms that black churches are a major institutional presence in the black community. Benjamin Mays and Joseph Nicholson (1969) declared that there was a certain "genius of soul" of the black church "that gives it life and vitality, that makes it stand out significantly above its buildings, creeds, rituals and doctrines; something that makes it a unique institution" (p. 278). Billingsley suggests that a key element in the genius of the church was complete ownership and control by African American people:

> It represented freedom, independence, and respect for leadership, as well as the opportunity for self-esteem, self-development, leadership, and relaxation. Moreover, they found that the black church was a community center and recreational center that encouraged education, business development, and democratic fellowship beyond its members. (1992, p. 354)

Theologian C. Eric Lincoln (1986) has called attention to the multiplicity of functions of the black church:

> Beyond its purely religious function, as critical as that function has been, the black church in its historical role as lyceum, conservatory, forum, social service center, political academy and financial institution has been and is for black America the mother of our culture, the champion of our freedom, the hallmark of our civilization. (p. 5)

The African American church is the only institution in the African American community that is supported and controlled by African American people. It is not an accident that African American churches have been burned and bombed during and after the modern Civil Rights movement. The African American pastor, in the words of my father, Reverend Phale D. Hale, "is the freest person in the African American community. He is the only person who is free of economic sanctions from the white power structure, because he is paid totally by African American people."

The African American church serves such a unique function in African American life that Anglo-Americans have recently sought to yank the chains of African American churches by threatening to withdraw their tax-exempt status if they engage in political activity. This effort at intimidation is analogous to the ban on African drumming during slavery, because messages were being sent via the drum that could not be interpreted or intercepted by the slave owners.

The role of the African American preacher is very different from the role of the Anglo-American preacher in American society. The African American preacher serves as a prophet or emissary, like Moses who spoke to Pharaoh on behalf of his people. African American preachers have tried to "call the Anglo preacher out," as Rev. Martin Luther King Jr. did in his letter from the Birmingham jail that was addressed to the white American clergy. King wanted to know, "Where are you?" As my father explained to me during the height of the Civil Rights movement, "when the white preacher preaches against the inequalities found in American capitalism or the moral decadence of racism, his coattails are pulled by the plantation owners and industrialists (capitalists) who sit on his Board of Trustees and pay his salary. They quietly suggest that he restrict his sermons to 'Jesus and him crucified'!"

C. Eric Lincoln (1970) asserts that the black church cannot depend on white theologians to provide theology for the black church:

> The black church has traditionally relied upon a "preached" theology . . . now that era may be past. The Blacks of this generation, and possibly for generations to come, are going to write their own theology in the light of their circumstances and their needs. A white Jesus, whether preached, taught or implied by cultural habits simply won't do. In a society like ours, he can't do anything for black folk!
>
> A white church that is painfully adjunctive to institutionalized racism— the consequences of which are devastating the whole society—can't do anything for black people. It can't do anything for itself.
>
> White theology suffers mortally from the sin of omission. It has sent its theologians to study in Europe where the problem isn't, or imported the best European theologians to bring us the light, but not for our darkness.
>
> In consequence, American theology has had few words to speak to our condition. White theology has not done anything for black people except ignore them. (p. 226)

There are some African Americans who declare that they don't want to hear about politics at church. To them I say that the African American church is still the "talking drum" in the African American community. At church, as no place else, parishioners can hear announcements, discussions of issues, and mobilizations that are critical to African American people.

In contrast, it is more difficult to hear alternative voices in the media. Often newspaper publishers in the African American community are capitalists who identify and belong to the party of the affluent political right. The editorial policies and politics of some African American newspapers do not render them a reliable source of information on some issues. Additionally, sometimes one person owns African American newspapers in several major cities. This one person becomes a very powerful, invisible molder of African American public opinion who can be influenced by forces outside the African American community. The same can be said about some civil rights organizations that are sustained by wealthy contributors who call the tunes.

The African American church stands alone as an institution in the African American community that is positioned to provide unfiltered information that, as former Congresswoman Shirley Chisholm said, is "unbought and unbossed."

J. Deotis Roberts (1980) identifies the mission of the African American church as one of ministering to black families. He identifies two aspects of that ministry, the priestly and the prophetic. "The priestly ministry of the black church refers to their healing, comforting, and succoring work. The prophetic ministry involves its social justice and socially transforming aspects." These are two sides of the same coin. "Personal concerns relate to social concerns and social realities determine the limits of personal freedom" (p. 110).

In *Learning while Black* (Hale 2001), a dual role is prescribed for the African American church in supporting the model of school reform that is outlined therein. The first role of the church is a nonsectarian function. The church is being called upon in this model, first and foremost, to supply a cadre of volunteers to enter the schools; serve on the *in loco parentis* committee, cultural enrichment committee, and others; and tutor children in the classroom. The church is also called upon in this model to supply men and women who can mentor children and create rites-of-passage programs. There is no religious dogma called for. There is no concern about separation of church and state because Christian education is not advocated for the school.

The second role is for the African American church to craft cutting-edge Christian education that will enrich the lives of the children who are in The Family (members of the church) and children who are in The Village (African American children wherever they are found).

It is important that the church conceptualize its mission as ministering to African American children wherever they are found. I shall never forget the church in Ohio that housed my child-care program, Visions for Children. The church evicted our program after firing the pastor. When I met with the board of trustees, they asked me how many children served by my program were members of their church. I looked at them in disbelief that they could even articulate such a question. I asked them how they could conceptualize their Christian mission as sending aid to Africa but could draw the line so close in this country that the poor African American child sitting on their doorstep did not fit into their definition of Christian mission and ministry unless he was a "member of their church." Their response was a telegram telling me to vacate in two days!

Fortunately, the perspective of that church is not typical for African American churches. Andrew Billingsley (1992) conducted a random sampling of black churches in the Northeast region of the United States. He discovered that most of the churches were actively involved in providing family-oriented community outreach programs. The average number of outreach programs operated by each church was four. His findings further revealed:

Taken together some 31 percent of these programs were aimed specifically at children and youth. Another 51 percent were of the more inclusive family support and assistance type; 8 percent were directed to adult and elderly individuals. Finally, 10 percent of these programs were more general community service and community development activities. (p. 374)

The challenge to school district administrators and teachers is to recognize the African American church as the major institution it is in the African American community. Every teacher and administrator should be on intimate terms with the pastors and parishioners in the churches that surround the school.

Billingsley (1992) studied seventy-one churches along the eastern seaboard and describes the community outreach programs of a significant sample in his book *Climbing Jacob's Ladder*. A large proportion of these programs involve education and assisting schools. The challenge for public school educators is to move beyond being a recipient of overtures from churches. They must create a vision of how the church can be involved as a key player in creating The Village as it is conceptualized in *Learning while Black* (Hale 2001). As I have discussed this idea with leaders of church organizations, they have always had a willingness to help public schools. However, when they approach the schools to adopt them, the schools don't give the churches anything meaningful to do. They assign them to lunchroom duty as monitors or some other such perfunctory task. The schools need to invite the churches to the table as collaborators in helping the school reach its goals.

Let me state clearly that the discussion in this chapter is also an action plan for churches as they examine their concept of ministry to children and youth in The Family and in The Village. The model of school reform outlined in *Learning while Black* (Hale 2001) *requires* the collaboration of churches ready to step up to the plate in supporting the development of the African American children in their community, whether they are church members or not.

The church should be a vehicle of change. The African American church is urged to become an advocate of change in the larger social systems that affect the socialization of black children and youth—particularly the public schools.

The African American church must address internal theological issues that are related to the Christian education of African American children and youth. Nannie Helen Burroughs (1927), an African American Baptist churchwoman, spoke of the need for black people to organize "inside," to reemphasize the moral and spiritual dimensions of life, and to teach black children "the internals and the eternals rather than the externals. Be more concerned with putting in than getting on. We have been too bothered about the externals—clothes or money. What we need are mental and spiritual giants who are aflame with a purpose."

The discussion in this chapter is designed to be an exploration of ways in which the African American church can construct its Christian education mission internally to complement its external mission as a change agent for all African American children in The Village.

There are some things that are unique about Christian education in the African American church, and if the African American church doesn't do them, they will not be done.

1. The program of Christian education must meet the needs of the African American community, whatever they are. Any need or concern within the African American community, individually or collectively, falls within the scope of the Christian educational ministry. This program should contribute to political action, economic development, and training in the cultural heritage of African American people.
2. The learning theory of the curriculum should reflect a relevant ministry to the needs and growth of each stage of the life cycle: the African American child, teenager, college student, older youth, young adult, middle adult, older adult, and senior adult. This education should develop naturally out of the lifestyles and experiences of African American people.
3. Christian education should enhance the development of a positive self-concept in children. This is important because the only way a person can construct a self-image is to see himself reflected in the eyes of others in his culture. This is the concept of the "looking-glass self." If everywhere African American children look they see negative concepts of what it means to be African American, they will develop negative self-concepts.

MISSION OF THE SUNDAY SCHOOL

According to Robert Lynn and Elliot Wright (1971) the Sunday school began in 1759 in England. Robert Raikes is known as the "Father of the Sunday School." There were two purposes for establishing a church school on Sunday.

First of all, the children of the poor were required to work in factories for long hours six days a week. On Sunday, their only day of leisure, they were often unsupervised and became involved in vandalism and crime. Raikes began to notice the relationship between inadequate schooling and criminal activity. He established the school on Sunday as a preventative measure of juvenile delinquency and to help youngsters who had inadequate schooling.

THE MISSION OF THE BLACK SUNDAY SCHOOL

There is an interesting parallel between the founding of the Sunday school in England and the function of the Sunday school in the African American community.

Sunday school in the African American community helped propel the African slave and freedmen toward literacy. It was in the Sunday school, often in secret, that African people learned to read the Bible, do mathematics, and eventually to write.

According to Olivia Pearl Stokes (1972), the Sunday school was also established for training in morals. White men used Sunday school to teach against drinking, war, and slavery. In America, the focus was entirely on the curse of liquor (p. 92).

Stokes points out that the African American Sunday school brought literacy to the former slaves after the Civil War. When the historically black colleges were founded in the South, they often included Sunday schools in which the faculty were required to teach. The Sunday school was designed to reach youths who did not have the educational background to qualify for college. The Sunday school provided the chance to be educated, an opportunity denied by the larger society, so that any opportunities outside servitude to whites could be circumscribed (pp. 92–93).

Many a church such as the one pastored for forty-three years by my father (Rev. Phale D. Hale), Union Grove Baptist Church in Columbus, Ohio, began as a Sunday school (in 1888) and grew into a church.

At its origin, the Sunday school was on the cutting edge of African American life. It met a critical need in the life of the African slave or freedman.

Theologian C. Eric Lincoln (Lincoln and Mamiya 1990) has described the dynamic interactive relationship between black families and churches:

> Families constituted the building blocks for black churches and the churches through their preaching and teaching, symbols, belief system, morality, and rituals provided a unity—a glue that welded families and the community to each other. (p. 311)

Lincoln has pointed out further that after the Civil War, black churches legitimated the informal marital relationships of former slaves. Parents often brought their children to church, sometimes often forcing them to go, because they deeply believed that the church would provide them with a moral education. Lincoln noted:

> Churches also provided Sunday school for children and adults, and for many black people for a long period of time the church was the place where they first began to learn rudimentary reading skills. (p. 312)

Both Carter G. Woodson and Charles S. Johnson have pointed to the molding influences of churches on rural youth. Although worship services were oriented toward adult members, special Sunday services were set aside for the participation of children and children's choirs. Carter G. Woodson (1930, 1969) uses the phrase "junior church," and Charles S. Johnson (1941, 1967) refers to "Children's Day" to describe the special activities of rural churches for youth.

Lincoln states that black churches also provide recreational events and sponsor athletic teams. Black churches have served as concert halls, art galleries, and public forums for African Americans. "The first public performance seen or given by many black children often occurred in the church" (1990, p. 312).

Lincoln states that a major problem for contemporary black churches is that there is not enough focus of their programs and efforts on black youth:

> While Sunday Schools continue as a traditional part of the typical black church, many perform functions more akin to babysitting than education and socialization. Too many black pastors do not concern themselves with this aspect of ministry, but tend to delegate the religious education of their youth to someone else. (1990, p. 316)

In his survey and study of black churches, Lincoln found that for the vast majority of black pastors, preaching was still seen as their major task. Lincoln's findings suggest that more attention needs to be paid to the education and socialization of black youth. He feels that black churches should begin with the religious education that is within their control, especially with Sunday school education and literature.

> The process of identity formation is a very subtle one, and the selection and presentation of Sunday school materials, as innocuous as they seem, send messages to young children about what is important and unimportant about themselves and their society, no less than what should have religious significance in their lives. (1990, p. 318)

Our task here is to consider ways of refocusing the ministry of the Sunday school so that it can continue to fulfill its mission in the future. There are a number of pitfalls we must avoid:

1. We must remove the socioeconomic barriers that separate the church's educational ministry from the masses of African American people. Most large churches in the African American community today are extremely middle-class in membership and orientation. (One gets the feeling that one is at a fashion show instead of worship service on Sunday morning.) The opulence on display is a deterrent to less-advantaged people in the community to participate in church activities. Sunday school in these settings is not an outreach activity; it is Bible study among the members.

My pastor, Dr. Charles G. Adams of Hartford Memorial Baptist Church, has structured a Saturday-evening worship service at 7:30 P.M. that is marketed to "Generation X," to which it is appropriate to wear casual attire. Also, during the summer casual wear is advocated for all parishioners at all services. This is a good trend for the Sunday school.

I have even seen some churches with a largely middle-class membership who have Sunday school and other children's and youth activities for their children (those in The Family) and then a separate track of activities for the children who live in the lower-income neighborhood surrounding the church (those in The Village).

Social barriers such as clothing expectations should be removed if the Sunday school is to fulfill its mission.

2. Attention must be given to training Sunday school teachers in child development, new trends in pedagogy, and also new trends in biblical interpretation and systematic theology.

In her book *Today's Children and Yesterday's Heritage*, Sophia Fahs (1952) discusses the problem of teaching a literal interpretation of the Bible to modern children. Many Sunday school teachers persist in confusing children when they discuss Bible stories about God literally talking to people from the heavens, parting the Red Sea, striking people dead, and so forth. Children become confused because they are taught about the laws of the universe at school in science classes. They have never seen such miraculous occurrences in their daily lives and are skeptical as to why we don't see God talking out loud now. Fahs recommends that we bring Christian education into harmony with the rest of education.

Our task in the Sunday school is to enrich our children's conceptualization of the universe by combing the insights of our religion with the theories of science.

In the Sunday school, we have a responsibility to teach the history of the African American church and the history of African Americans. We must help African American people understand their role as leaders in the struggle for liberation and justice in America and the world.

We have a responsibility to include illustrations of African American people in the Sunday school literature as well as content that reflects the culture and experience of African Americans.

It is critical that the Sunday school address the economic practices that accompany Protestant Christianity. Our children must understand the manner in which capitalism and Protestantism go hand in hand. White Anglo-Saxon Protestants read the same Bible we read, sing the same anthems we sing, and pray to the same God we pray to. However, they interpret the oppression they have perpetrated against African people to amass their fortune as a blessing from God for hard work. A table in an article in *Newsweek* titled "Christianity across the Ages" (March 29, 1999, p. 62) reveals the disparity between the "religious" beliefs of mainstream Christians and the priority they assign to applying the principles of Christianity to matters of social justice. Respondents were asked, "In the next millennium, which one of the following do you think should be organized Christianity's top priority?" Thirty-eight percent answered "Returning to traditional moral values"; 32 percent, "Spreading the faith"; 13 percent, "Increasing tolerance"; and a mere 7 percent, "Right social ills."

It is clear that the Christians who responded to this survey see very little correlation between embracing moral values and righting social ills. This is one of the reasons that the eleven o'clock hour at Sunday-morning worship services can be the most segregated hour of the week.

In discussions of Christian missionary activities, we must correct the misconceptions about Africa that are perpetuated by white denominations. First of all, we must dispel the notion that Africans are primitive, cannibalistic heathens who need to be converted to Christianity in order to be civilized. This notion was at the root of African enslavement and is a cloak for present-day colonialism and economic exploitation.

Africa should be presented in all of its complexity. Crises in Africa, such as famines and civil wars over resources such as oil, gold, and diamonds, should be presented in the context of Western domination and exploitation, and not from the perspective of African poverty. In the words of Olivia Pearl Stokes (1972):

> Christian education in the Black churches is that ministry of the Church which provides the educational undergirding for mission as seen from the Black perspective—meaning, the struggle for liberation and equal justice in the spirit of the teachings of Jesus Christ in our worship, relationships with all men, our witness, and daily work in the American society. (p. 100)

ELEMENTS OF A BLACK YOUTH MINISTRY

Charles Foster (1989) has pointed out that a primary purpose of black youth ministry is to call youth into discipleship. This purpose embodies the identity and vocation central to the experience of adolescence. Identity has to do with allegiance and commitment—"Whose am I?" The first task is to clarify one's relationship to Jesus Christ and the church that was formed in loyalty to him. The second task involves clarifying one's relationship to one's cultural heritage—the heritage of African Americans (p. 103). In the interplay of call and commitment to Christ, heard and responded through the medium of the African American experience, the identity of black youth takes form (Foster 1989, p. 104).

Vocation has to do with the expression of that commitment to Christ in service to the community as an agent of Christ. Vocation is political activity. Vocation is engaging the values and ideals of Christ shaped in the crucible of the African American experience for the sake of that community and the welfare of all humankind (Foster 1989, p. 104).

Discipleship is consequently both the *aim* and the *means* of African American youth ministry. There should be no confusion about whether youth are viewed as the church of tomorrow or participants in the church's ministry today. The call to discipleship is *life-long*. Both new disciples and old disciples are disciples (Foster 1989, p. 104).

Jacquelyn Grant (1989) has set as a goal for youth ministry the *nurturing of a sense of somebodiness in youth*. The youth ministry must be *evangelical*. When youth are confronted with many options for their commitments, churches are faced with the task of presenting the gospel of Jesus Christ in a way that makes it relevant to their experience. We must reach out to youth where they are.

Foster (1989) states further that the call to discipleship must reveal the *viability* of the gospel for the lives of African American children and youth. The viability of the gospel is most evident in ministries that are *hope-filled*. Especially for African American youth trapped in cycles of poverty and frustration, the call to discipleship is essentially a call to hope in the face of what often appears to be absolute hopelessness. A gospel of otherworldly escape does not serve these youth well (pp. 105–6).

The call to discipleship comes as a call to *liberation*. Liberation is experienced as *respect, dignity, freedom,* and *responsibility* (Foster 1989, p. 106). J. Deotis Roberts

(1980) defines the mission of the black church as liberation of the family. "While many white theologians are preoccupied with the unborn and the dying, the black theologian must be concerned about the abundant life for black folk between birth and death" (p. 131). Roberts states further that the primary task of the black church is the strengthening of black families:

> While the liberation of black men, women, and children, separately, must move forward, priority must be given to black families. Families are the "moral schools" for children. Our future as a people will be determined by how well we meet the needs of healthy black families. The relation of black families and churches is mutual. Failure of the black church to minister appropriately and urgently to black families will hasten its own death. (p. 132)

References

Billingsley, Andrew. 1992. *Climbing Jacob's Ladder: The Enduring Legacy of African-American Families.* New York: Simon and Schuster.

Burroughs, Nannie Helen. 1927. "Unload Your Uncle Toms." In Gerda Lerna, ed., *Black Women in White America: A Documentary History.* New York: Vintage Press, 1972, pp. 551–53.

Fahs, Sophia. 1952. *Today's Children and Yesterday's Heritage.* Boston: Beacon Press.

Foster, Charles R. 1989. "Elements of a Black Youth Ministry." In Charles R. Foster and Grant S. Shockley, eds., *Working with Black Youth: Opportunities for Christian Ministry.* Nashville: Abingdon Press.

Grant, Jacquelyn. 1989. "A Theological Framework." In Charles R. Foster and Grant S. Shockley, eds., *Working with Black Youth: Opportunities for Christian Ministry.* Nashville: Abingdon Press.

Hale, Janice. 1994. *Unbank the Fire: Visions for the Education of African American Children.* Baltimore: Johns Hopkins University Press.

———. 2001. *Learning while Black: Creating Education Excellence for African American Children.* Baltimore: Johns Hopkins University Press.

Johnson, Charles S. 1941, 1967. *Growing Up in the Black Belt: Negro Youth in the Rural South.* New York: American Council on Education. Reprint, New York: Schocken Books.

King, Martin Luther, Jr. 1964. "Letter from Birmingham Jail." In *Why We Can't Wait.* New York: Harper and Row.

Lincoln, C. Eric. 1970. "Black Church." *Christianity and Crisis* 30, no. 18 (November 16): 226.

———. 1986. "The Black Church and Black Self-Determination." Paper read before the Association of Black Foundation Executives, April 15, Kansas City, Missouri.

Lincoln, C. Eric, and Lawrence H. Mamiya. 1990. *The Black Church in the African American Experience.* Durham, N.C.: Duke University Press.

Lynn, Robert W., and Elliot Wright. 1971. *The Little Big Sunday School.* New York: Harper and Row.

Mays, Benjamin, and Joseph Nicholson. 1969. *The Negro's Church.* New York: Arno Press.

Raboteau, Albert. 1995. *A Fire in the Bones: Reflections on African-American Religious History.* Boston: Beacon Press.

Roberts, J. Deotis. 1980. *Roots of a Black Future: Family and Church.* Philadelphia: Westminster Press.

Schneider, Iris. 1992. "Refuge and Strength: Black Church Life in Southern California." *Los Angeles Times*, 9 February, E–1.

Stokes, Olivia Pearl. 1972. "The Black Perspective: Christian Education in Today's Church." In Riggins R. Earl Jr., ed., *To You Who Teach in the Black Church*. Nashville: National Baptist Convention Publishing Board.

Woodson, Carter G. 1930, 1969. *The Rural Negro*. New York: Russell and Russell.

Chapter 13

Black Pastoral Theology as Psychological Liberation

Edward P. Wimberly

Psychological liberation is a precondition for political freedom. Historian Carter G. Woodson once observed that if a person's mind is enslaved, there's no need to have a back door (traditionally required for blacks to use in entering or leaving white homes and businesses in the South). A person with an enslaved mind will create a back door out of necessity.[1]

The contemporary African American community is more vulnerable today to the reality of racism and oppression than at any other time in our pilgrimage in the United States of America. The source of our fragility is the inability of our extended family and our church ties to provide a buffer against unjust racial realities. At one point in our pilgrim journey, the extended family and African American churches mediated a spirit-filled, faith-filled worldview that formed a solid wall of protection from the negative stereotypes and images of black people held by wider society. This spiritual reservoir provided support for a positive sense of self for African Americans despite the negative information that came their way. As a result, our parents and grandparents had the stuff to make it in a hostile environment of nullification.

Today the capacity of the countercultural positive mediating worldview to provide the same protection as it once did to African Americans is crippled. We are more susceptible to the negative racial stereotypes today because the village life that sustains a viable extended family and relational church environment has all but deteriorated and collapsed.[2] Made up of extended family and church relational ties, the village once helped African Americans maintain physical, emotional, spiritual, interpersonal, and communal integrity in the midst of oppression and racism. Now, however, these support systems have dwindled under the weight of a different kind of public valuing system that runs unchecked in contemporary society. More precisely, the cultural roots that supported our meaningful survival in a hostile environment have been undermined. Rather than publicly supporting those communal ties that have supported African American development and identity for several centuries, such ties are often viewed as hindrances by our high-tech, urban, market-driven, and individualistic culture. We are more vulnerable, then, to racism not only because of the collapse of the village but also because of the devaluing of the legacy of communal ties.

By way of further elaboration, there has been a shift away from the values that support the significance of communal activities toward noncommunal values. For example, increasing the return on our investments, managerial attention to profits, tax and housing public policies, and failure of government and the entertainment industry to support communal values have diminished the role once played by community in the lives of African Americans.[3] In fact, public valuing and morality impact our private decision making more directly today than they did when there were strong support systems. Nonmarketing values such as care, nurture, commitment to family, and cherishing community relationships are viewed as unnecessary or at least peripheral in our market-driven economy. The end result of market valuing is that we are more prone to be recruited into identities and personalities that serve the market economy and that undermine communal sources of sustained identity and personality development. What Erich Fromm described as the "marketing oriented personality," through which people experience themselves cut off from relationships and as commodities, seems to be a common personality pattern for upwardly mobile African Americans. They obey the laws of supply and demand and uncritically embrace marketplace values.[4] Such a market-driven orientation separates us from our historical legacy, and we feel more directly the impact of racism, discrimination, and oppression.

This brief essay in honor of my theological mentor, J. Deotis Roberts, is about exploring the way in which adopting marketing identities makes us more vulnerable to racism and facilitates psychological bondage to internalized racism. Our buying into marketing values uncritically makes us prime candidates for being recruited into self-destructive psychological bondage. Such bondage undermines our ability to grow and develop into people who value themselves as well as others.

CONTEMPORARY CASES

Contemporary African American novelists provide significant case-study material for viewing how we are recruited into marketing identities as well as into self-images that undermine our ability to become full human beings. Gloria Naylor's novel *The Men of Brewster Place* provides a graphic glimpse into how the lure of marketplace values makes African Americans more vulnerable to racism.[5]

This novel is about men who have been recruited into identities of wider society that are either market-driven or not highly valued. These men are often burdened with personal problems that render them ineffective in making contributions to their own lives and the lives of others. They are often portrayed as unproductive and dysfunctional, and the wider society not only is often comfortable with these portrayals but also reinforces them. This is to say that black men are often recruited into deviant roles so that they can be dealt with through recovery clinics or the prison and justice systems.

The clearest example (which also turns out to be the most tragic) is a clergyman who is pulled away from communal values by the promise of power, position, and prestige in holding political office. The preacher's name is the Reverend Moreland T. Woods, and Naylor portrays him as a man angry with God because he felt held back from his self-chosen destiny of fame, power, and fortune. He desired all the spoils of being the first black man to hold the political office of city councilman. He felt that in order to achieve his lifelong dream he had to grow his already ample congregation to more than twice its current size before people would take him seriously as a viable political candidate. He overcame the initial opposition from within his own congregation through being a shrewd church politician. He was able to take advantage of some of his head deacons' moral frailty and ethical missteps. Eventually he achieved his dream of being elected to the city council.

His church was only two blocks from Brewster Place, a residence for many of his congregation. His church and Brewster Place were stable symbols of the village and small community life that characterized much of urban black life at one period of African American history. Yet political success, like any success in a market-driven economy, comes with a price. His first vote on the city council turned out to be his last. Rev. Woods was the swing vote on whether they would tear down Brewster Place to make room for the marketing and profit interests of those with a great deal of money. He ignored the fact that Brewster Place was a symbolic community fixture to which people attached feelings of stability and permanence. With his one and only vote, he voted Brewster Place out of existence. He was driven from office because his own extracurricular sexual activity was exposed in a very graphic way.

Rev. Woods's demise was not because of his sexual indiscretions; rather, it was because he betrayed a community trust. He sold the community's symbols of continuity and familiarity for his own personal gain. In other words, his character flaw was that he over-bought into the marketing values of the wider culture that had no concern for the values that sustained black life. Thus, one of Naylor's messages is a reminder that the recruiting lure of the marketplace undermines the values needed for black survival.

Another novel that highlights the significance of black communal values is Pearl Cleage's *What Looks Like Crazy on an Ordinary Day*.[6] This book is about a black woman who contracted AIDS but found a home base and romantic love, despite the loss of the village and the threat of AIDS in her life. The book chronicles how she found community despite life's pain and suffering. Her secret was that she returned home to a small community and began to contribute to the lives of others. In other words, she discovered service and committed herself to nonmarketing values. She found vocation and purpose for her life. As a result, community and love found her. The heroine ran from commitment and relationships, but the real point is that when she stopped running and committed herself to others, her life changed for the better.

The heroine in this novel was a relational refugee. She avoided closeness out of fear that she would end up like her mother, who committed suicide. She felt that if she avoided close relationships and intimacy, she would be spared her mother's self-denying fate. Therefore, she allowed herself to be recruited into a self-oriented role, pursuing pleasure in the big city. Hers was the perfect personality to be driven by marketing values, because she was disconnected. In the end, however, because she was vitally connected to community, she was less vulnerable to being recruited into market-driven values and negative identities.

With regard to the work of pastoral theology and pastoral counseling, these characters' roles imply that we must help people find the vital community links that support, sustain, and transform lives. Such linkages provide the kinds of protection people need to transcend the negative images and roles into which many African Americans are being recruited. Moreover, such community linkages help African Americans put marketing attractions into proper perspective, and pastoral counseling plays a significant role in helping people make these important linkages to community. Pastoral counseling, then, contributes significantly to the liberation ministry of the church.

THE CONNECTION OF PASTORAL THEOLOGY TO LIBERATION

The role of pastoral counseling and therapy in the liberation process of individuals, marriages, and families has not been always clear. In fact, pastoral counseling and therapy have often been thought to be an instrument of oppression, in which people were urged to accept or adjust to their oppression. In other words, some viewed pastoral counseling and therapy as a tool of social accommodation rather than as an instrument of liberation. This was the perspective of sociologists who viewed psychotherapy as a legitimating tool of wider culture.[7] Some African American colleagues in social ethics and sociology of religion held this view of pastoral counseling and felt that it was irrelevant to the cause of justice and liberation.

J. Deotis Roberts was the first contemporary black theologian to visualize the appropriate role of pastoral counseling in the liberation struggle. Unlike other black theologians, he envisaged a connection between the prophetic and the priestly and took seriously the fact that the priestly and the prophetic must be held in creative tension, or in a dialectical relationship. As early as 1971, Roberts was speaking of the inseparable link between personal and social ministry.[8] About this social and personal dimension of Roberts's theology, I conclude the following in my doctoral dissertation:

> Deotis Roberts . . . united both the social and the personal in black theology; therefore, he established a broad base for another ministry of liberation. Moreover, he attempts to systematically apply the Christian theological doctrine of experience. As a result, his conclusions reflect a concern for the total dimensions of Black experience. In his way of thinking, a Black theology must be prophetic as well as priestly; "the slums must be cleaned up, but the heart must be purified also."[9]

More than twenty-three years later, Roberts expanded his view of personal and social liberation to include a theological anthropology in which he linked psychological liberation and social liberation.[10] His theological anthropology grew to include the transformation of society as well as the transformation of personality. He turned his prophetic attention toward internalized racism and the need for people to be free from such internal bondage. He says that "psychological liberation is a precondition for political freedom."[11] He interprets this to mean that African Americans must believe in and embrace their freedom psychologically before they can take advantage of the political, social, and economic rights under God and the U.S. Constitution.

Discussions of internalized racism and the need for psychological liberation may not be new, but what is new in the conversation is that the concept of internalized racism is dominating contemporary African American pastoral theology and counseling. Pastoral counselors are including in their writing an awareness that internalized racism is devastating the lives of many who come for counseling. For example, Homer Ashby points out that it is time for pastoral theology and counseling to address the cycle of racial conditioning known as "internalized oppression."[12] His point of view is that internalized racism is a reality caused by political conditioning. Political conditioning, in his mind, is a process whereby the mistreatment of a targeted minority group by a majority group is internalized so that the minority group believes in its inferior status. When internalized oppression takes place, the majority group does not overtly have to oppress the minority group members, because the members of the minority group carry the oppressive system in their psyches.

Ashby points out that the task of black pastoral theology is to address the problem of internalized racism. He recommends that pastoral counseling take deinternalization of racism seriously and that black pastoral counselors focus on Afrocentric themes in helping black counselees understand their experience of oppression and bondage. He also urges pastoral counselors and those who carry out ministries of caring in general to begin to help people explore their thoughts and actions in order to be sure that they are not driven by negative, passive, and shame-based internalized oppression.[13]

By way of summary, Roberts's theology set the stage for both black theology and liberation theology to address the social as well as the personal dimensions of liberation. More recently, his attention has shifted to the need to address psychological liberation that, in his thinking, precedes political liberation. His concern for addressing psychological liberation parallels the concern of pastoral theology to deal with internalized racism and liberation from it. Here, pastoral theology refers to the reflection that the pastoral counselor does on his or her practice of pastoral counseling in light of psychology and the behavioral sciences as well as in light of theology, for the purposes of improving intervention in the lives of the counselees. Therefore, pastoral theologians must do a theological, as well as a psychological, analysis. Consequently, pastoral theologians will continue to take important theological anthropological cues for their work from the conceptualization of theologians such as J. Deotis Roberts.

PASTORAL COUNSELING AND LIBERATION FOR INTERNALIZED RACISM

In the introduction to this essay, the point was made that African Americans are more vulnerable to racism today than they were in the past, primarily because the traditional support systems and structures of the black community have been weakened. This section explores how contemporary racism manifests itself through the process of internalized racism. Further, this section provides a language for assessing how public valuing heavily influences the self-devaluation that drives internalized racism.

We live in a market-driven economy in which certain things are valued more highly than other things. Such valuations take on racial connotations. In this section, the central role of racial valuations and marketing values in facilitating internalized racism is examined.

The Meaning of Racism

Racism is understood as the power to define the nature of reality as well as the power to implement these definitions politically through public policy and decision making. Racism is driven by the belief that certain groups are inherently inferior to other groups and, by virtue of this, are not worthy to be accorded access to the same level of social, economic, political, and educational privileges and rewards as others. To reinforce racial superiority and inferiority, the devalued racial group is recruited into certain negative racial definitions in ways that negative views of self are internalized and form the core of internalized oppression.

The Reality of Racial Recruiting

The phenomenon of recruiting people into negative identities that lead to internalized racism has been explored by family psychotherapist Michael White. To understand what he means by recruiting, several key and related terms must be defined first. For example, White believes that interpretation of human experiences is linked to the dominant practices and knowledge of the use of power in wider society.[14] More precisely, knowledge and techniques of living are *contextual*, and how families and other institutions deal with intimate relationships is linked with messages and practices that dominate public conversations.

A related concept is that of *torture*. Taken from his understanding of abuse in intimate relationships, White believes that torture is the process of "breaking down identity, breaking down a sense of community," isolating people from each other, destroying self-respect, demoralizing, and depersonalizing.[15]

Given these definitions of context and torture, White believes that they are public phenomena that impact on close and intimate relationships, and the public aspect is what he calls *recruiting*. Recruiting refers to the process of drawing people into stories not of their own creation, which lead them to self-subjugation, self-surveillance, self-punishment, self-denial, and personal exile.[16] Recruiting leads to practices of self-abuse through the internalization of conversations with oneself and with others. In this way, self-subjugation is linked to public conversations taking place in wider society. Such public conversations influence the private conversations. When people are isolated from supportive community, the public conversations take on more power in defining the reality to which they subscribe. As a result, isolated persons are more vulnerable and are prone to internalize conversations that can undermine their identities.

Racial conversations at the public level are political discussions. As such, these conversations are defining the nature of reality and shaping public policy, knowledge, and practices in the private sphere. The concept of torture helps us envisage how being isolated from community makes us more vulnerable to such conversations. It also helps us to visualize how such conversations contribute to negative identity formation.

With regard to the two literary characters introduced earlier, close and intimate connections to communities represented for them the key to personality growth and development, as well as to the ability to overcome public negative conversations. The more Rev. Woods got caught up in the pursuit of political gain, the more vulnerable he became to the influence of racial conversations taking place behind the scenes in city council chambers. While overt torture is not obvious in Rev. Woods's case, it was very much present subtly. He felt that he would lose something if he did not abandon his community in order to achieve what he thought was a higher goal.

Naylor's heroine discovers the error of being isolated from community in enough time to build a new community. As a result, she was not as vulnerable to torture because she was a committed participant in community. Her community afforded the protection that she needed from the political and racial conversations at the public level.

For White, the mechanisms of recruiting include institutional subjugating practices. Black people and other ethnic populations, White says, are overrepresented in the prisons and psychiatric systems in Britain, where he works.[17] Such institutions force occupants to internalize racist conversations that reinforce racism. Inequality, abuse of power or privilege, policies of admissions, confinement, and police profiling contribute to the internalization of oppression. White calls such mechanisms practices of technologies of power that encourage negative comparisons, inconsistency, and surveillance.[18]

The valuable contribution White offers to pastoral theology is a language for linking public conversations about race to private and personal meaning systems. The concept of contextual conversation and torture contributes to our understanding of how public conversation and public mechanisms that isolate contribute to the internalization of racism.

TOWARD A MODEL OF PSYCHOLOGICAL LIBERATION

Overcoming psychological oppression, self-subjugation, and internalized racism is a narrative process known as *externalization*.[19] The process of externalization deals with those stories into which people have been recruited in such a way that these stories have less impact on the individual's attitudes toward himself or herself. Much of my own work has been an attempt to help people reedit the stories that have shaped their lives and their interactions with others in a negative way. In this section, the attempt is made to present a model I have been utilizing for years that is grounded in the principle of externalization.

Before presenting my own ideas, however, I want to present Michael White's concept of *re-membership* as central to understanding how to overcome internalized racism. Basically, this concept means reconnecting to sources of one's original knowledge and understanding of the world, which is one's original birth home and community. More precisely, re-membership is reclaiming and privileging, if only temporarily, significant historical and local associations and stories that first provided meaning for people's lives, for the purpose of upgrading, downgrading, editing, or discarding them.[20]

Alienating people from their relational roots is a reality of professional training in the United States. It assumes that one's upbringing, which is the source of one's initial understanding of the world, is inferior and therefore must be marginalized or disqualified. White calls this *dis-membership*.[21] It is a disconnection from our original meaning-making environment. The end results of such disconnection are the loss of meaning, loss of a sense of identity, and loss of a sense

of purpose and legacy. Such losses make us more vulnerable to the internalization of dominant cultural images, particularly if such cultural images negatively
portray one's racial and ethnic group. Moreover, such disconnection makes one
vulnerable to being recruited into negative identities by the dominant group.

For White, *externalization* is the process of deconstruction of the negative identity into which we have been recruited.[22] It is bringing the cultural conversation
about race that has been internalized into our awareness and examining its impact
on our lives. Externalization also includes a process of re-membership, or returning to our original meaning-making environment and reconnecting with it in
order to upgrade, downgrade, privilege, discard, edit, reauthor, or relinquish our
original meaning, knowledge, and skills. It short, externalization involves examining the impact of being recruited into negative identities as well as countering the
recruiting based on reconnecting with our original sources of meaning making.

White does not assume that returning to one's original meaning-making context automatically means undoing the negative recruiting. In fact, one's original
meaning-making environment could have aided in the process of disconnecting
and made one vulnerable to being recruited. White is a family therapist, and he
recognizes that the family of origin or family of birth often facilitates recruiting
by wider society.

Turning to my own work, I have drawn on White's understanding of externalization in my publication titled *Recalling Our Own Stories: The Spiritual Renewal
of Religious Caregivers*.[23] Applying the way my own father reconnected with his call
periodically in his preaching, I was able to fashion a model of reediting the convictions and beliefs that people have about themselves, their relationships with others, their family relationships, their ministry, and the world in general.

My emphasis was on the fact that it is in recalling our own stories that we recon-
nect with our original meaning-making contexts. In returning to our original stories, we get a chance to revisit and renew old important meanings and at the same
time externalize the early conversations and identities into which we were
recruited. If our early recruiting was into positive stories, our returning to our original stories allows us to be nurtured by those early stories of positive identity formation. Such reconnecting and re-membering can lead to liberation from those
negative, wider cultural conversations we have internalized since becoming adults.

A good case example of the role of recalling our own stories in psychological
liberation comes from a recovering drug addict named Clifford Harris. He chronicles his recovery process and psychological and spiritual liberation in his autobiography *Death Dance: A True Story of Drug Addiction and Redemption*.[24]

The original family context for Clifford was a Christian home composed of
both parents and brothers and sisters. It was a close-knit family with its own share
of problems, but there was a caring environment and all felt genuinely loved.

Clifford's problem developed because of the frequent moves his family made
in order for his father to find work. He changed schools many times and often
felt out of place when he had to attend different schools. Often he was the only
black person in his class. He frequently encountered discrimination from his

teachers, but not his classmates. He often felt singled out by his teachers in negative ways. He said, "The prejudice I encountered from my teachers made me hate school. Slowly the bad taste in my mouth turned into a bad attitude. Had it not been for the students, I would have exploded long before I did."[25] He felt the adults in school made his life a living hell. In short, he was being recruited into a negative identity. He said he was the best example of a poor student with inferior learning abilities. He felt like teachers battered his already weak self-esteem. A series of events led him into a rebellious identity, and as a result, he ended up with a very serious drug addiction.

He went through his young adulthood and up to midlife with a serious drug problem. He had been imprisoned several times, but at the age of forty-four, transformation began to take place in his life. While in prison, he began to reflect on his earlier life, and later he attributed this to spiritual prompting by God's Spirit. He proclaimed that God's Spirit was present in his life as a child, and it stayed with him despite his addiction.

The inner spiritual prompting led him to re-member and connect with early memories of his family. This was long before he felt recruited into his rebellious identity by school officials. He reports one story that is very instructive. While in prison in midlife, he would make a daily pilgrimage to the library to be in the presence of an attractive female librarian.[26] To justify his trips to the library, he had to browse the shelves, pretending to look for books. His pretense, however, became God's opportunity.

On one occasion, he spotted a book that he recalled being in his parents' home when he was a child. Flashbacks about how his parents read this particular book to him and his brothers and sisters when he was a child began to flood his memory. The book was about Jesus, and the stories his parents read were about Jesus' love. Positive memories began to flood his awareness. He checked out the book but never opened it. Instead, the mere presence of the book allowed past memories and positive conversations to enter his mind, and the pain of his present life began to diminish. He felt himself going through a cleansing period, and he would renew the book just because its presence continued to trigger these healing memories.

Clifford was reconnecting with his original meaning-making environment and giving it initiative in his life. Simultaneously, he was externalizing negative conversations into which he had been recruited earlier and was replacing them with healing conversations from the past. This process was not of his own making but a gift that he felt came from God. He did, however, have to make a decision to cooperate with the cleansing process that was unfolding in his life. At the end of the cleansing process, he had successfully overcome the psychological bondage to the negative conversations he had internalized from his teachers. He was hearing new voices, voices that affirmed his divine worth as well as his membership in God's family. He is in full recovery from his addiction to substances.

In summary, recalling our own stories, particularly if it is part of a Spirit-led renewal process, facilitates psychological liberation. The concepts of externalization of negative conversations and of reconnecting with one's original meaning-making environment are helpful in understanding how the process of psychological liberation takes place. In the next section, I talk about how comprehensive mentoring contributes to psychological liberation.

COMPREHENSIVE MENTORING

My newest publication, *Relational Refugee: Alienation and Reincorporation in African American Churches and Communities,* presents a model of comprehensive mentoring that facilitates psychological liberation.[27] Mentoring is explicated from a pastoral counseling perspective, which involves the mentor's making himself or herself available to the one needing mentoring in order for the one who needs mentoring to draw specific things from the mentor. These things needing to be drawn are attitudes, scenes, roles, and plots.[28] For example, the person needing mentoring grows and develops as he or she internalizes the positive attitude of the mentor. The person also grows by internalizing positive scenes that occur with the mentor. Third, the person needing mentoring internalizes the plot, or narrative direction, emerging out of the counseling process, and this plot internalization contributes to meaning, purpose, and direction in the life of the person being mentored. Finally, the person needing mentoring internalizes the possible roles that he or she sees emerging out of interaction with the mentor. These four dimensions of mentoring make up comprehensive mentoring.

The connection between mentoring and psychological liberation is that through internalization in the mentoring process, the negative conversations into which one has been recruited in the wider culture are silenced and replaced by more positive conversations. First, internalization of positive attitudes counteracts the negative voices of self-condemnation stemming from negative recruiting. Second, the internalization of positive scenes occurring between the person being mentored and the mentor help counteract those negative scenes of recruiting similar to the ones that Clifford Harris (in the case study) had with his teachers. Third, the internalization of positive plots as the result of the mentoring process helps the person overcome the negative-outcome plots that can lead to substance abuse and criminal activity. Finally, persons needing mentoring learn to play liberating roles rather than roles of bondage when they internalize the roles emerging out of the counseling.

CONCLUSION

This essay is my tribute to the theologian who mentored my academic writing in pastoral care. I drew on his early writings as a doctoral student in order to provide theological bases for pastoral care in the black church. More recently, his theological anthropology as related to liberation from psychological bondage provides a basis for my understanding of pastoral counseling and internalized racism. I am greatly indebted to J. Deotis Roberts.

This essay also correlated the therapeutic political thinking of Michael White with the psychological understanding of internalized racism. His concepts of recruiting, re-membering, and externalization all correspond to my mentoring work and spiritual renewal writing. I concur with J. Deotis Roberts's conclusion that psychological liberation and sociopolitical and economic liberation are closely related.

In summary, pastoral theology as presented in this essay utilizes both psychological liberation and sociopolitical and economic liberation. The mentoring dimension of psychological liberation contributes to a more sociopolitical and economic understanding of liberation, particularly through the concepts of role, plot, and scene. Both the awareness of public policies and the influence of racism on the inner life of black people are things that persons being mentored can internalize. Moreover, the mentor leads the person being mentored into discovering liberating roles, scenes, and plots that he or she can enact in public as well as private life. In other words, comprehensive mentoring can lead to holistic liberation.

Chapter 14

Theological and Spiritual Empowerment of Black Women in Ministry

Delores Carpenter

ESTHER

Esther is a Tennessee woman who was ordained a United Methodist deacon in 1979 and an elder in 1984. She is married and her husband is a state government employee. Sometimes his career has prevented her career advancement, and sometimes her career has interfered with her husband's career advancement. Esther's husband shares in the housecleaning, cooking, and getting the children ready for school. Their children are ages eleven, twelve, and sixteen. This dual-career couple has not worked in the same geographic area for the past six years. Esther is a full-time, salaried pastor who earns $20,000 to $29,000 a year. She pastors three small churches that have a combined membership of 150. Two of the churches are growing while one is "static." Esther has been pastoring churches for the past twelve years. When asked if she finds her M.Div. education helpful, she said, "I guess I'm using it," but she adds that she has had "very few opportunities" to gain experience since seminary. One of the places where her education is used is on a denominational leadership team for spiritual formation. In this capacity she gets to address African and African American spirituality.

Regarding her acceptance as a woman pastor, Esther has faced some opposition. At the denominational levels of district superintendent, bishop, and other clergy, she said, some have been accepting and some have not. As a United Methodist, she is under the itinerant appointment system and admits, "I did not accept an appointment. That has inhibited me from getting a more challenging appointment." She feels her career is considered second-class when compared to those of male M.Div. graduates.

Most of Esther's interaction with other clergy is at district clergy meetings. She has been part of two support groups, one for clergypersons and one for clergywomen, but at present she is not an active member of either group. She currently has no mentor, but when she did they met once a month. She admits that she has not been mentoring other women.

Male participation in Esther's churches is "very low," and she believes that men need to be encouraged to participate in church more than women do. She has given extensive community service serving as president of the NAACP and sitting on the board of directors of a local day-care center and adult learning center. She also challenges other people to be active in both the local church and the community. In her leisure time, Esther reads and listens to music and plays the piano. Given an opportunity for gaining greater competency in ministry through continuing education, she would pursue a degree in pastoral counseling. She is in the process of applying to a Ph.D. program. Her most effective gifts for ministry have been in the areas of pastoral counseling and liturgy

Esther feels that the system she is in is in need of change. While there are strategies on paper to improve it, these are not actually happening. The church system, in her view, is not inclusive, and women pastors need more challenging positions. What sustains her through these challenges are prayer and daily devotions. Her favorite theological image is "being rooted and grounded," being reminded that Jesus is the "root of Jesse." Most often she portrays God as just and gracious, and her most cherished image of Christ is of him speaking with the woman at the well. Here Christ demonstrates that he is inclusive of people who are different. Jesus gave the woman at the well a message and she carried the word. Ultimately, Esther worries that a larger percentage of women are preparing for a church system that is not ready to include them. She said women are viewed as "last-class, not even second-class" within the church. She perceives a hierarchy where white clergymen come first, white women come second, black clergymen come third, and black clergywomen come last.

Clearly this woman has identified the problems of both sexism and racism. She has also pointed to the difficulties of dual-career couples. After twelve years, her experience in pastoring does not seem to be challenging. She would like to see black clergywomen placed in more challenging situations. She is an example of highly educated women who are being placed in small, unchallenging situations with nowhere else to go. Fortunately, she is able to serve on denominational task forces and community boards that use her expertise, but this is usually without compensation. Most clergywomen do not have this luxury, and when they do, they often find this pattern of work for no pay to be exploitive.

Before becoming a pastor, I used all the vacation time from my job as a college administrator to travel to church-related meetings as a resource person. I was never compensated for this activity. Once, an executive of a major philanthropic foundation informed me that I had been an adviser on an unprecedented number of their grants to religious organizations, more than any other consultant. He noted that he thought I had never been adequately compensated for these services, whereupon he proceeded to offer me a lucrative contract, which I continued for three years. Although I was greatly appreciative, this scenario is rare for most women. More frequently I observe seminary-trained women who give enormous numbers of hours and years in regional and national church deliberation, and only occasionally does such activity translate into salaried positions.

Once as a student, when I conducted a large regional survey on the needs of women in our denomination, my professor, who reviewed the statistical work, asked if I was being paid for my services. When I answered no, he remarked, "The church is the most exploitative institution I know." Understandably, the church is a volunteer organization; but why should persons who have been professionally trained to give leadership to the church, and for whom there is no other profession that will pay them on a professional basis, have to render service uncompensated? One pastor friend informed me that she used to perform weddings free of charge until her associate informed her that he was paid $300 to sing two or three solos per wedding. He suggested that her services were even more valuable than his. He said, "Why not ask for more pay?" and she did. The notion that ministers should not be paid for their services comes to us from the Catholic vows of poverty for the priesthood, and from a time when black ministers were not professionally trained. In the former case, the Catholic Church provides amenities and care for its priests, which the black Protestant church has never done. And now that black clergy are professionally trained, both men and women should be paid on a level commensurate with their training.

The "rooted and grounded" image of God is very reminiscent of my grandmother's spirituality, which was illustrated in the song "I Shall Not Be Moved"—"like a tree planted by the waters, I shall not be moved." It declares that the singer has a determination to triumph over adversity. Nothing will be able to take Esther away from the place where God has called and planted her. Regardless of the measure of human success that one feels, there remains the need to be faithful over the things entrusted to her hands. There is a quality of staying power here that sustains this woman as it did my grandmother, even in the face of adversity. Thus, black women have certainly been among "the called, the chosen, and the faithful."

METHODOLOGY

The case study that appears above is one of several recorded from telephone interviews that were a part of three national studies on black female Master of Divinity graduates. Esther is a fictitious name. Methods used to collect data included also a sixteen-page questionnaire. The first data (1985 study) were collected as part of a doctoral dissertation at Rutgers University in 1986 titled "The Effects of Sect-Typeness upon the Professionalization of Black Female Master of Divinity Graduates 1972–1984." The second study (1992) was an update of the first and included five additional graduating classes (1972–1989). Although they were seven years apart, the two surveys sought to measure similar information about black female Master of Divinity graduates. The data for the 1992 study were collected in the summer and fall of 1999. The participants included both male and female Master of Divinity graduates. In each case, potential respondents were identified by a staff person at the Association of Theological Schools. ATS provided the names of member schools that had enrolled African American M.Div. students between 1972 and 1998. A letter was sent to the executive officer of each school. A sixteen-page questionnaire was sent to the names and addresses submitted to the researcher by the schools. New questions were added to previous ones used in order to allow some comparisons with the Hartford Theological Seminary studies that were published in both *Women of the Cloth* (1983), by Jackson W. Carroll, Barbara Hargrove, and Adair T. Lummis, and its follow-up study by Zikmund, Lummis, and Chang, *Clergywomen: The Uphill Climb* (1998).

Unless otherwise noted, the results reported here come from an analysis of the 1992 returned questionnaires, which had a return rate of 34 percent. The participants were female Master of Divinity graduates for the years 1972–1992; 203 of 605 responded.

As in other areas of social change, women ministers have experienced both positive elements that are propelling and negative elements that are discouraging. This chapter examines and interprets some of the women's perceived sources of power. Such power has helped them to prevail even when the negatives seem to outweigh the positives. Specifically, the conversation revolves around womanist theology and the spirituality of black women. Both are important promoters of confidence and competence in ministry.

THE PARTICIPANTS

A glance at black clergywomen's predecessors in ministry sheds some light on ancestral inheritance and a sense of responsibility among the present generation to prevail. Three waves of pioneer black women ministers are recognized. The subjects of this study compose the third wave.

The first wave of black clergywomen were the preaching, praying, and singing evangelist women of the late nineteenth century. The second wave were the twentieth-century black female leaders who headed churches that were small and either self-established or inherited through the ministry of a male relative, usually a husband or father. The third wave is going where black women ministers before them have not gone, that is, into positions of leadership in the center of the church. No longer ministering from the margins, they have stepped into the pastoral arena of the dominant institutional church. These contemporary black clergywomen are leading larger, historic churches which were founded by persons other than themselves or their family members. Parallel to all these groups are the active laywomen who served in church positions as missionaries, educators, social workers, counselors, church administrators, and staff. Black women form the majority and backbone of the church in that they are the strongest constituency of the church in every way—numerically, financially, and programmatically. This makes them important allies of the pastor.

THEOLOGICAL ORIENTATION

In response to the inquiry regarding their theological orientation, "womanist" led all other designations among the survey respondents. It is most remarkable that so many women chose "womanist." None of the women in 1985 wrote "womanist" as the response to a similar, open-ended question. The term itself was then in its infancy stage.

Its origins can be traced to Alice Walker's *In Search of My Mother's Garden* (New York: Harcourt Brace Jovanovich, 1983). Walker affirmed the history and importance of the experience of black women. She turned the spotlight on the uniqueness and complexity of black women's lives as they continually struggle to maintain life and to make it better for themselves and their families.

A womanist, according to Alice Walker, is one who is "outrageous, courageous, and willful in behavior" (p. xi). Usually a black mother charged her female daughters with this kind of assertiveness. Invariably, the child is seeking to know more and in greater depth than what is considered "good" for her. Walker says that a "womanist is responsible, in charge, serious." However, a womanist is not a "separatist" but "one who is committed to the survival and wholeness of an entire people, male and female, regardless" (p. xii).

The womanist tradition is identified with such notables as Harriet Tubman, Sojourner Truth, Maria Stewart, Anna Jones Cooper, Mary McLeod Bethune, Rosa Parks, and Fannie Lou Hamer, along with countless other women who have molded and shaped the womanist consciousness that now pervades twenty-first-century North America. This consciousness has resulted in a social and political praxis that is characterized by struggle, survival, self-determination, and freedom for others and themselves.

A womanist ideal cannot be understood apart from its historical context. The impulse for liberation has been a perennial struggle from the forcible removal of female slaves from West Africa and their exportation to American shores up to the present time. Responsibility, wholeness, and resistance illustrate a womanist tradition of struggle among black women in overcoming the brutality of slavery, the dehumanization of segregation, and the injustice of discrimination to forge a new world for succeeding generations.

With the recent emergence of the womanist concept in the African American community, black women are unashamedly claiming their place in the development of black history, culture, and religion. They are affirming their ability to struggle against a pyramid of oppression that consists of racism, sexism, and classism. They are doing this while maintaining their families, churches, communities, and themselves. Womanist religious dialogue is contextualized in the life experiences of black women who have utilized the faith tradition for ontological affirmation, salvific regeneration, and social transformation.

Dr. Jacquelyn Grant, professor of theology at the Interdenominational Theological Center in Atlanta, Georgia, emphasizes that black women are among the poorest and the most oppressed people of the United States. Therefore, womanist theology speaks a liberating message to the lives and struggles of black women. When black women affirm that God is on the side of the oppressed, they are saying that "God is in solidarity with the struggles of those on the underside of humanity; those whose lives are bent and broken from the many levels of assault perpetrated against them" (*African American Religious Studies*, p. 124).

The fabric of black women's lives has been woven with the threads of spirituality, human compassion, and suffering.

The term *womanist* first emerged in black women's theological writing in 1985, when Katie Cannon adapted Alice Walker's definition of a womanist for theological interpretation in "The Emergence of Black Feminist Consciousness," which was published in *Feminist Interpretation of the Bible* (Sanders 1994). In the spring of 1986, Jacquelyn Grant published "Womanist Theology: Black Women's Experience as a Source for Doing Theology, with Special Reference to Christology" in the *Journal of the Interdenominational Theological Center*. In March 1987, Delores Williams published her article "Womanist Theology: Black Women's Voices" in *Christianity and Crisis*. These earliest pieces offered sources and methods for doing womanist theology and ethics as a discipline focused on the experiences of black women. In 1988, Dean Lawrence Jones of Howard University School of Divinity provided the necessary funds to include a consultation of womanist scholars. The result of this meeting was a continuation of the discussion at the American Academy of Religion. In 1989 the womanist group held its first consultation, and it was officially recognized in 1990. Each year a variety of papers have been presented and panel discussions held. In 1989 the *Journal of Feminist Studies in Religion* printed a roundtable discussion initiated by Dr. Cheryl J. Sanders on "Christian Ethics and Theology in Womanist Perspective." Dr. Kelly Brown Douglas teaches a course on womanist theology at Howard University School of Divinity. In response to the intergenerational dialogue between a mother and daughter found in Walker's definition of womanism, Douglas says, "This dialogue suggests three essentials for womanist pedagogy: it must provide students with an opportunity to dialogue with black women's history, with ordinary black women, and with each other."

The fact that only 2 percent of the women in the 1992 study chose "feminist" exclusively, and only 8 percent in combination, is interesting. It documents to a large extent the rejection of the white women's struggle as their own. On one hand it affirms the urgency of the imperative for a distinct, female imaging of God, while on the other hand it demonstrates the determination of black women to hallow out a space for the voice of God to speak through their unique experience. With the creation of black liberationist theology and feminist theology, books were written according to black men's and white women's understandings of faith, in addition to white men's theologies. Yet none of them spoke directly to the concerns of African American women. Until womanist theology, black women had little opportunity to hear or read about theology from a black woman's point of view.

The rapid identification with this term *womanist*, which was imported from secular black women's literature into theological circles, testifies to the richness of black female spirituality and the long tradition of black women preachers and evangelists. The acceptance came also because of the profundity of Sojourner Truth's "Ain't I a Woman" and black women's familiarity with the cultural audacity of being "womanish." Not without its problems, "womanist" seems to have appeal and endurance. Because it encompasses the well-being of gender, race, and class, it may prove to be sufficiently particular and universal at the same time. If so, it will be a helpful construct for speaking about God in an increasingly diverse society.

"Liberationist theology," which encompasses black theology, remains strong, as it was in the 1985 study. This probably means that these women have a passion for the uplift of black people. If so, the denominations into which they have switched have gained additional social justice advocates. "Liberal theology" reflects the majority of graduate theological schools in America, particularly those associated with large universities.

SPIRITUALITY: IMAGES AND ATTRIBUTES OF GOD

These contemporary womanists "love the Spirit."
(Walker 1983)

Creator God who gives Purpose.

Spirit God who gives Freedom.

Wisdom God who gives Revelation.

Friend God who gives Nurture.

Healer God who gives Forgiveness and Restoration.

Liberator God who gives Power.

Helper God who gives Strength and Courage.

Regarding the image of God the survey respondents thought of "most of the time and much of the time," "Creator" and "Spirit" tied at 97 percent. "Wisdom" was at 95 percent, "Healer" at 94 percent, "Friend" at 93 percent, and both "Liberator" and "Help" at 91 percent. Certain life-giving themes emerge from these most frequently chosen images. One way of construing these images is to conclude that they represent God as Presence, which not only offsets the existential loneliness of persons but also gives to persons good gifts that are valuable and eternally enduring.

In the 1985 study, an overwhelming majority checked the image of God as "Creator." In 1992, "Creator God" and "Spirit God" tied for first place. The emergent theme of purpose and freedom ties these two together.

In creation, God's purpose for one's life is limitless and not to be circumscribed by human assignment. Rather, God has the freedom in creating any woman to invest her with gifts and callings that are unlimited and unchallengeable. "God made us and not we ourselves" (cf. Psalm 100). No human being can say for sure what purpose each man and woman is called to fulfill. This belief about God grants freedom of being and expression, which no human hierarchy can dismantle. With God all things are possible. It is God's prerogative to choose and appoint whomever God wills, irrespective of gender, race, or class. This strengthens the assertion on the part of women that it is God who called them. What person can with certainty question another's calling? This applies equally to male ministers. If we can limit God's choice in any way, it sets the stage for someone else to challenge whether or not God has called anyone, male or female. The essential issue is one of God's freedom and the free will given to all human beings by God.

The second number-one image of God selected was that of Spirit. "Now the Lord is Spirit, and where the Spirit of the Lord is, there is freedom" (2 Cor. 3:17). Historically, black women have fared better and gained far more acceptance in those churches that emphasize the free-flowing movement of the Holy Spirit. Such openness builds upon the belief that it is the Spirit that animates and uses the man or woman of God, not the person alone. Therefore, what is required is a willing, yielding, obedient, righteous vessel. In religious communities where these are higher principles than the principle of gender, followers acknowledge the free movement of God's Spirit in anointing one for the mission and giving one the gifts necessary for the task. Both the passion and the competence for the work are from the Spirit, not from doctrine or education alone. Emphasis upon the Holy Spirit allows for and invites innovation within worship and ministry. There is no set order that defies the possibility of God's doing a new thing. For many years, therefore, the largest acceptance of black women ministers was in certain Pentecostal and Holiness churches. These churches emphasized the Spirit.

As a seminarian in 1968, I documented that there were more black female pastors than black male pastors in the Shaw neighborhood of northwest Washington, D.C. I counted the many house and storefront churches that displayed the pastor's name as a female name. While these churches were much smaller than most of the churches pastored by men, their numerical count was higher (Causion 1969). The power of these women to carry on these community-based min-istries is almost always attributed to the assurance that the Holy Spirit is with them. They preach, minister, and evangelize, frequently in spite of the stigma and scorn of public opinion, because of the freedom of the Spirit. The Spirit authen-ticates their charisma as God-given and themselves as God-sent. As a young girl, I observed my grandmother participate with groups of black women ministers who aligned themselves with Women Ministers Alliances, as a network along the East Coast from Washington, D.C., to New York. Later, as a youthful preacher, I often ministered in their storefront churches, where grandchildren and other family members gathered to sing, pray, raise an offering, and hear the Word of God delivered by women ministers. They supported each other, fellowshipping together. They were tenacious, often spending enormous time and resources over-coming transportation and financial problems to dress in the proper attire and to ensure that the programs were beneficial to all concerned. Their goal was to help get the unsaved saved, starting with their own families and the individuals and families who lived near their churches. These women's collectives had a life of their own, almost invisible to dominant religious circles. There was one excep-tion, however: they were often called upon by large churches and even govern-ment officials to offer prayer, since their prayers were almost always heartfelt and believed to reach heaven. On rare occasions, one of them was asked to bring a Women's Day message to a large church. But more often they went to the nurs-ing homes and the hospitals with music and words of exhortation. Creator and Spirit meant freedom from constraint so that they could respond to the call of God in their own way. They published religious tracts and took their ministry very seriously, irrespective as to whether others took them seriously or not. They ministered in the tradition of nineteenth-century black preaching women such as Jarena Lee, Maria Stewart, and Lucy Smith (Carpenter 1989). They exempli-fied in the late twentieth century the four survival strategies suggested by Delores Williams in her book *Sisters in the Wilderness*: "1) an art of cunning 2) an art of encounter 3) an art of care, and 4) an art of connecting" (Williams 1993).[1] When women ministers could not be ordained elsewhere, these groups organized them-selves and held ordinations. A number of large Baptist Ministers Conferences would label such ordinations "clandestine."

The attributes of God that rated highly or "much of the time" in the survey were "faithful," "loving," "forgiving," "all-knowing," "all-powerful," "every-where," "close," "understanding," "dependable," and "nurturing." When "some of the time" responses were added, attributes such as "mysterious," "transcen-dent," "awesome," "peaceful," and "joyful" joined the list. All of these attributes were checked in 90 percent or more of the responses. Of first importance seems to be the God who intersects with human need. Of second importance is the deis-tic, remote God. From these attributes, one can begin to outline certain con-structs of thought related to the spirituality of black women.

It needs to be pointed out that Christian spirituality is much more than images and attributes of God. Spirituality is a given. It is not something separate from persons that has to be sought. It is who a person is in his or her deepest moments. Spirituality encompasses a broad set of meanings, including religious experiences. It also covers a broad set of social-psychological factors, including religious biography, cognitive development, and personality. Spirituality relates to the inner, deep longing of the human spirit for a connection to and a relationship with God that can be experienced through an all-encompassing presence. The availability of these dynamics produces a process that integrates one's whole being and all one's life experiences and life situations into a soulful center. Spirituality seeks the absolute fullness of creative love, found only in God.

Spirituality is a belief and hope that one can be a part of the habitation of God, a sanctuary for God, a touchstone. It is the part of a human being that invites the Holy Spirit with a welcoming reception. It emanates from an ontological center that moves on a continuum of equilibrium–disequilibrium. There are several constructs helpful in describing how the human spirit and Holy Spirit intersect: (1) order and purpose, which offer meaning that we are made in the image of God with a special purpose; (2) the guidance and instruction of Scripture, reason, and tradition, which elicit the obedience that leads to a godly life, one filled with mercy, justice, and truth; (3) provision for protection from evil, which offers survival for life; and (4) worship and celebration, which offer a dwelling place for God's habitation among human beings, a place for the low-burning flame of peace and security.

Spirituality gives meaning, purpose, and perspective to how one sees oneself, others, and the world and how one organizes one's life. Further, spirituality is a yearning to understand, to be understood, to belong, and to have inner peace.

While images and attributes of God do not constitute a totality of spirituality, they do reveal some of the concepts through which God is experienced. They give insight into the brokenness, recovery, and salvation that people of faith encounter on their human journey. Thus they are important.

The listing below has been organized in such a way as to tie the most frequently selected attributes of God to various dimensions of spirituality that emerge from them.

> Spirituality of Identity (all-knowing)
>
> Spirituality of Survival (faithful, everywhere)
>
> Spirituality of Relationship (close, loving, forgiving, nurturing)
>
> Spirituality of Empowerment (all-powerful, understanding)
>
> Spirituality of Mystery (mysterious, transcendent, awesome)
>
> Spirituality of Celebration (peaceful, joyful)
>
> Spirituality of Productivity (dependable)

We can compare the images of God with the dimensions of spirituality that emerge from the attributes of God. A pattern of conceptualization comes into focus accordingly. In this presentation, the image of God is related to a dimension of God. God gives to believers a quality that assures safety, security, meaningfulness, and significance.

Image of God	Relates to	Dimension of Spirituality
Creator God gives	purpose, which assures order	identity vocation obedience
Spirit God gives	freedom, which assures unity intuition	celebration community discernment
Friend God gives	nurture, which assures companionship	relationship compassion
Healer God gives	restoration, which assures salvation	survival sustenance
Liberator God gives	power, which assures freedom	empowerment justice
Helper God gives	strength, which assures courage victory	productivity generativity fulfillment completion

CONCLUSION

Creator God gives purpose to these women, which leads to a spirituality of identity, assuring these women that God made them and knows all about them. Spirit God gives them the freedom to be whatever God has called them to be, which causes them to celebrate and count all their suffering as joy, for what they do is under the anointing of the Holy Spirit. Wisdom God gives them the revelation of the nature of God's holiness and salvation, so that their spirituality consists of a special knowledge of God that informs their thinking and action. Although God is awesome and transcendent, they have been given a glimpse of God's mystery and glory. Friend God gives them the nurture to rely on their relationship with God, who is close, loving, and forgiving; thus they are never alone. God is always with them wishing them well, even when family and others do not support them in ministry. Healer God gives them the recovery and salvation they need when they are broken and weak, thus sustaining them in God's healing stream and renewing within them the good and ultimate intention God has for them and their ministry. Since God is faithful and everywhere, there is no circumstance, event, or feeling that is beyond the reach of God, and there is nothing that is too hard for God. They bounce back; they survive because of who God is. God is a good God all the time. Liberator God gives them power to overcome adversity and accomplish the goals they set for themselves, whereby their spirituality is not timid or weak but one of empowerment. Helper God gives them the strength to endure whatever comes until the victory is won and the assigned task is completed.

From the seven images of God and the fifteen attributes of God that rated highest among the female graduates, seven theological concepts can be postulated to form the core understanding of their spiritual power: *purpose, freedom, nurture, power, strength, revelation,* and *restoration.* Each of these can be explored more fully in later reflection. These findings lend credence to womanist construction as a particularistic theology. The fact that these concepts parallel major topics within systematic theology in general hints at the potential universality of womanist theology. Womanists contend that they are for women, men, and community. Certainly, these seven themes are life-giving for everyone.

THEOLOGICAL EDUCATION

Chapter 15

African American Baptists

Prolegomenon to
a Theological Tradition

William H. Brackney

African American Baptist experience is an important theological category not only for the Baptist tradition but far beyond. African American Baptists span a history beginning at the least in the mid-eighteenth century and continuing to the present. The Baptist persuasion in one form or another constitutes the largest single category of Christians among African Americans. The priority of identifiably Baptist themes and emphases among other African American Christians is unmistakable, because of both the chronological contribution of Baptists in establishing churches and institutions and the prominence of black Baptist leaders in the evolution of black theology.[1] It is a theological tradition that encompasses the slave and free churches as well as mainstream, evangelical, and liberation theologies. However, the African American Baptist tradition has suffered from inadequate analysis.[2] New perspectives need to be devised, inclusive of many different strains and personalities. I offer this interpretive overview as a prolegomenon to that task, in honor of J. Deotis Roberts, one of the major contributors to this tradition over much of the past century.

FOUNDATIONS

Across its history, African American Baptist thought has been dominated by pastor figures. Miles M. Fisher, W. E. B. Du Bois, and later historians have pointed out the connections between slave preachers and African priests. Whether slave exhorters or recognized clergy, the preacher/pastors were the theologians of the black communities.[3] Early in the development of an African American Baptist identity, John Jasper was an important leader. A former slave, Jasper (1812–1901) was regionally known as a great orator who exploited the metaphors of Scripture by the employment of a "black vernacular," sometimes with outlandish results.[4] He served as pastor of Richmond, Virginia's Sixth Mount Zion Baptist Church for over three decades, and his sermon "De Sun Do Move" was a remarkable piece of slave idiom. Jasper showed his hearers that black Baptist thinking was richly experiential, and he created the foundation for theology growing out of biblical narrative.[5] David George in South Carolina and Nova Scotia, Andrew Bryan in Georgia, Lott Carey in Virginia, and Thomas Paul in New England and later New York also exemplified this role.

Following the War between the States, a new breed of leaders emerged under the nurture of the American Baptist Home Mission Society. Chief among these was William James Simmons. Simmons (1849–1890) was educated at Madison University (later Colgate), the University of Rochester, and Howard University. He took up a career in school teaching and also worked as a dental apprentice and served in the Civil War. Simmons's motto was "God, my race, and denomination." He managed to be placed in positions of significant leadership as black Baptist life took shape after the Civil War. In 1880 he became president of the Normal and Theological Institute of Louisville, Kentucky, where, historian James Washington pointed out, "he awarded numerous Doctor of Divinity degrees, ministered to a local church, trained leading clergy, organized political events, edited a newspaper and presided over a denomination . . . in short Simmons was an ecclesiastical politician with a powerful patronage system."[6] In 1886 he began to build support for his dream of a united Negro Baptist organization. Behind his simple congregational eccelesiology was a conviction of the church as an agent of much-needed social transformation.[7] As an agent of morality, he held that the theological underpinnings of the church would reach into every area of life.

Simmons's dream was realized in short order when he was elected president of the American National Baptist Convention (1886–1890), and no one left more of an impress on this body. Under his leadership the convention embarked on a course that emphasized "self-elevation" of blacks through social and educational renovation. For him, "the Baptist host is like a cube; throw them aside and they always land on an equal side, and you need never despair when in your trials and doubts in your several churches; remember the God of battles is on your side and that the ages have only increased his glory."[8] He also recognized early that within the African American experience was an inherently unique spirituality that was not diminished in slavery. His desire was therefore "to exalt his people, snatch their lives from obscurity to become household matter for conversation."[9] He himself wrote countless essays on Baptist polity and thought, as well as compiling a hagiographic dictionary for "Men of Mark."

Other black leaders in the Progressive Era were Elias Camp Morris and Lewis G. Jordan. Morris (1855–1922) was born in slavery and attended Roger Williams University in Nashville. He built educational institutions to improve the future of Negro Baptists and joined the chorus in favor of a Negro Baptist ecclesiology. Jordan (1860?–1940) likewise was reared in slavery and used his narrative to create an appreciation of the Negro's pilgrimage and unique spirituality. He, too, was educated at Roger Williams University, and he served congregations in Texas and Pennsylvania. Jordan was also convinced that the future of Negro Baptists was to develop their own identity and resources. Against conservatives who favored a slower course recognizing the gains of religious freedom, he moved along the same course as Simmons. Among others who favored a separation from white structures, and eventually white thought, were Walter H. Brooks of Washington, D.C., and Richard H. Boyd of Texas. These men would sow the seeds of a black consciousness.[10] Historian James Washington has also noted the importance of black women among African American Baptists of the later nineteenth century.[11]

Importantly, the later nineteenth century witnessed the emergence of schools and colleges to train Christian leaders for Negro churches and denominational roles. Here, Baptists made a significant contribution, establishing more institutions than any other denominational tradition. Some of these were concerned with training persons for skills in the southern labor market, while others specifically trained ministers and missionaries for both the American and African contexts. As Sandy Martin and Edward Wheeler have shown, some were diligent about upgrading the status of the black ministry.[12] Of the fifteen or so collegiate-level institutions founded, five locations were formative in creating parts of an emerging theological tradition.[13] Perhaps the first was State University (later Simmons University) in Louisville, under the careful and far-sighted vision of W. J. Simmons, discussed above. Atlanta, the original home of Spelman and Morehouse Colleges, evolved with other traditions into the Interdenominational Theological Center.[14] Richmond, Virginia, became the permanent location of Wayland Seminary and the National Theological Institute (Washington, D.C.), Richmond Theological Seminary, Hartshorn Memorial College, and Storer College,[15] by the twentieth century to become Virginia Union University and School of Theology.[16] Yet another was Raleigh, North Carolina, the location of Shaw University, its divinity school, and Leonard Medical College, arguably the most comprehensive attempt at a university among African American schools.[17] Of the so-called independent schools, Lynchburg (later Virginia) Theological Seminary (1887), National Baptist Theological Seminary (1916), and National Baptist Training School (1918) stand out.[18] Careful studies of faculty and curricula of these school traditions need to be made in order to profile the evolution of African American Baptist thought and theologian-educators.[19] Other institutions, such as Roger Williams University in Nashville, Benedict College in South

Carolina, and Leland College in New Orleans,[20] provided a foundation for key leaders such as A. W. Pegues, E. C. Morris, Calvin Brown, and L. G. Jordan, and later Gardner C. Taylor, to pursue advanced studies at such seminaries as Crozer and Rochester and graduate schools such as Harvard, Boston, and Chicago.

ACORNS TO OAKS

Miles Mark Fisher (1899–1970) was one of the first nationally recognized African American Baptist scholars. Educated at Morehouse College, he later received his theological degree from Northern Baptist Theological Seminary. At the University of Chicago he wrote a Ph.D. dissertation under William Warren Sweet, "Negro Slave Songs in the United States." He taught at Richmond Theological Seminary and Shaw University Divinity School in North Carolina and for many years was pastor of White Rock Baptist Church in Durham, North Carolina.

Fisher followed in the footsteps of his distinguished father, Elijah John Fisher (1858–1915), who was pastor of Olivet Baptist Church in Chicago for eight years. The elder Fisher was born and raised in slavery in LaGrange, Georgia. He became a "floor preacher" and taught himself rudimentary theology from reading J. R. Boyd's *Eclectic Moral Philosophy*, Adam Clarke's *Commentaries*, and the *Works of Josephus*. Later he studied at Atlanta Baptist Seminary (Morehouse College) and the University of Chicago. At an early stage in ministry, Elijah published essays on "The Influence of Baptist Principles on Other Denominations" and "A Regenerated Church Membership and Why."[21] He would become well known for his love of Scripture, writing, "The fundamental principle is our belief in the supreme authority and absolute sufficiency of the Word of God." "Relying on God's Word," he went on, "we believe in a scriptural church, hence a regenerated membership . . . and we believe that our religion should be spiritual, direct, and practical, instead of formal, meditative and creedal."[22]

Miles Mark Fisher carried his father's accomplishments several steps further. His work on slave songs opened new insights into African American experience. Fisher pointed out that Negro spirituals reflected the harsh social conditions under which the slaves were forced to live. He demonstrated that the slave song was a kind of index to the mentality of the slave. The source of Baptist thought among the slaves, he concluded, came from the teaching of the missionaries and white publications. Behind the missionary context, however, lay a solid foundation in African expression. In identifying this character, Fisher brought to black theology a pursuit of its African heritage, and this would find expression in black liturgics and black hermeneutics.[23]

Fisher believed that the Negro church as an appendage of white organizations obscured the religious history of Negro Baptists. In tracing the development of Negro organizations, he created a foundation for race consciousness. Insightfully, he showed appreciation for the social gospel, the lyrics and tunes of evangelical Protestantism, and primarily the theological approach of the northern Baptists in defining Negro Baptist identity. Of particular note was the publication of his *The Freedman's Book of Christian Doctrine* (1865) by the American Baptist Publication Society, first of its kind. He was especially appreciative of Colgate, Rochester, and the University of Chicago divinity schools, while also stressing the importance of Negro schools operated by Negro leaders.

After World War I, black Baptists took new departures, reflecting currents of thought among American Christians generally. One of these was traceable to social thought in the liberal Baptist community. Howard Thurman, for instance, made a major impact on African American and Baptist thought. Thurman (1899–1981) was educated at Morehouse College, Columbia University, and Rochester Theological Seminary. In his autobiography he painfully recounted how he was denied admission to Newton Theological Institution on the grounds of race. Like Mordecai Johnson and Benjamin Mays, Thurman sought theological studies elsewhere, finally being cordially received at Rochester Theological Seminary.[24] There he encountered the social gospel, liberal theology, and a comparative approach to the study of religion, reflective of the approach of the University of Chicago. After seminary he was a pastor and taught at Morehouse and Spelman Colleges, after which he became dean of the chapel at Howard University in Washington, D.C. Later he held a similar post at Boston University. In 1943 he founded the Church for the Fellowship of All Peoples in San Francisco, the first multiracial, intercultural congregation in the United States. During his early career he cultivated the friendship of emerging African Americans such as Mary McLeod Bethune, Nannie Helen Burroughs, and A. Philip Randolph. His Howard University intellectual elite circle included Mordecai Johnson, E. Franklin Frazier, and Alain Locke. Thurman was for several decades an important mentor for many black Baptists.

There were three important sources to the thought of Howard Thurman. The first was his seminary orientation at Rochester Theological Seminary, primarily guided by George Cross, Henry B. Robins, and Conrad H. Moehlman. Cross, characterized as an "evangelical liberal," sought to establish the "essence" of Christianity apart from the entire overlay of history and cultures. He taught Thurman to look for spiritual qualities, as seen in Jesus Christ. It was an applied form of religion, realized in human fellowship that has a power for social redemption. Christian salvation, Thurman learned, is to be found in a "perfect community." Owing to his University of Chicago training, Cross emphasized to Thurman the evolutionary character of Christianity. He urged Thurman to be a "sensitive Negro," turning away from social questions to "the timeless issues of the human spirit." Thurman later said of Professor Cross that he had a greater influence on his thinking than anyone else.[25]

Two other faculty colleagues at Rochester also influenced Thurman. Henry Robins taught religious education and missions at the seminary, as well as philosophy of religion. Following the theme that Cross had commenced, Robins showed Thurman that there was a single spiritual essence underlying all world religions. Understanding this religious essence would enable him to appreciate other religious traditions. Robins also utilized Walter Rauschenbusch's terminology of the kingdom of God to characterize the perfect community. Moelhman was a tow-ering scholar who introduced Thurman to a historical understanding of theol-ogy, noting particularly the creedal battles of the church.[26]

Like many twentieth-century African American thinkers, Thurman preferred to work in ethics rather than theology per se. He often quoted Walter Rauschen-busch that it is safer to be eloquent about the immortality of the soul than the ethical demand the soul makes for a living wage. For him, therefore, the task of the Negro minister was "to interpret life in terms of a creative expansive ideal-ism. . . . He must be aware of the findings in all of human knowledge and inter-pret their meaning in terms of the Kingdom of God."[27] His own interpretation was greatly enhanced in 1935–36 when he made a trip to India, where he saw firsthand how poorly Christianity related to other world religions. During that trip he was especially attracted to Bhakti mysticism. He met Gandhi personally and introduced the saga of the American Negro to the Indian philosopher. Thur-man was profoundly impressed with the interchange.

What constituted a doctrine of God for Howard Thurman was mediated through his slave background. His ancestors once had no identity and with eman-cipation achieved their first sense of self. Hence Thurman would write, "To be known, to be called by one's name, to find one's place and hold it against all the hordes of Hell . . . It is to honor an act as one's very own, it is to live a life that is one's very own."[28] Thurman's Christology was unique and influential. In his search for a proper interpretation of Jesus, he found traditional theologians defin-ing Jesus as an object of worship and devotion. But he saw Jesus as a religious subject in quest of moral community and spiritual dignity. Jesus' solution for the evils of his world was to work for the redemption of all the cast-down people in every generation. The similarity of the social position of Jesus in his context to that of the American Negro could not be missed in Thurman's thought. Recon-ciliation became for Howard Thurman a major doctrine. He defined it as the sim-ple human desire to understand others and to be understood by others. "Every man," he wrote, "wants to be cared for and . . . this is essential to the furtherance and maintenance of life in health." Of primary importance to Thurman's idea of reconciliation was nonviolence. Here he was indebted to Mahatma Gandhi as much as to the teachings of Jesus. Nonviolence for him created an attitude that inspired wholeness and integration.[29] Thurman was convinced that the primary obstacles to reconciliation were the existence of "tight circles of security" like those found in religious faith, political ideology, or social purity.

Ecclesiologically, Howard Thurman behaved like a Baptist. His ministry was directed through his local church, which he envisioned as a genuine experiment in Christian community. In his youth he had been exposed to rigorous Baptist dis-cipline, where doctrinal matters were highly specified and church process was of the essence. He reacted negatively to both.[30] In his project, membership was typ-ically open to any who shared the commitments and responsibilities. He wanted to work within the framework of historical Protestantism, though without refer-ence to a denomination. Within the congregation itself, there were sufficient integrative activities and programs to emulate what Edward Judson referred to as an "institutional church."[31]

Thurman brought both challenge and distress to many black Baptists, mostly because of their concern for his perceived universalism. His stance in support of reconciliation and dialogue led him to say that he was not interested in converting people of another faith to Christianity. Instead, he encouraged all to discover their own heritage and "affirm its revelation of the divine." Martin Luther King Jr. was one who much appreciated Thurman as a great thinker and friend. Thurman had a profound impact on King, beginning at Boston University. (Thurman and Daddy King had been students at Morehouse.) According to Lerone Bennett, King read and reread Thurman's widely published book *Jesus and the Disinherited* during the 1956 boycott.[32] It is very tempting to posit a significant genetic dependency here, though Thurman retreated from such a claim.[33] What is unmistakable is that Thurman certainly reinforced Gandhi's thought in King's mind, which King later credited as a major point of transformation. Through his writings and his heritage at Rochester Seminary, Thurman continued to be a model for young black leaders.

Close to Thurman in age and style was Mordecai Wyatt Johnson. Johnson (1890–1976) rose from poor circumstances in Tennessee to attend Roger Williams University, Howe Institute, and Morehouse College. Later he earned a second bachelor's degree in social science at the University of Chicago. Johnson served in the pastoral ministry in Ohio and West Virginia, during which time he championed the rights of coal miners and helped organize for the NAACP. His dream to enter theological studies at Newton Theological Institution was denied—another casualty of racial discrimination. This led to a future disenchantment with denominations and to a commitment to the social tenets of the gospel.[34] Johnson earned two theological degrees, one from Rochester Theological Seminary, the other from Harvard University. At Rochester he developed an affinity for Walter Rauschenbusch and his work on the social gospel and graduated at the head of his class. He was ordained there, with seminary president Clarence Barbour participating in the service. A few short years later, at thirty-seven, he became America's youngest black college president at Howard University.

In his youth, Johnson signaled some new departures in understanding the church and the possibilities of a black theology. In his Harvard University commencement address of 1922, he declared a growing differentiation between "white man's religion and white man's understanding of democracy." He saw segregation as a national, not just a southern, problem, and he called for laying the foundations of "a black empire, a black religion, and a black culture."[35] He seemed convinced that the Negro could not expect to acquire economic, political, and spiritual liberty in the United States, and religion must address that reality. Upon graduation, Johnson assumed a Baptist professorship and worked with Baptist students at Howard. His vision became nonsectarian; the school of religion he founded at Howard was to enable the entire Negro church: "The simple, unsophisticated, mystical religion of the Negro cannot continue to endure unless it is reinterpreted over and over to him by men who have a fundamental and far-reaching understanding of the significance of religion in its relation to the complexities of modern civilized life."[36] His models were Harvard and the University of Chicago.

As president of Howard, Johnson developed a stellar faculty of Ph.D.s and encouraged several young scholars in their career development, notably J. Deotis Roberts, Howard Thurman, and Richard McKinney. Under his leadership, Howard University Divinity School and Department of Religion became accredited centers of theological training for black Baptist ministers. Congregations in the Middle Atlantic states in particular benefited from Howard's programs, and Benjamin Mays sent many prized Morehouse graduates to Howard for theological studies. In 1978, Colgate Rochester Divinity School recognized the important contribution of Johnson by establishing the Mordecai Wyatt Johnson Institute of Religion.

J. Deotis Roberts was an exception to Benjamin Mays's observation that the Negro group has produced few theologians because Negro thinkers are not much interested in fine theological or philosophical discussions about God.[37] Roberts was influenced by both Miles Mark Fisher and Mordecai Johnson. He became a leading philosophical theologian, bridging a dialogue between black theology and other major categories of Christian discourse. Roberts (b. 1927) was educated at Johnson C. Smith College, Shaw University Divinity School, Hartford Seminary, and the University of Edinburgh in philosophical theology. His doctoral dissertation, "The Rational Theology of Benjamin Whichcote: Father of the Cambridge Platonists," was under the direction of John Baillie and Charles Duthie.[38] Roberts taught at Georgia Baptist College and Shaw University before he accepted an invitation from Mordecai Johnson at Howard University to be professor of religion. He later served on the faculties of Virginia Union School of Theology, Interdenominational Theological Center, George Mason University, and the Eastern Baptist Theological Seminary. While a student at Shaw Divinity School, Roberts was a student of Miles Fisher, and his longest teaching post was at Howard under Johnson, who recruited him as one of the young Ph.D.s for the faculty.

In his own scholarly and ecclesial development, Roberts has made an important statement about black thinkers and black themes. He sought the best education he could attain, and his work among classical theologians has been hailed by American and continental theologians as a genuine contribution. His contribution to black theology has been to describe and contextualize. He is particularly interested in black theology as an intellectual and spiritual endeavor that will open dialogue with other theological traditions. Given his priority for experiential theology, Roberts has been active in various parts of the black Baptist denominational traditions and with local churches. He has contributed energetically to interpreting the life and work of Martin Luther King Jr. in various church programs.

Like Thurman, Roberts has affirmed highly the concept of reconciliation. He saw himself as an ameliorating force: "I will not go into a tirade," he wrote, "regarding the confusion and omission of White scholars. I am pro-Black and not merely anti-White." He believed that James Cone had done the necessary decon-structionist work and that someone had to take up the task of reconstruction. He wrote that "reconciliation is the more excellent way. Christ the Liberator is like-wise Christ the Reconciler. . . . We are called forth as agents of reconciliation. Reconciliation has to do with overcoming estrangement, mending fences, break-ing down walls of separation between men."[39]

Another black Baptist leader in the tradition of Mordecai Johnson and Deo-tis Roberts was Benjamin E. Mays. Mays (1894–1984) held degrees from South Carolina State College, Bates College, and the University of Chicago, where he received the Ph.D. Like Thurman and Johnson, Mays's original plan to enter Newton Theological Institution was set aside because of racial discrimination. While a student at Bates, a Newton recruiter had told Mays to apply to Virginia Union School of Theology because of his race, and he permanently set aside sem-inary studies.[40] He went on to teach mathematics at Morehouse College while also serving a local Baptist church and completing graduate school. He worked for the Urban League and conducted sociological research for the Institute of Social and Religious Research. In 1934, Mays was named dean of the School of Religion at Howard University and president of Morehouse College in 1940. While at Morehouse and through his chapel talks he encouraged countless young black men, inspiring future leaders toward excellence. An ecumenist among black Baptists, Mays was a major speaker at the Evanston (Illinois) Assembly of the World Council of Churches in 1954.

An important facet of Mays's theological outlook was his own realism about social change and theology in general. Mays believed that the Negro's ideas of God grew out of his social situation, and particularly they develop at the point of social crisis. He also observed that the Negro's life has been too unstable and precarious and too uncertain for him to become sufficiently objective to theolo-gize or philosophize about God.[41] He could only urge would-be theologians to look at a school such as the University of Chicago, whose application of the social sciences to religious disciplines helped the Negro transcend the classical scholar-ship of the mainstream Baptist community. But Mays also recounted in his auto-biography that he experienced more discrimination in Chicago and while at the university than perhaps anywhere else in his youth. That experience certainly shaped his theological outlook.[42]

Mays pointed out in his groundbreaking study on the Negro church that Negroes first achieved freedom in the Christian churches, the first one of which to be entirely Negro was Baptist. He further pointed out that a segregated church was a boon to Negro development and identity, for it fostered self-expression and leadership. Negro churches and pastors thus enjoy "unrestrained freedom" in Baptist churches, where "four laymen and three ordained ministers can start a Baptist church." Mays and his cohort found that the minister is God's ambas-sador on earth, that the minister and the church are sacred, even if his conduct is not exactly what it might be. The idea that the church is God's house and the minister is God's prophet are leading expectations of the Negro churches.[43] As

Mays's thought about the church matured, he became much more cooperative as a Negro Baptist. At the level of enabling a theological school primarily for black Baptists to survive, he fostered a plan to unite Gammon Theological Seminary and Turner Theological Seminary with Morehouse School of Religion, to become the Interdenominational Theological Center in Atlanta. With this development black Baptists had a fully accredited, ecumenical institution on a par with other ecumenical centers in California, Chicago, Rochester, and Boston.[44]

GIANTS AMONG GIANTS IN THE LAND

Three figures are responsible for the largest contributions and influence thus far in the black Baptist tradition: Joseph H. Jackson, Martin Luther King Jr., and Adam Clayton Powell Jr. Through their organizational, social, and political networks, thousands were in their respective debt.

Joseph H. Jackson (1900–1991), a life-long pastor and denominational leader, was devoted to the denominational vision of E. C. Morris, described earlier. Part of the heritage of the Olivet Baptist Church in Chicago, begun by Elijah Fisher, Jackson was educated at Jackson College and Colgate Rochester Divinity School and did further study at Creighton University, the University of Pennsylvania, and the University of Chicago. He served pastorates in Omaha, Philadelphia, and Chicago, where his congregation, Olivet, became a leading black church in the denomination and the United States.

For Jackson, black Baptists were first evangelical, meaning there can be no great preaching without faith in God. "If theology can successfully be reduced to merely 'God-Talk,' it will have no substance or reality." What all National Baptists had in common, he believed, was "an idea of God that they inherited from Jesus Christ."[45] This christological approach led Jackson to argue that God is essentially "spirit." As spirit, God is an invisible principle, a living force or being, a personality or an entity that is not limited to time and space. He mixed his evangelical perspective with the social gospel, which displayed his indebtedness to Colgate Rochester. His "Rauschenbuschian" tendency on the doctrine of the kingdom showed clearly: "The National Baptist Convention USA, Incorporated is an example of what can happen when an organization will be both active for the growth of itself and for its fellowmen in obedience to God our maker and to our Lord, Jesus Christ."[46] The contributions to the cause of the relief of the poor and the oppressed and the progressive influence of the lovers of the nation were manifestations of the kingdom.

Theologically, Jackson made much of the doctrine of freedom. "Freedom is the right of all human beings and should be granted to all God's people. All human beings who have tasted bondage and have known the bitter experience of servitude must hate the chains that bind their bodies. The Christian Church cannot ever become less than a fellowship of believers dedicated to the ideals and principles of Jesus Christ."[47] But the church cannot be divorced from the need to eliminate human affliction and suffering. Baptists, Jackson thought, must be interested in civil rights and cooperate with legitimate organizations through finances, words of encouragement, and fellowship.[48] Jackson was concerned when protest went out of control, and he felt that organizations such as NAACP and the Southern Christian Leadership Conference (organized by the NBC-USA [National Baptist Convention-USA]) could be the vehicles of addressing social ills. He also saw value in organizing the National Baptist Convention for all sorts of social and political engagement, believing that the time would come when "out of our own genius and experience we may help to supply the psychology for the disconsolate, and the creative philosophy for the oppressed and teach men in all walks of life the correct use of all available resources in the spirit of love without being poisoned by the incubus of hate."[49] He was an active ecumenist who fully engaged Vatican II, where he served as an observer to the official proceedings and heralded its changes.[50] Here Jackson's understanding of the church was manifest. Rather than tearing down the organized church, Jackson believed the church should embody unity. This unity should also be evident in denominational plurality.

Jackson's leadership drew increasing opposition from younger members of the denomination. At Philadelphia in 1960, there was an organized attempt to unseat him as president in favor of Gardner C. Taylor. A "Baptist sit-in" was organized that held up the convention business in order to get the number of votes necessary to elect Taylor. Those organizing the opposition to Jackson included Martin Luther King Jr. The Taylorites lost, Jackson continued to control the convention presidency, and Taylor eventually left to form the Progressive National Baptist Convention.[51] What was really at stake was an understanding of Christian activism that differed markedly between Jackson and King and Taylor. Beginning in 1956, when Jackson called for steps to be taken to achieve civil rights for Negroes, he thought he was in the vanguard of the movement. Gradually, however, King built new bases of support in the Deep South. Jackson was identified with the NAACP, while King wanted more immediate approaches. Repeatedly, Jackson moved the NBC away from the independent Civil Rights crusade, and a serious breach with King was inevitable. The convention, he wrote, "has not reduced its worship to a cult of race, or nationality, and has not put the gospel of color above the Christ of God."[52] Particularities of race, nationality, or rank that might demand compromise or negate the universality of the love of God were out. In some of his strongest language, Jackson said, "Negroes will not—and cannot—be blessed by those eloquent speakers who counsel their Negro brothers to curse white people on whom such hypocrites secretly rely for finance, aid, and support."[53] At the ecclesial level, Jackson opposed dual alignment with predominantly white conventions of Baptists, because they were not permitted to exercise the freedoms that were taken for granted in the Negro conventions. "Many of us have made supreme sacrifices to make our own churches and conventions as great and meaningful as possible."[54] Here was a sense of black Baptist identity that William J. Simmons or Elias Camp Morris could have articulated a century before.

Martin Luther King Jr. (1929–1968), a Baptist minister and thinker, was the outstanding protégé of Benjamin Mays. King's influence on Baptist life and thought has yet to be fully assessed. He was the son of a prominent Georgia black Baptist pastor, Martin Luther King Sr.; he was educated at Baptist-related More-house College and Crozer Theological Seminary; and he assumed the pastorate at Dexter Avenue Baptist Church in Montgomery, Alabama. Another important Baptist "gene" in King was the influence of J. Pious Barbour (1894–1974), pas-tor at Calvary Baptist Church in Chester, Pennsylvania, for four decades, under whose watchful eye young Martin interned for his seminary years. Barbour was the first Negro graduate of Crozer, who completed an M.A. at the University of Pennsylvania on theories of religious knowledge. Barbour was convinced that socialism was a means of reversing economic exploitation, and his pulpit often echoed this type of pro–African American social theory.[55]

"Daddy King" was first among influences on his son. A literalist in doctrinal understanding and baptistic to the core of his ecclesiology, Martin Sr. came from a poor family, graduated from Morehouse College, and assumed the pastorate of Ebenezer Baptist Church in Atlanta, where he remained until his death. He was typical of black preachers who remained within the congregation, affirming the authority of Scripture, relating the Bible to life, and active in the community. His advocacy of equal rights and human dignity was the bedrock of his son's social concern. He also bequeathed to Martin Jr. a yearning for excellence in school.[56]

Beyond his father, King's Morehouse College mentors were George D. Kelsey and Benjamin E. Mays. Kelsey, the head of the Department of Religion, was King's favorite teacher. He led Martin out of a rigid literalism to a critical understanding of the Bible. "The shackles of fundamentalism were removed from my body, thanks to Prof. Kelsey," King recalled.[57] Martin Jr. revered President Mays as a towering black thinker who dismissed black accomodationism for an educational philosophy of "liberation through knowledge." His chapel talks were filled with encouragements to engage social realities rather than find "socially irrelevant pat-terns of escape."[58] As an undergraduate, King often lingered to debate or discuss Mays's topics, and a life-long friendship ensued. After King completed his Boston University doctorate, Mays offered him a teaching position at Morehouse, which King declined to become pastor at Dexter Avenue Baptist Church.[59]

The Crozer influences on King have suffered inadequate explanations. In the three-year Bachelor of Divinity course two Crozer professors stood out: George Washington Davis and Kenneth L. Smith. In Davis's theology courses King encountered the thought of neo-orthodox theologians, especially Reinhold Niebuhr, plus Nietzsche and Karl Marx. Davis also had an intense interest in Mahatma Gandhi and his concept of *satyagraha*.[60] In Smith's ethics class, Mar-tin again encountered Walter Rauschenbusch, Paul Tillich, and the social gospel. He was troubled by the optimism of Rauschenbusch, on the one hand, and Niebuhr's desire to identify with oppressed peoples and to confront evil with the power of love, on the other. He was also in constant conversation with Crozer president Sankey Lee Blanton, a gentle liberal North Carolina Baptist. As impor-tant as the courses he took were the lectures he attended at other institutions in the Philadelphia area. On one occasion he met A. J. Muste, executive secretary of the Fellowship of Reconciliation and founder of the Congress of Racial Equality, who emphasized nonviolent organization. At the University of Pennsylvania, he heard Mordecai Johnson of Howard University lecture on Gandhi's spiritual leadership and its results in India. As young Martin left Crozer, a prize-winning student at the head of his class, he was a self-confessed liberal, sympathetic to oppression and discrimination and intent on engaging issues of social justice.

King's full impact on Baptist thought was of course supplemented by his work with the Southern Christian Leadership Conference and the Atlanta Improvement Association. He would still profess, however, that he was "fundamentally a clergyman, a Baptist preacher."[61] That identity was the basis of his 1961 revolt, with Gardner Taylor and other prominent civil rights–oriented ministers, from the National Baptist Convention and President Joseph H. Jackson, to form the Progressive National Baptist Convention. Its understanding of the church was ecumenical, interracial, and assertive. King's final theological and personal legacy was his following of young black Baptist ministers, including Ralph Abernathy, Wyatt T. Walker, Jesse Jackson, and Andrew Young.

Adam Clayton Powell Jr. was the most radical black Baptist thinker in the twentieth century and heir to a unique black Baptist tradition. Powell (1909–1972) represented congregational leadership applied to a political agenda, and he opened opportunities for his successors. Adam Jr., like Martin Luther King Jr., was the son of a nationally prominent black Baptist pastor. Powell Sr. was educated at Howard University and Wayland Seminary (later Virginia Union School of Theology) and later spent a year of studies at Yale. He served several churches in Minnesota, Philadelphia, and Connecticut before Abyssinian Baptist Church in New York City. He saw himself in the conservative tradition of Booker T. Washington.[62] At Abyssinian he built a congregation dedicated to community service and spiritual ministry, a powerhouse congregation in the National Baptist Convention.

Adam Jr., like King, received an excellent education, graduating from Colgate University with further study at Union Theological Seminary in New York. Fulfilling his father's fondest dream, he succeeded his father as pastor in the prestigious Abyssinian pulpit. Soon the church became the political headquarters for Adam Jr.'s four-decade political program. In his Harlem neighborhood were shapers of black American activism: W. E. B. Du Bois, A. Philip Randolph, Roy Wilkins, and Ben Davis. Powell's thought was enriched and empowered by their presence.

Powell's doctrine of the church suggested that it was a gathering of significant power, prestige, and money to respond to economic injustice. In contrast to his father, he was uninvolved in the larger black Baptist organization arena; he attended no meetings as a representative of the Abyssinian congregation. As his own future took shape, he became critical of other civil rights leaders, notably Martin Luther King Jr. He had difficulty identifying with "black" leaders because of his lighter skin color, and this proved a problem among blacks in Harlem. He became, for all purposes, a solitary leader in the black Baptist community.

Powell considered himself a mystic, which meant linking the powerful influence between the spirit of humanity and the absolute Spirit that rules the universe.[63]

God was ultimate truth and knowable through ideals of truth, beauty, and love. Powell moved far beyond the bounds of orthodoxy, rejecting specific teaching about the afterlife and establishing a kind of Marcionite political canon: "We do not believe in the Bible as the word of God. It is too filled with contradictions. We believe in the Thomas Jefferson Bible. Carefully that brilliant Founding Father cut from the New Testament only those words that Jesus spoke. Then in logical order he put them together until he had created a new Bible, a new Bible of old words."[64] Powell understood Christ as a bearer of God's absolute truth, the mandate of Scripture. But he rejected orthodox notions of human depravity. He developed a theory of two kingdoms, one the kingdom of God, the other a kingdom of humanity, the two of which are in conflict. Not unlike Walter Rauschenbusch, whom he undoubtedly read at Colgate, the kingdom of God was to be realized in history as human beings submit to God's will. His ecclesiology included the metaphor that the church is a family and yet a transforming agent to usher in the kingdom of God with healing and reconciliation.

Powell's career ended in political investigations and unresolved legal problems that greatly hampered his contribution to black Baptist life. He did, however, cast a long shadow. There were those who served with him at Abyssinian, notably David Licorish, a fiery West Indian preacher, and Wyatt Walker, a more conservative brand of Powell who was put off by Powell's lifestyle. Second, there was the group of Baptist ministers who coveted his application of ethics to politics. These included Jesse Jackson from Chicago and William Epps, a student activist who had attended Andover Newton Theological School. Gardner Taylor admired him as a friend, and Samuel D. Proctor, a nationally recognized educator, actually succeeded him as senior minister at Abyssinian and carried forth his oratorical reputation.

IN SUMMARY

The African American Baptist theological heritage is unique. It has definite genetic traces of baptistic identity, while within its own context producing arguably the most creative forms of Baptist thought. Historical and theological analyses confirm the priority of Scripture, a strong Christology, the power of religious experience, the dignity and worth of all persons before God, and an activist understanding of the kingdom of God. Of all the influences on various black Baptists discussed here, the slave experience and liberal Baptist thought—the latter as encapsulated in the period 1890–1930—were determinative. Of all the institutions, white and black, Rochester Theological Seminary, later Colgate Rochester, was foremost in fostering black Baptist thinkers and ideas.

This essay is a beginning. Much work needs to be done in identifying original sources and other historical subjects and in tracing the next generation of black Baptist leaders. The Baptist tradition overall will be greatly enriched as that work continues. Men like Deotis Roberts are models for us all.

Afterword

J. Deotis Roberts

This afterword is written to express my thanks to all contributors to this important collection of essays in my honor. A *Festschrift* is always uplifting to the honoree. Words are not adequate to fully express my gratitude for all those who shared in this project.

This brief statement is my honest attempt to reflect on how my life and experience have been enriched by dialogue with several persons who have shared in this cherished volume of essays. The memory and gratitude for what they have shared with me will be remembered for the rest of my life. And now I extend to each writer my word of thanks.

It has been a privilege to be a colleague of Professor Michael Battle for a brief period of time, when I concluded a career of theological teaching at Duke Divinity School. As research professor of theology, I was pleased to welcome a youthful colleague in the field of theology with so much promise. His zeal for the witness of the church is balanced by his passion for vigorous scholarly work. In this regard, we share a common outlook on ministry.

Battle has been well received in both church and academy, and he begins an exciting lifetime of service. As my retirement approached, Professor Battle offered to edit this *Festschrift*. He received an excellent response from religious scholars at home and abroad, in the church and the academy, men and women, from diverse religious, racial, and ethnic groups.

The quality of this collection has been for me both an informative and an inspirational treat. This brief response is a hearty thank-you for what has been completed. I wish for Battle a productive future in a field of scholarship and ministry that has been my passion for many years.

The memory of Desmond Tutu as a dialogue partner, when African and black theologies were in a formative stage, is vivid and precious. He was very amenable to our Pan-African religious, theological, and ecumenical conversations. Black theology owes much to his input. After being satiated with thought from Europe and Asia, Tutu introduced African American theologians to the richness of African thought, belief, and culture. In his own words, he viewed us as "soulmates."

Since those early years, Tutu has been exalted to the archbishopric in South Africa and has become a leader in the liberation of his home country. His Nobel Prize has established his status as an international peacemaker. He has become an authentic voice for goodwill everywhere and among all people.

Thus this volume has the blessing of one of the leading church theologians of our time. It also has the touch of one of the most promising of the theologians of a new generation, who has already an international reputation to his credit.

Jürgen Moltmann's theology of hope has been an inspiration since I heard him lecture at Duke University in 1968. He spoke on the night that M. L. King Jr. was assassinated. He was deeply touched by that tragic event.

In 1977, I was hosted by Moltmann and his colleagues at his home university in Tubingen, Germany. The ninety days I spent in his company and with his theological colleagues throughout the then Federal Republic of Germany made a deep impact on my venture into political and liberation theologies. His essay "Religious Dialogue or Social Justice?" sets the stage for the section titled "Theological Reflection" in this volume. I appreciate his willingness to put his imprint on this volume through a moving plea for the uplift of the victims of injustice and poverty in theological context.

John Macquarrie has pointed out our encounters and friendship over many years. Our experiences in Scotland, England, and the United States have been mutually beneficial. As a specialist on existentialism, he provided insights that helped me use this philosophy in religious and theological discourse. I recall that we were seated side by side at the "Theology of Hope" conference at Duke when the somber announcement came that M. L. King Jr. had been killed. His compassion across the racial divide was very moving at that time.

The choice of reflection upon "faith and reason" is very appropriate for this volume. This subject matter pinpoints my intellectual struggle as a theologian. The problem of religious knowledge has been crucial for my work as a theologian. The question "What can we know and believe?" has been central to my vocation. It antedates another question: "What must we do to be Christian disciples?" I must also say that my encounter with Kierkegaard, together with Pascal, led me to appreciate the significant contribution of Macquarrie to my personal understanding of the Christian faith. This essay deepens my appreciation for our dialogues through the years.

Norbert M. Samuelson has presented an important reflective essay on the relationship between science and spirituality. This essay reflects dialogue between us as we taught in the same city, Philadelphia. I was at Eastern Baptist Seminary and he was at Temple University. Our most significant exchange of ideas was as members of the American Theological Society in its annual meetings at Princeton Theological Seminary. He always had significant input of ideas from the Jewish religious tradition. This was important since most members are Protestant, Roman Catholic, or Orthodox. He represented religious and cultural diversity in our scholarly exchanges.

In this splendid essay, Norbert has shared with us his thoughts on the life and thought of one of the greatest intellectuals of the late nineteenth and the first half of the twentieth century. Albert Einstein contributed much to our understanding of the physical universe as well as to the relationship of science and religion. Einstein's work is coming to its own in the strides being made in the exploration of outer space. This is a subject in which I have interest.

However, he has also contributed much to our knowledge of Judaism as well as anti-Semitism—what it means to be the Other. Here Norbert and I share common ground. His sharing has put us in his debt. I am grateful that he has shared his thoughts at length and in a most profound way. The essay has greatly enhanced the section on philosophical theology and philosophy of religion.

Frederick Ferré correctly applies my initial reflections to my midlife emphasis on the black theology movement. He has reflected upon my epistemological and ethical outlook and the balance I have sought in a "holistic" stance.

Ferré's own work in process thought is very intense. I have not ignored this view entirely. My teaching at Claremont for a term, at the invitation of John Cobb, supports my attempt to come to terms with this theological movement. This attempt came at a time when my focus was on liberation theology. His suggestions are much appreciated. Perhaps now would be a good time to take a closer look. I appreciate his helpful suggestions.

Alistair Kee provides an analytical and critical essay that is helpful. He speaks from my alma mater, Edinburgh University. He is concerned that black theology has not made adequate use of Marxist analysis. Cornel West and other younger theologians in the black community have suggested that the first generation of black theologians did not give adequate attention to social and economic issues of justice. He has also pointed out the close connection between black theology and liberation theologies.

As one with interest in the future of black theological scholarship and its impact on churches and communities, I am grateful for Kee's perspectives. I welcome a continuing conversation with him. Since the theological faculty at Edinburgh is becoming more and more concerned about dialogues in the non-Western world, our dialogue could be mutually beneficial. It is important, however, that liberation theologies always need a contextual reference.

In some ways the essays by Cone and Hopkins are at the heart of my attempt to contribute insights for the black theology movement. Since James H. Cone is a mentor, I place my comments on his insights first in chronological and logical order. Hopkins represents the future of the project and its promise for new generations of African American theologians, women as well as men.

The essay by Professor James H. Cone is much appreciated. It indicates that the conversations we have shared have enriched our programs of theology. He recaptures much of the passion and insight that gave birth to the black theology movement in which I entered as an exponent and dialogue partner. I appreciate the manner in which the self-reflection by Cone leads to my own self-understanding. This essay is in many ways a centerpiece for this honorary volume. I owe Cone a cordial vote of thanks for this splendid contribution.

The essay by Dwight Hopkins is much needed. He is a representative of the second generation of black theologians. Though he is a mentee of Professor Cone, he illustrates a different approach to the project as he defines and applies the concept of culture. In addition, he is looking carefully at the contribution to religious, ethical, and theological thought by Africans. He also includes serious dialogue with black women theologians. Cone and I looked back to our omissions of the riches of black women in theological discourse. Dwight is able to move forward with them. His contribution is illuminating and anticipates developments to come in the black theology movement.

Charles Curran and I were colleagues in Washington, D.C., for several years. He was at Catholic University of America while I was at Howard University's Divinity School. We were fellow theologians in the Washington Theological Consortium. In addition, we have been associates in several professional groups. We both have served as president of the American Theological Society. I have learned much from the ecumenical dialogue with him.

Curran has captured the "both-and" holistic character of my theological outlook. The theological foundation for ethics has been important to both of us in the context of our reflection. It is helpful that he has brought a personal touch to his reflection on my writing, to which he has given such careful examination, both analytical and critical. A significant Protestant–Roman Catholic dialogue is the result. I am deeply grateful for his careful reflection upon my thought.

The essay by Peter Paris is very much appreciated. Peter and I have been close friends and colleagues throughout most of our professional life. He is a fellow Baptist as well as a scholar with common interests. We were both professors at Howard University during our formative years. Thus we have shared many important experiences in the church and the academy.

As an African Canadian, Peter has spent much of his life serving in Africa, Canada, and the United States. The richness of his background is present in his several writings. He has excelled in the academy not merely as professor but as president of the Academy of Religion and the Society for the Study of Black Religion. Peter has been fully "adopted" by African Americans. He has done much to facilitate dialogue between persons of African descent internationally—in the

United States, Canada, Africa, and the Caribbean Islands. During his life he has provided leadership in religious studies in the tradition of W. E. B. Du Bois on more secular subjects. What I have learned from Peter is invaluable. This makes his essay very significant for this honorary volume.

Kosuke Koyama, a Japanese theologian, was professor of ecumenics at Union Theological Seminary in New York City when I first encountered his *Water Buffalo Theology*. I found his writings to be informative and inspirational. I soon arranged for him to lecture at Howard Divinity School. This initiated years of dialogue with his unique theological reflections.

As early as 1964, I had been on a study tour of Japanese religions, including the Christian church. Koyama brings the flavor of the Japanese mind to theology. In this essay he has brought his personal experience of cross-cultural insight together with his Christian reflections to the text. His contribution to ecumenical theology is considerable. I have read his words with deep appreciation for his friendship and the fellow feeling expressed through his reflections upon my thought.

Professor Tinyiko S. Maluleke has made a unique contribution to this collection. We have never met, but we share much common ground as church theologians.

My interest in the racial climate in South Africa began decades ago, when I heard Father Trevor Huddleston review his book *Naught for Your Comfort* at Cambridge University in the late 1950s. In the 1970s, I joined the Reverend Leon Sullivan's project and wrote a commentary on the "Sullivan Principles." Sullivan advocated a program of affirmative action for American businesses operating in South Africa. In the late 1980s, I visited that country while the apartheid period was still present. During that visit, I lived in Soweto with a wonderful family and traveled countywide in conversation with leaders in church, state, and academy. My last visit was in the early 1990s, after the apartheid government was no longer in power. This visit was to attend and provide a lecture at the meeting of the International Bonhoeffer Society, hosted by Professor John DeGruchy at the University of Cape Town. The visit was limited in scope; nevertheless, I did visit Johannesburg, where I was able to visit friends in Soweto.

The climate seemed much more positive for Africans during this time. However, I was concerned that many theologians I had met earlier were now in leadership positions in education and politics. While this is progress, I was concerned about the absence of theologians in the academy and the education of pastors from such a limited pool of scholars.

Professor Battle, the editor of this volume, who studied Desmond Tutu's life and thought, has introduced me to a significant person who is involved in the life of the African churches. He is also involved in the academy. I am greatly encouraged by his ministry and status. He is in a crucial position during this transition period in his country. He introduces us to the present situation in South Africa and has outlined his theological agenda. I find his message informative and inspirational. I am grateful that he was able to respond to Battle's request to offer this splendid essay. We wish him much success and look forward to future dialogue with him as he pursues his important mission.

It was a privilege to meet Professor Janice Hale during my tenure as president of the Interdenominational Theological Center (ITC) in Atlanta. Her father was a distinguished pastor and she studied at ITC, earning a master's degree there. Her passion has been the education of black children from an Africentric perspective. Her doctorate is in education from Georgia State University. Janice has provided leadership on the family that brings religion and education together. She is at Wayne State University, but she is proud of her participation in the ministry of the Hartford Avenue Baptist Church in Detroit, where Charles G. Adams is pastor.

This important essay has put my concern for ministry to families in a good context. She dwells on the cooperation between schools and churches in the nurture of children and parents in moral values and issues of social justice. She has made a unique contribution to this study by her passion for reforming the Sunday school for the benefit of entire families and the black community. I am grateful for her unique outlook and witness.

Professor Edward P. Wimberly has emerged as a leading scholar in his discipline of pastoral care. He has specialized in ministry to those in the African American community, but his outreach is to all who suffer anxiety.

Our association and dialogue covers several decades, beginning during his graduate studies. He has referred to the impact of my theological program in black theology on his development. When I was president of the Interdenominational Theological Center, Wimberly was a valuable faculty member. Edward and his wife, Anne, participated in a consultation on the black family and church at the Ecumenical and Cultural Institute at Collegeville, Minnesota. Thomas Hoyt was codirector of that consultation. Bishop Hoyt is at present (2004) president of the National Council of Churches and a bishop in the Christian Methodist Episcopal Church.

My own reflections on theology and ministry have been greatly enriched by reading Wimberly's mature writings. I consider myself as a pastor who became a theologian. In the words of another ITC faculty person who reviewed one of my books: "Roberts is a theologian with a pastor's heart." This being so, the mentee (Wimberly) has become a mentor to me in the field of pastoral care. I am pleased to be one of his greatest admirers and thank him sincerely for his essay in my honor.

In the essay by Professor Delores Carpenter, we have a unique witness to the experience of women in ministry. Her message comes out of an adult life dedicated to ministry and family. Her specialization is religious education. Nevertheless, she has been a pastor as well as a theological educator for many years.

I knew Delores as a seminary student at Howard University's Divinity School in the late 1960s. She pursued a doctorate under the late Samuel Proctor at Rutgers University and has not taught at Howard for many years. Her quest for knowledge and spiritual growth and her role as parent, teacher, pastor, and denominational leader have been outstanding. It has been a privilege to observe her ministry. I have also read her publications and held personal dialogues with her through the years.

Called to minister in her mid-teens, with her grandmother as a role model in ministry, she has risen to a first-class minister-servant in church and academy. Her powerful essay in this volume is a splendid testimony to her work. I, of course, am extremely proud of how God has used her and the manner in which she has developed and exercised her gifts. Along with thanks for her essay, I wish her a blessed future.

Professor William H. Brackney has been a Baptist colleague over many years. He has been a Baptist historian and theological administrator. He was my academic dean for a brief period at Eastern Baptist Seminary in Philadelphia. He served for a number of years as principal of MacMaster Divinity College in Canada. After I retired from Duke Divinity School, Brackney became chair of the Department of Religion at Baylor University. In that location, he invited me for one academic year as a distinguished visiting scholar. This provided me with the opportunity for campus-wide dialogue and several preaching events.

In this essay, he has explored for us his interest in the tradition of black Baptists. His essay is very informative. He has placed me in the august tradition of Baptist ministers and scholars. I acknowledge my debt to him for the research he has put into this important contribution to this honorary volume. We have much in common, as we have served the Baptist denomination as pastors, professors, and theological education administrators. I wish him well as he continues his important mission.

A final word of thanks is due to Michael Battle, our editor. He planned, organized, collected, and edited an unusual assemblage of religious and ethical reflection on proximate and ultimate issues of life and social transformation. He and his dutiful assistants prepared this "moveable feast" of global religious reflection. Words are inadequate to express my personal gratitude to him. It is my wish that his future will be productive and blessed.

Brief Biography
and Bibliography

J. Deotis Roberts, the founder of the Foundation for Religious Exchange (FREE), has taught at a number of universities and seminaries, including Howard University, Yale University, Duke University, and the Eastern Baptist Theological Seminary.

He was educated at Johnson C. Smith University (A.B.), Shaw University Divinity School (B.D.), Hartford Seminary (B.D./S.T.M.), and the University of Edinburgh (D.Litt./Ph.D.).

Closed in 1994, FREE served from 1974 as an invaluable exchange between religious scholars, ministers, and laypersons through cultural immersion experiences in economically developing countries. The organization conducted study and travel seminars abroad for religious scholars. FREE's banner project was in Argentina, during which twenty black Americans shared with European groups for ten days. Roberts remained in that country as a guest professor for ninety days, as adjunct professor of liberation theology (black and Latin American) at the International Baptist Theological Seminary in Buenos Aires, at which time dialogue with José Míguez Bonino also took place.

Roberts was the first and only black president of the American Theological Society and one of its earliest African American members. Several persons of color have been elected to membership in this society because of Roberts.

Most noted for his book *Liberation and Reconciliation: A Black Theology*, Roberts is also the recent author of *The Prophethood of Black Believers* and *Africentric Christianity*. In the latter work, Roberts provides a theological assessment of Africentrism and its relationship to Christianity. Roberts explores the origins, history, and principles of Africentrism for those who have only a general sense of this movement and reveals how its influences have affected how people practice their Christian faith. In *The Prophethood of Black Believers,* Roberts shows how knowledge gained through black theology can be applied to specific areas of ministry such as education, pastoral care, and political and economic issues. In his book *Quest for a Black Theology*, Roberts outlines the need for a theology capable of expanding to accommodate other worldviews in order to avoid the bifurcation of racism and violence.

For a more complete reference to the works of J. Deotis Roberts, including his essays and articles, see David Goatley's edited work *Black Religion, Black Theology: The Collected Essays of J. Deotis Roberts*. For a listing of Roberts's books only, see the following chronological listing.

Faith and Reason: A Compartive Study of Pascal, Bergson and James. Boston: Christopher, 1962.

From Puritanism to Platonism in Seventeenth-Century England. The Hague: Martinus Nijhoff, 1968.

Liberation and Reconciliation: A Black Theology. Philadelphia: Westminster Press, 1971. Rev. ed., Maryknoll, N.Y.: Orbis Books, 1994.

[Coeditor with James J. Gardiner.] *Quest for a Black Theology*. Cleveland: Pilgrim Press, 1971.

Extending Redemption and Reconciliation. St. Louis: Christian Board of Publication, 1973.

A Black Political Theology. Philadelphia: Westminster Press, 1974.

The Roots of a Black Future. Philadelphia: Westminster Press, 1980.

A Theological Commentary on the Sullivan Principles. Philadelphia: International Council of Equality of Opportunity, 1980.

Christian Beliefs. Atlanta: John Colton & Associates, 1981. Rev. ed., Silver Spring, Md.: J. Deotis Roberts Press, 2000.

Black Theology Today: Liberation and Contextualization. Lewiston, N.Y.: E. Mellen Press, 1983.

A Philosophical Introduction to Theology. London: SCM Press; Philadelphia: Trinity Press International, 1991.

The Prophethood of Black Believers: An African American Political Theology for Ministry. Louisville, Ky.: Westminster John Knox Press, 1994.

Africentric Christianity: A Theological Appraisal for Ministry. Valley Forge, Pa.: Judson Press, 2000.

Notes

Introduction

1. J. Deotis Roberts, *Liberation and Reconciliation: A Black Theology* (Philadelphia: Westminster Press, 1971), p. 56.
2. Ibid., p. 57.
3. Ibid., p. 58.
4. J. Deotis Roberts, *A Philosophical Introduction to Theology* (London: SCM Press; Philadelphia: Trinity Press International, 1991).
5. It is of note that Roberts trained under Miles Mark Fischer, pastor and church historian at Shaw University.
6. See David Goatley, ed., *Black Religion, Black Theology: The Collected Essays of J. Deotis Roberts* (Harrisburg: Trinity Press International, 2003).
7. Roberts's handwritten letter to the author, September 8, 2003.
8. Ibid.
9. J. Deotis Roberts and James J. Gardiner, eds., *Quest for a Black Theology* (Cleveland: Pilgrim Press, 1971); and Roberts, *Liberation and Reconciliation* (rev. ed., Maryknoll, N.Y.: Orbis Books, 1994).
10. Roberts letter, September 8, 2003.
11. James H. Cone, *Black Theology and Black Power* (New York: Seabury Press, 1969).
12. Roberts, *Liberation and Reconciliation*.
13. James H. Cone, *A Black Theology of Liberation* (New York and Philadelphia: J. B. Lippincott Company, 1970).
14. For an example of the importance of black theology in the church, see African Methodist Episcopal Church General Conference, *The Doctrine and Discipline of the African Methodist Episcopal Church 2000* (Nashville, 2000).
15. See Roberts, *Liberation and Reconciliation*.
16. Cone, *Black Theology and Black Power*.
17. Roberts, *Liberation and Reconciliation*.
18. See Dwight N. Hopkins, "Black Theology and a Second Generation: New Scholarship and New Challenges," in *Black Theology: A Document History*, vol. 2: *1980–1992*, ed. James H. Cone and Gayraud S. Wilmore (New York: Orbis Books, 1993), pp. 61–70.

Chapter 2. The Problem of Religious Knowledge

1. Blaise Pascal, *Pensées* (Paris: Garnier-Flammarion, 1973), pp. 90, 92.
2. William James, *Selected Papers in Philosophy* (London: Dent, 1917), p. 206.
3. William James, *The Varieties of Religious Experience* (London: Longmans, Green, 1952), pp. 506–7.
4. J. D. Roberts, *Faith and Reason* (Boston: Christopher Publishing House, 1962), pp. vii–viii.
5. Pascal, *Pensées*, p. 48.
6. I. Kant, *The Critique of Judgement* (Oxford: Oxford University Press, 1952), p. 195.
7. J.-F. Lyotard, *Postmodern Fables* (Minneapolis: University of Minnesota Press, 1997), p. 37.
8. J. Milbank, "The Sublime in Kierkegaard," *Heythrop Journal* 37, no. 3 (1996): 298.

Chapter 3. Science and Spirituality

1. *Mishnah Torah*, Hilchot Talmud Torah chap. 1, paras. 3 and 7.
2. See ibid., chap. 1, paras. 11–12, and chap. 2, para. 1.
3. Ibid., chap. 1, para. 12.
4. The idea is not new in the twentieth century. It is also central in Shakespeare's Shylock, which was written in an Elizabethan England that was, for all practical purposes, *Judenrein.*
5. The *London Times*, November 28, 1919.
6. Einstein's view of religion, for example, excluded the possibility of revelation. In this case his views were close to (but probably more superficial than) the views of liberal Christian German theologians of his time, such as P. Wilhelm Schmidt (in *Der Ursprung der Gottesidee*) and Ludwig Büchner (in *Kraft und Stoff*). Einstein believed that religion was at its most basic level a product of fear, at a higher level a projection of a social and moral conception of a deity based on a desire for personal "guidance, love, and support," and, at the highest level, simply the result of a human "cosmic religious feeling." For Einstein, science was about reason and religion was about emotion; he felt at home with the first and utterly uncomfortable with the latter.
7. Dagobert Runes asked Einstein in September 1932 to write an essay about Spinoza for a volume commemorating the three hundredth anniversary of Spinoza's birth. Einstein declined, saying that all he knew about Spinoza could be expressed in a few words, *viz.* that Spinoza was a strict determinist (from the Einstein Archives, reel 33–286) and Spinoza conceived of the soul and the body as a single entity (from G. S. Viereck's *Glimpses of the Great* [Macauley N.Y., 1930]). Concerning Maimonides, Einstein said that he "exerted a crucial and fruitful influence on his contemporaries and on later generations" (*New York Times*, April 15, 1935), but he did not say that he (Einstein) had read him (Maimonides).
8. Brian Denis, *Einstein: A Life* (New York: J. Wiley, 1996), p. 193.
9. Albert Einstein, "What I Believe," *The Forum and Century* 80 (1930): pp. 193–94.

Chapter 4. Faith and Reason

1. *Quest for a Black Theology*, ed. James J. Gardiner and J. Deotis Roberts Sr. (Philadelphia: Pilgrim Press, 1971), xi.
2. Published a decade later as *Faith and Reason: A Comparative Study of Pascal, Bergson and James* (Boston: Christopher Publishing House, 1962).
3. Ibid., p. 81.
4. Ibid.

5. Ibid.
6. Ibid.
7. Ibid., p. viii.
8. Ibid., pp. 14–15.
9. Ibid., p. 38.
10. Ibid., p. 61.
11. James Deotis Roberts Sr., *From Puritanism to Platonism in Seventeenth-Century England* (The Hague: Martinus Nijhoff, 1968).
12. Ibid., p. 121.
13. Ibid., p. 56.
14. Ibid., p. 59.
15. Ibid., pp. 153–54.
16. Ibid., p. 154.
17. Ibid.
18. Ibid.
19. *Quest for a Black Theology*, p. xi.
20. Ibid., p. 65.
21. *Puritanism to Platonism*, p. 83.
22. Ibid.
23. *Quest for a Black Theology*, p. 67.
24. J. Deotis Roberts, *Liberation and Reconciliation: A Black Theology* (Philadelphia: Westminster Press, 1971; rev. ed., Maryknoll, N.Y.: Orbis Books, 1994), p. 24.
25. Ibid., p. 25.
26. Ibid., p. 24.
27. Ibid., p. 25.
28. Ibid, pp. 25–26.
29. Ibid., pp. 6–7.
30. Ibid., p. 7.
31. J. Deotis Roberts, *A Black Political Theology* (Philadelphia: Westminster Press, 1974), p. 123.
32. Ibid., p. 138.
33. James Deotis Roberts, *Black Theology Today: Liberation and Contextualization* (New York and Toronto: Edwin Mellen Press, 1983), p. 42.
34. Ibid.
35. Ibid.
36. Ibid.
37. Ibid., p. 43.
38. *Quest for a Black Theology*, p. 71.
39. J. Deotis Roberts, *Roots of a Black Future: Family and Church* (Philadelphia: Westminster Press, 1980), p. 22.
40. *Black Theology Today*, p. 13.
41. J. Deotis Roberts, *Black Theology in Dialogue* (Philadelphia: Westminster Press, 1987), p. 23.
42. Frederick Ferré, *Being and Value: Toward a Constructive Postmodern Metaphysics* (Albany: State University of New York Press, 1996).
43. *Black Theology in Dialogue*, p. 18.
44. Ibid., p. 19.
45. Ibid., p. 35.
46. Frederick Ferré, *Knowing and Value: Toward a Constructive Postmodern Epistemology* (Albany: State University of New York Press, 1998).
47. J. Deotis Roberts, *The Prophethood of Black Believers: An African American Political Theology for Ministry* (Louisville, Ky.: Westminster John Knox Press, 1994), p. 38.

48. Frederick Ferré, *Living and Value: Toward a Constructive Postmodern Ethics* (Albany: State University of New York Press, 2001).

49. *Roots of a Black Future*, esp. chap. 7.

50. *Prophethood of Black Believers*, p. 97.

51. *Black Theology in Dialogue*, p. 17.

52. *Prophethood of Black Believers*, p. 136.

53. *Liberation and Reconciliation*, p. 95.

54. Ibid.

55. *Prophethood of Black Believers*, p. 141.

Chapter 5. "The Criticism of [Black] Theology Is Transformed into the Criticism of Politics"

1. Alice Walker, *In Search of Our Mothers' Gardens* (London: Women's Press, 1984), p. 212.

2. Albert Cleage, *Black Christian Nationalism* (New York: William Morrow and Co., 1972), p. 158.

3. James H. Cone, *For My People: Black Theology and the Black Church* (Maryknoll, N.Y.: Orbis Books, 1984), p. 175.

4. Karl Marx and Frederick Engels, *Collected Works* (London: Lawrence & Wishart, 1975), 1:400.

5. Ibid., 3:176.

6. Ibid., 3:151.

7. Ibid.

8. Ibid., 3:154.

9. Ibid., 3:162.

10. Ibid., 3:164.

11. Walker, *In Search of Our Mothers' Gardens*, p. 168.

12. Simon S. Maimela and Dwight N. Hopkins, eds., *We Are One Voice* (Braamfontein, South Africa: Skotaville Publishers, 1989).

13. "In France, [Proudhon] has the right to be a bad economist, because he is reputed to be a good German philosopher. In Germany, he has the right to be a bad philosopher, because he is reputed to be one of the ablest French economists." Foreword to the *Poverty of Philosophy*, in Marx and Engels, *Collected Works*, 6:109.

14. Lebamang Sebidi, "The Dynamics of the Black Struggle and Its Implications for Black Theology," in *The Unquestionable Right to Be Free: Essays in Black Theology*, ed. Itumeleng J. Mosala and Buti Tlhagale (Johannesburg: Skotaville Publishers, 1986), p. 22.

15. Mokgethi Motlhabi, "Black Theology and Authority," in *Black Theology: The South African Voice*, ed. Basil Moore (London: C. Hurst & Co., 1973), p. 119.

16. Ibid.

17. Ibid., p. 120.

18. Ibid.

19. Ibid., p. 122.

20. Ibid., p. 121.

21. Ibid., p. 129.

22. Ibid., p. 123.

23. Sebidi, "Dynamics of the Black Struggle," p. 19.

24. See, for example, Anthony B. Pinn, *Varieties of African American Religious Experience* (Minneapolis: Fortress Press, 1998); Albert J. Raboteau, *A Fire in the Bones: Reflections on African-American Religious History* (Boston: Beacon Press, 1995); Gayraud S. Wilmore, ed., *African American Religious Studies: An Interdisciplinary Anthology* (Durham, N.C.: Duke University Press, 1989).

25. See, for example, Russell T. McCutcheon, ed., *The Insider/Outsider Problem in the Study of Religion: A Reader* (London: Cassell, 1999).
26. Timothy Fitzgerald, *The Ideology of Religious Studies* (Oxford: Oxford University Press, 2000).
27. Ninian Smart, *The Phenomenon of Religion* (Oxford: Mowbrays, 1973), pp. 12–13.
28. Anthony B. Pinn, *Terror and Triumph: The Nature of Black Religion* (Minneapolis: Fortress Press, 2003), pp. 139–42.
29. Compare "XIth Thesis on Feuerbach," in Marx and Engels, *Collected Works*, 5.8.

Chapter 6. Martin, Malcolm, and Black Theology

1. Theologian Langdon Gilkey of the University of Chicago made that observation to me in a private conversation. It is unfortunate that he never made a disciplined argument about King's theological importance in his published writings. If he had done so, perhaps American white theologians would not have been as hostile as they were to the rise of black liberation theology.
2. *Malcolm X Speaks*, ed. George Breitman (New York: Grove Press, 1965), pp. 107–8.
3. See *Washington Post*, 23 January 1994, p. G6.

Chapter 7. Black Theology

1. Randwedzi Nengwekhulu, "The Dialectical Relationship between Culture and Religion in the Struggle for Resistance and Liberation," in *Culture, Religion, and Liberation*, ed. Simon S. Maimela (Pretoria: Penrose Book Printers, 1994), p. 19. At the printing of this book, Dr. Nengwekhulu was lecturer at the Institute of Development Management in Gaborone, Botswana.
2. Stuart Hall, "Cultural Studies: Two Paradigms," in *Culture/Power/History: A Reader in Contemporary Social Theory*, ed. Nicholas B. Dirks, Geoff Eley, and Sherry B. Ortner (Princeton, N.J.: Princeton University Press, 1994), pp. 522 and 524.
3. Ibid., p. 522.
4. Ibid., pp. 523 and 524.
5. W. Emmanuel Abraham, "Crisis in African Cultures," in *Person and Community: Ghanaian Philosophical Studies I*, ed. Kwasi Wiredu and Kwame Gyekye (Washington, D.C.: Council for Research in Values and Philosophy, 1992), p. 13.
6. Edward P. Wimberly and Anne Streaty Wimberly, *Liberation and Human Wholeness: The Conversion Experiences of Black People in Slavery and Freedom* (Nashville: Abingdon Press, 1986), explore some of the emotional and psychological realities of black culture. Similarly, see William H. Grier and Price M. Cobbs (two psychiatrists), *Black Rage* (New York: Basic Books, 1968), and Ellis Cose, *The Rage of a Privileged Class* (New York: HarperCollins, 1993).
7. Abraham, "Crisis in African Cultures," p. 14.
8. See Melville J. Herskovits, *Myth of the Negro Past* (1941; reprint, Boston: Beacon Press, 1990); E. Franklin Frazier, *The Negro Family in the United States* (1939; reprint, Chicago: University of Chicago Press, 1966); William Bascom, *African Folktales in the New World* (Bloomington: Indiana University Press, 1992); and Richard M. Dorson, "African and Afro-American Folklore: A Reply to Bascom and Other Misguided Critics," *Journal of American Folklore* 88 (1974): 151–64.
9. See Sterling Stuckey, *Slave Culture* (New York: Oxford University Press, 1977); Roger D. Abrahams, ed., *Afro-American Folktales: Stories from Black Traditions in the New World* (New York: Pantheon Books, 1985); Jacob Drachler, *African*

Heritage: Stories, Poems, Songs, Folk Tales and Essays from Black Africa Revealing the Rich Cultural Roots of Today's Black Americans (London: Collier Books, 1969); William D. Piersen, *Black Legacy: America's Hidden Heritage* (Amherst: University of Massachusetts Press, 1993); and Molefe Kete Asante, *The Afrocentric Idea* (Philadelphia: Temple University Press, 1987).

10. See Angela Y. Walton-Raji, *Black Indian Genealogy Research: African American Ancestors among the Five Civilized Tribes* (Bowie, Md.: Heritage Books, 1993); William Loren Katz, *Black Indians: A Hidden Heritage* (New York: Aladdin Paperbacks, 1997); and Jack D. Forbes, *Africans and Native Americans: The Language of Race and the Evolution of Red-Black Peoples* (Urbana: University of Illinois Press, 1993).

11. In my *Down, Up, and Over: Slave Religion and Black Theology* (Minneapolis: Fortress Press, 1999), I argue for black culture being constituted by three strands, one of which is a reinterpretation of the negative slave master culture and white supremacist Christian doctrines. In retrospect, it would have been helpful to acknowledge the Native American/American Indian influence on the making of African American culture.

12. Abraham, "Crisis in African Cultures," p. 29.

13. Amilcar Cabral, "National Liberation and Culture," in *Return to the Source: Selected Speeches of Amilcar Cabral* (New York: Monthly Review Press, 1973), p. 41.

14. Ibid., pp. 41–42.

15. Ibid., pp. 43–44 and 50.

16. Ibid., p. 55.

17. Lucius T. Outlaw, "Race and Class in the Theory and Practice of Emancipatory Social Transformation," in *Philosophy Born of Struggle: Anthology of Afro-American Philosophy from 1917*, ed. Leonard Harris (Dubuque, Iowa: Kendall/Hunt Publishing Company, 1983), p. 122.

18. Ibid., pp. 122–23.

19. Barry Hallen, *The Good, the Bad and the Beautiful: Discourse about Values in Yoruba Culture* (Bloomington: Indiana University Press, 2000).

20. Ibid., pp. 114–15.

21. Ibid., p. 115.

22. Ibid., p. 117.

23. Ibid., pp. 118–19.

24. Ibid., pp. 120–21.

25. J. P. Odoch Pido, "Personhood and Art: Social Change and Commentary among the Acoli," in *African Philosophy as Cultural Inquiry*, ed. Ivan Karp and D. A. Masolo (Bloomington: Indiana University Press, 2000), pp. 111–12.

26. Ibid.

27. Ibid.

28. Innocent C. Onyewuenyi, "Traditional African Aesthetics: A Philosophical Perspective," in *The African Philosophy Reader*, ed. P. H. Coetzee and A. P. J. Roux (New York: Routledge, 1998), p. 398.

29. Ibid., p. 399.

30. Kwame Gyekye, *African Cultural Values: An Introduction* (Accra, Ghana: Sankofa Publishing Company, 1998), p. xiii.

31. Ibid., pp. 4–5.

32. Patrick A. Kalilombe, "Spirituality in the African Perspective," in *Paths of African Theology*, ed. Rosino Gibellini (Maryknoll, N.Y.: Orbis Books, 1994), p. 115.

33. Ibid., pp. 118–19.

34. Ibid., p. 122.

35. Ibid. Kalilombe quotes John Pobee, *Toward an African Theology* (Nashville: Abingdon Press, 1979), p. 49.

36. Ibid.

37. For a detailed and interesting look at how the spirituality of the living dead ancestors, the unborn, and reincarnation play into the notion of contemporary culture, see Kofi Asare Opoku, *West African Traditional Religions* (Accra, Ghana: FEP International Private Limited, 1976), pp. 25–39; and Ogbu U. Kalu, "Ancestral Spirituality and Society in Africa," in *African Spirituality: Forms, Meanings, and Expressions*, ed. Jacob K. Olupona (New York: Crossroad Publishing Company, 2000), pp. 54–55. In my present argument, these contributions are not by necessity germane to my claims; hence I omit a full treatment at this time.

38. Kalilombe, "Spirituality in the African Perspective," pp. 132–33.

39. Mercy Amba Oduyoye, "Spirituality of Resistance and Reconstruction," in *Women Resisting Violence*, ed. Mary John Mananzan, Mercy Amba Oduyoye, Elsa Tamez, J. Shannon, Mary C. Grey, and Letty M. Russell (Maryknoll, N.Y.: Orbis Books, 1996), p. 163.

40. Ibid., p. 167.

41. Kwame Gyekye agrees with Oduyoye when he states: "In talking about cultural values, I do not imply by any means that there are no cultural disvalues or negative features of the African [traditional] cultures. There are, of course; and they are legion" (*African Cultural Values*, pp. 171 and 174). Likewise, Kalilombe challenges traditional spirituality by stating that the seeds of negative spirituality preexisted foreign contact, particularly the failure to allow for some forms of "individualistic ambition, aggressiveness, and self-interested acquisitiveness" ("Spirituality in the African Perspective," p. 129).

42. From J. N. K. Mugambi's lecture given at the Pan African Consultation on Religion and Poverty in Nairobi, Kenya, July 20, 2002. Notes in author's possession.

Chapter 8. J. Deotis Roberts and the Roman Catholic Tradition

1. James H. Cone, *Speaking the Truth: Ecumenism, Liberation, and Black Theology* (Grand Rapids, Mich.: Wm. B. Eerdmans Publishing Co., 1986).

2. The issue of *Theological Studies* 61, no. 4 (December 2000) is dedicated entirely to "The Catholic Reception of Black Theology," with articles by Diana L. Hayes, M. Shawn Copeland, Cyprian Davis, Jamie T. Phelps, and Bryan N. Massingale and a final piece by James H. Cone.

3. James J. Gardiner and J. Deotis Roberts, eds., *Quest for a Black Theology* (Philadelphia: Pilgrim, 1971), p. xi.

4. J. Deotis Roberts, *Black Theology in Dialogue* (Philadelphia: Westminster Press, 1987), pp. 48–51; idem, *The Prophethood of Black Believers: An African-American Political Theology for Ministry* (Louisville, Ky.: Westminster John Knox Press, 1994), pp. 9, 49.

5. J. Deotis Roberts, "Status of Black Catholics," *Journal of Religious Thought* 48 (1991): 74–75; see also idem, *Black Theology Today: Liberation and Contextualization* (New York and Toronto: Edwin Mellen Press, 1983), p. 153.

6. J. Deotis Roberts, *Africentric Christianity: A Theological Approach for Ministry* (Valley Forge, Pa.: Judson Press, 2000), pp. 81–82.

7. Ibid., p. 100.

8. Roberts, "Status of Black Catholics," p. 77; *Black Theology Today*, pp. 23ff.

9. Roberts, *Black Theology in Dialogue*, p. 47.

10. From a Roman Catholic perspective, see Hans Urs von Balthasar, *The Theology of Karl Barth* (New York: Holt, Rinehart, and Winston, 1971), pp. 40ff.

11. Andrew M. Greeley, *The Catholic Imagination* (Berkeley: University of California Press, 2000); David Tracy, *The Analogical Imagination: Christian Theology and the Culture of Pluralism* (New York: Crossroad, 1981).

12. Will Herberg, introduction to Karl Barth, *Community, State, and Church: Three Essays* (Garden City, N.Y.: Doubleday/Anchor Books, 1960), pp. 22–38.
13. Roberts, *Prophethood of Black Believers*, p. 110.
14. J. Deotis Roberts, *A Philosophical Introduction to Theology* (Philadelphia: Trinity Press International, 1991), p. 14.
15. Ibid., pp. 6–7.
16. J. Deotis Roberts, *A Black Political Theology* (Philadelphia: Westminster Press, 1974), pp. 19–20.
17. Ibid., pp. 122–24; Roberts, *Black Theology Today*, pp. 38–42, 118; J. Deotis Roberts, "Black Theological Ethics: A Bibliographical Essay," *Journal of Religious Ethics* 3 (1975): 69–109; idem, *Roots of a Black Future: Family and Church* (Philadelphia: Westminster Press, 1980), pp. 12–14.
18. Roberts, *Black Theology Today*, p. 118.
19. Roberts, *Philosophical Introduction to Theology*, pp. 110–12.
20. Ibid., p. 7.
21. On one occasion (*Black Theology in Dialogue,* p. 28), Roberts criticizes an older Catholic theology for being too exclusive, based on its axiom of no salvation outside the church. However, the traditional recognition of baptism by desire and of the universal salvific will of God gave a universalizing interpretation to this axiom.
22. J. Deotis Roberts, *Liberation and Reconciliation: A Black Theology* (Philadelphia: Westminster Press, 1971), pp. 13–48.
23. Charles E. Curran, *Catholic Social Teaching 1891–Present: A Historical, Theological, and Ethical Analysis* (Washington, D.C.: Georgetown University Press, 2002), pp. 137–59.
24. Roberts, *Black Political Theology*, pp. 91–92.
25. Roberts, *Roots of a Black Future*, pp. 90–93.
26. Roberts, *Prophethood of Black Believers*, pp. 104, 91–92.
27. Ibid., p. 104.
28. Ibid., p. 97.
29. Ibid., pp. 107–8.
30. For his most developed discussion of the family, see Roberts, *Roots for a Black Future.*
31. Roberts, *Black Theology in Dialogue*, p. 51.
32. Ibid., pp. 43–52.
33. Roberts, *Prophethood of Black Believers*, pp. 1–10.
34. Roberts, *Roots for a Black Future* and *Africentric Christianity.*
35. Roberts, *Roots for a Black Future*, pp. 80–109.
36. Roberts, *Black Theology in Dialogue*, pp. 15–19.
37. Roberts, *Black Political Theology*, pp. 221–22.
38. Roberts, *Liberation and Reconciliation*, pp. 137–40.
39. Roberts, *Black Political Theology*, pp. 127–29.
40. Roberts, *Black Theology Today*, pp. 106–8.
41. Curran, *Catholic Social Teaching*, pp. 85–91.
42. Roberts, *Liberation and Reconciliation*, pp. 20–25.
43. Roberts, *Black Political Theology*, pp. 139–55; idem, *Black Theology Today*, pp. 151–61.
44. Roberts, *Black Theology in Dialogue*, pp. 65–92.

Chapter 9. African Contributions and Challenges
to the Ecumenical Movement

1. It is important to note that the SCM of Nigeria was begun by Nigerians in the 1930s and that it had always been completely autonomous from foreign control.

2. E.'Bolaji Idowu, *Olodumare: God in Yoruba Belief* (London: Longmans, 1962).
3. See Gayraud S. Wilmore and James H. Cone, *Black Theology: A Documentary History, 1966–1979* (Maryknoll, N.Y.: Orbis Books, 1979), pp. 17ff.
4. Effiong Utuk, *Visions of Authenticity: The Assemblies of the All Africa Conference of Churches, 1963–1992* (Nairobi: All Africa Conference of Churches, 1997), p. 16.
5. F. Eboussi Boulaga, *Christianity without Fetishes: An African Critique and Recapture of Christianity* (Maryknoll, N.Y.: Orbis Books, 1984), p. 44.
6. Ibid., p. 61.
7. Ibid.
8. See Ans J. van der Bent, ed., Foreword to *World Council of Churches' Statements and Actions on Racism, 1948–1979* (Geneva: Program to Combat Racism, World Council of Churches, 1980), p. v.
9. Ibid.
10. See Wilmore and Cone, *Black Theology*, pp. 74ff.
11. Ibid., pp. 103ff.
12. Ibid., p. vi.
13. Ibid., p. vii.
14. Ibid., p. 76.
15. Ibid., p. 4.
16. Ibid., p. 77.
17. "Address by Nelson Mandela to the WCC on the Occasion of Its 50th Anniversary, Harare, 13 December 1998," in "Extract of the Official Report of the Eighth Assembly of the World Council of Churches," Harare, Zimbabwe, December 1998, p. 16.
18. Utuk, *Visions of Authenticity*, p. 33.
19. Ibid., p. 108.
20. Ibid., pp. 116–18.
21. Ibid., p. 173.
22. Ibid., p. 171.
23. Ibid.
24. Ibid., p. 172.
25. The author of this essay was privileged to attend that assembly while teaching for a semester at Trinity Theological College in Legon, Ghana. That assembly elected the Ghanaian scholar and church leader Kwesi Dickson to succeed Bishop Tutu as president of the AACC.
26. In November 2002, the Society for the Study of Black Religion (SSBR) held a one-day conference in Toronto in conjunction with the annual meeting of the American Academy of Religion and the Society of Biblical Literature. A large part of its agenda was a discussion with African Canadians about the legacy of the underground railroad in Canada. Later the Black Theological Scholars Consultation hosted the SSBR at a special celebration at an African Methodist Episcopal Church founded in the 1820s by those who had come to Canada via the underground railroad. Earlier that fall, the author of this essay was the principal speaker at the 175th anniversary of the First Baptist Church in that city—a church that also dates back to the period of the underground railroad.

Chapter 10. Centrality of Periphery

1. *Sabbath,* 1951, p. 3.
2. Lawrie Balfour, *The Evidence of Things Not Said* (Ithaca: Cornell University Press, 2001), p. 73.
3. Deotis Roberts, *Black Theology in Dialogue* (Philadelphia: Westminster Press, 1987), p. 38.

4. *ad deum contra deum confugere,* Weimar edition, 5.204–26.
5. Paul Tillich, *Systematic Theology* (Chicago: University of Chicago Press, 1951), 1:133.
6. James Baldwin, *Nobody Knows My Name* (New York: Dell, 1954), p. 66.
7. From "Devotions upon Emergent Occasions" (1623), XVII: *Nunc Lento Sonitu Dicunt, Morieris*—"Now, this bell tolling softly for another, says to me: Thou must die."
8. John Mbiti, *African Religions and Philosophy* (Porstmouth, NH: Heinemann, 1990), p. 117.
9. Derrick Bell, *Faces at the Bottom of the Well* (New York: Basic Books, 1992).
10. Howard Thurman, *Jesus and the Disinherited,* 1949, p. 86.
11. Balfour, *Evidence of Things Not Said,* p. 30.
12. James P. Wind and James W. Lewis, eds., *American Congregations* (Chicago: University of Chicago Press, 1994), p. 257.
13. Balfour, *Evidence of Things Not Said,* p. 2.
14. From "Statement of the Fourth Assembly of the World Council of Churches in 1968."
15. James Cone, *A Black Theology of Liberation,* 1970, p. 39.
16. Walter E. Fluker and Catherine Tumber, eds., *A Strange Freedom,* 1988, p. 29.
17. Delores S. Williams, *Sisters in the Wilderness,* 1993, p. 201.
18. Donald Senior and Carroll Stuhlmueller, *The Biblical Foundations for Mission* (Maryknoll, N.Y.: Orbis, 1983), pp. 211, 340.
19. Baldwin, *Nobody Knows My Name,* p. 58.
20. Aelred Stubbs, *Steve Biko—I Write What I Like* (San Francisco: Harper Collins, 1978), p. 45.
21. Fifth Assembly of the World Council of Churches, Nairobi, 1975.

Chapter 13. Black Pastoral Theology as Psychological Liberation

1. J. Deotis Roberts, *The Prophethood of Black Believers: An African American Political Theology for Ministry* (Louisville, Ky.: Westminster John Knox Press, 1994), p. 72.
2. The sources for this insight are from Andrew Billingsley, "Changes in the African American Family Structure since 1960" (paper presented at the Conference on Black Families, National Council of Churches, Atlanta, Georgia, February 2000); Cornel West, *Race Matters* (New York: Vintage Books, 1993), p. 15; and Edward P. Wimberly, *Pastoral Counseling and Spiritual Values: A Black Point of View* (Nashville: Abingdon Press, 1982), pp. 9–16.
3. See Sylvia Ann Hewlett and Cornel West, *War against Parents* (New York: Houghton Mifflin, 1998), pp. 29–30.
4. Salvatore R. Maddi, *Personality Theories: A Comparative Analysis* (Homewood, Ill.: Dorsey Press, 1976), p. 663.
5. Gloria Naylor, *The Men of Brewster Place* (New York: Hyperion, 1998).
6. Pearl Cleage, *What Looks Like Crazy on an Ordinary Day* (New York: Avon Books, 1997).
7. This was the view of Peter Burger and Robert Luckmann in *The Social Construction of Reality* (New York: Anchor Books, 1963), pp. 112–16.
8. J. Deotis Roberts, *Liberation and Reconciliation: A Black Theology* (Philadelphia: Westminster Press, 1971), pp. 73–74.
9. Edward P. Wimberly, "A Conceptual Model of Pastoral Care in the Black Church, Utilizing Systems and Crisis Theories" (Ph.D. diss., Boston University Graduate School, 1976), p. 33.
10. Roberts, *Prophethood of Black Believers,* p. 3.
11. Ibid., p. 72.

12. Homer Ashby, "Is It Time for a Black Pastoral Theology?" *Journal of Pastoral Theology* (1996): 2–5.
13. Ibid., p. 13.
14. Michael White, *Re-authoring Lives: Interviews and Essays* (Adelaide, South Australia: Dulwich Centre Publications, 1995), p. 89.
15. Ibid., p. 90.
16. Ibid., p. 48.
17. Ibid., p. 53.
18. Ibid., p. 67.
19. Ibid., p. 48.
20. Michael White, *Narratives of Therapists' Lives* (Adelaide, South Australia: Dulwich Centre Publications, 1997), pp. 3–4, 12, and 23.
21. Ibid., p. 17.
22. White, *Re-authoring*, pp. 21–34.
23. Edward P. Wimberly, *Recalling Our Own Stories: The Spiritual Renewal of Religious Caregivers* (San Francisco: Jossey-Bass, 1997).
24. Clifford Harris, *Death Dance: A True Story of Drug Addiction and Redemption* (Grand Terrace, Calif.: Drug Alternative Program, 1999).
25. Ibid., p. 40.
26. Ibid., pp. 230–34.
27. Edward P. Wimberly, *Relational Refugee: Alienation and Reincorporation in African American Churches and Communities* (Nashville: Abingdon Press, 2000).
28. Ibid., p. 34.

Chapter 14. Theological and Spiritual Empowerment of Black Women in Ministry

1. See the following issues of the *Journal of Religious Thought* for published lectures from the Feminine in Religious Traditions Lecture Series: (1) *JRT* 43, 1 (Spring–Summer 1968): Delores Causion Carpenter, "The Professionalization of the Ministry of Women"; Delores Williams, *Sisters in the Wilderness: The Challenge of Womanist God-Talk* (Maryknoll, N.Y.: Orbis Books), 1993.

Chapter 15. African American Baptists

1. See, for instance, *Afro-American Religious History: A Documentary Witness*, ed. Milton C. Sernett (Durham, N.C.: Duke University Press, 1985), pp. 43–50, 337–48; 423–64; and Gayraud S. Wilmore, *Black Religion and Black Radicalism: An Interpretation of the Religious History of Afro-American People* (Maryknoll, N.Y.: Orbis Books, 1983), pp. 5, 128.
2. For instance, Owen Pelt and Ralph Smith, *The Story of the National Baptists* (New York: Vantage Press, 1960); Leroy Fitts, *A History of Black Baptists* (Nashville: Broadman Press, 1985); Joseph H. Jackson, *A Story of Christian Activism: The National Baptist Convention, USA, Inc.* (Nashville: Townshend Press, 1980).
3. Milton C. Sernett, *Black Religion and American Evangelicalism: White Protestants, Plantation Missions, and the Flowering of Negro Christianity, 1787–1865* (Metuchen, N.J.: Scarecrow Press, 1975), pp. 94–101.
4. Walter F. Pitts, *Old Ship of Zion: The Afro-Baptist Ritual in the African Diaspora* (New York: Oxford University Press, 1993), p. 67.
5. On Jasper, see William E. Hatcher, *John Jasper: The Unmatched Negro Philosopher and Preacher* (New York: Fleming H. Revell, 1908); and Richard Ellsworth Day, *Rhapsody in Black: The Life Story of John Jasper* (Philadelphia: Judson Press, 1953), esp. pp. 95–111.

6. James Melvin Washington, *Frustrated Fellowship: The Black Baptist Quest for Social Power* (Macon, Ga.: Mercer University Press, 1986), pp. 159–60.

7. Pelt and Smith, *Story of the National Baptists*, pp. 88–91.

8. William J. Simmons, *Men of Mark: Eminent, Progressive, and Rising* (Nashville: Rowell Co., 1887), p. 16.

9. Ibid., pp. 2–3.

10. See James D. Tyms, *The Rise of Religious Education among Negro Baptists: A Historical Case Study* (New York: Exposition Press, 1965), pp. 150–51.

11. Washington, *Frustrated Fellowship*, p. 139n. See also Evelyn Brooks, "The Feminist Theology of the Black Baptist Church, 1880–1900," in *Class, Race, and Sex: The Dynamics of Control*, ed. Amy Swerdlow and Hanna Lessinger (Boston: G. K. Hall, 1983), pp. 31–59; and her other article, "Nannie Helen Burroughs and the Education of Black Women," in *The Afro-American Woman: Struggles and Images*, ed. Sharon Harley and Rosalyn Terborg-Penn (Port Washington, N.Y.: Kennikat Press, 1978), pp. 97–108.

12. Sandy Dwayne Martin, "The American Baptist Home Mission Society and Black Higher Education in the South, 1865–1920," *Foundations* 24:4 (December 1981): 313–19; Edward L. Wheeler, *Uplifting the Race: The Black Minister in the New South 1865–1902* (Lanham, Md.: University Press of America, 1986), pp. 97–118.

13. There were over twenty-five schools of all kinds founded by the American Baptist Home Mission Society and the Freewill Baptists. Most of these institutions focused on skills training and primary education. A few were targeted for advanced studies and training Christian leaders. Two issues of the *American Baptist Quarterly* (*ABQ*), 11:4 and 12:1 (December 1992 and January 1993), were devoted to these schools.

14. On Morehouse, see Edward A. Jones, *A Candle in the Dark: A History of Morehouse College* (Valley Forge, Pa.: Judson Press, 1967).

15. Storer College, unique among the institutions founded by Freewill Baptists, until 1955 survived at Harper's Ferry, West Virginia, related to the American Baptist Convention.

16. Ralph Reavis Sr., "Black Higher Education among American Baptists in Virginia: From the Slave Pen to the University," *ABQ* 11:4 (December 1992): 357–74.

17. William C. Turner, "African-American Education in Eastern North Carolina: American Baptist Mission Work," *ABQ* 11:4 (December 1992): 290–308; and Wilmoth Annette Carter, *Shaw's Universe: A Monument to Educational Innovation* (Raleigh, N.C.: Shaw University, 1973).

18. On the heritage of the Lynchburg institution, consult Ralph Reavis, *Virginia Seminary: A Journey of Black Independence* (Bedford, Va.: Print Shop, 1989).

19. Among the existing works, the following are useful: W. A. Daniel, *The Education of Negro Ministers* (New York: J. & J. Harper Editions, 1969); Ronald E. Butchart, *Northern Schools, Southern Blacks, and Reconstruction: Freedmen's Education, 1862–1875* (Westport, Conn.: Greenwood Press, 1970); J. M. Stephen Peeps, "Northern Philanthropy and the Emergence of Black Higher Education: Do-Gooders, Compromisers, or Co-Conspirators?" *Journal of Negro Education* 50 (1981): 251–69.

20. On Roger Williams University (RWU), see Eugene TeSelle, "The Nashville Institute and Roger Williams University: Benevolence, Paternalism, and Black Consciousness, 1867–1910," *Tennessee Historical Quarterly* 41:4 (December 1982): 360–79. Another institution in Nashville, the American Baptist College, rose from the foundations of RWU and was jointly sponsored by the Southern Baptists and National Baptists.

21. Miles Mark Fisher, *The Master's Slave: Elijah John Fisher* (Philadelphia: Judson Press, 1922), p. 43.

22. Ibid., p. 91.

23. J. Deotis Roberts, "Thurman's Contributions to Black Religious Thought," in *God and Human Freedom: A Festschrift in Honor of Howard Thurman,* ed. Henry James Young (Richmond, Ind.: Friends United Press, 1983), 145.

24. Howard Thurman, *With Head and Heart: The Autobiography of Howard Thurman* (New York: Harcourt, Brace, Jovanovich, 1979), p. 45; Richard I. McKinney, *Mordecai: The Man and His Message: The Story of Mordecai Wyatt Johnson* (Washington, D.C.: Howard University Press, 1997), pp. 30–31.

25. Luther E. Smith Jr., *Howard Thurman: The Mystic as Prophet* (Lanham, Md.: University Press of America, 1981), pp. 19–23; Thurman, *With Head and Heart,* pp. 55, 60–61. Cross, a white man, attempted to empathize with Thurman as a Negro and planned a mentorship for his protégé that never happened because of Cross's untimely death.

26. Thurman, *With Head and Heart,* p. 54.

27. Walter Earl Fluker and Catherine Tumber, eds., *A Strange Freedom: The Best of Howard Thurman on Religious Experience and Public Life* (Boston: Beacon Press, 1998), p. 199.

28. Howard Thurman, *The Inward Journey* (San Diego: Harcourt, Brace, Jovanovich, 1984).

29. Ibid., p. 172.

30. As a student at Rochester Seminary, Thurman worked at First Baptist Church of Roanoke, Virginia, where at the time of his ordination he answered questions about the Trinity unsatisfactorily, and he objected to the laying on of hands until he rationalized the act in his own mystical thinking. See *With Head and Heart,* pp. 55–58.

31. Edward Judson, *The Institutional Church: A Primer in Pastoral Theology* (New York: Lentilhon, 1899), pp. 29–31.

32. Lerone Bennett Jr., *What Manner of Man: A Biography of Martin Luther King, Jr.* (Chicago: Johnson Publishing Co., 1964), pp. 74–75.

33. Thurman stated, "We did not ever discuss in depth the progress, success, or failure of the movement itself," referring to the Civil Rights crusade in *With Head and Heart,* p. 255.

34. McKinney, *Mordecai,* pp. 30–31.

35. Carter G. Woodson, *Negro Orators and Their Orations* (Washington, D.C.: Associated Publishers, 1925), pp. 146–48.

36. Quoted in McKinney, *Mordecai,* pp. 257–58.

37. Benjamin Mays, *The Negro's God as Reflected in His Literature* (Boston: Chapman & Grimes, 1938), p. 225.

38. Duthie awakened in Roberts an interest in Blaise Pascal, about whom Roberts had written at Hartford Theological Seminary.

39. J. Deotis Roberts, "Black Theology in the Making," *Review and Expositor* 70:3 (Summer 1973): 324, 327.

40. The incident is described in Benjamin E. Mays, *Born to Rebel* (New York: Charles Scribner's Sons, 1971), p. 61.

41. Mays, *Negro's God,* p. 255.

42. Mays, *Born to Rebel,* p. 65.

43. Benjamin Elijah Mays and Joseph William Nicholson, *The Negro's Church* (New York: Negro Universities Press, 1933), pp. 10–11.

44. Mays, *Born to Rebel,* pp. 234ff.

45. Jackson, *Story of Christian Activism,* pp. 582–83.

46. Ibid., p. 591.

47. Ibid., p. 235.

48. Ibid., p. 237.

49. Ibid., p. 256.

50. See his book *Many but One: The Ecumenics of Charity* (New York: Sheed and Ward, 1964), p. 40. Pope John XXIII personally invited Jackson to attend.

51. Unfortunately, the only published version is Jackson's in *Many But One*, pp. 406–37. The Taylorites emphasized dual affiliation with white Baptists, an ecumenical vision, and a commitment to various forms of the Civil Rights crusade. There is a brief historical sketch in Clarence Taylor, *The Black Churches of Brooklyn* (New York: Columbia University Press, 1994), pp. 147–49.

52. Ibid., p. 491.

53. Jackson, *Many But One*, p. 493.

54. Ibid., p. 494.

55. The most detail yet found on Pius Barbour is in Richard Lischer, *The Preacher King: Martin Luther King, Jr., and the Word That Moved* (New York: Oxford University Press, 1995), pp. 67–70.

56. For a warm-spirited insight into the elder King, see *Daddy King: An Autobiography* (New York: William Morrow, 1980), esp. pp. 80–102.

57. Quoted in ibid., p. 19.

58. Ibid.

59. Mays, *Born to Rebel*, 266.

60. *Satyagraha* (*satya* = truth and love; *graha* = force) was a program of nonviolent activism espoused by Gandhi. Compare King's explanation in *Strength to Love* (New York: Walker and Company, 1984), p. 151. Davis had devoted his Ph.D. dissertation to Indian spirituality.

61. Quoted in Lischer, *Preacher King*, p. 5.

62. On Powell Sr., see *Against the Tide: An Autobiography* (New York: Richard R. Smith, 1938).

63. Paris, *Black Religious Leaders* (Louisville, Ky.: Westminster/John Knox Press, 1991), 145.

64. Adam Clayton Powell, *Adam by Adam: The Autobiography of Adam Clayton Powell, Jr.* (New York: Dial Press, 1971), p. 43.

List of Contributors

Michael Battle
Vice President, Associate Dean for Academic Affairs, and Associate Professor of Theology, Virginia Theological Seminary

William H. Brackney
Director of the Program in Baptist Studies and Professor, Religion Department, Baylor University

Delores Carpenter
Associate Professor of Religious Education, Howard Divinity School

James Cone
Briggs Distinguished Professor of Theology, Union Theological Seminary

Charles Curran
Elizabeth Scurlock University Professor of Human Values, Southern Methodist University

Frederick Ferré
Professor Emeritus, University of Georgia

Janice E. Hale
Professor of Early Childhood Education, Wayne State University

Dwight Hopkins
Associate Professor of Theology, University of Chicago

Alistair Kee
Professor Emeritus of Religious Studies, University of Edinburgh

Kosuke Koyama
John D. Rockefeller Jr. Emeritus Professor of Ecumenical Studies, Union Theological Seminary

John Macquarrie
Professor Emeritus of Theology, Christ Church, Oxford University

Tinyiko Samuel Maluleke
Professor of Black and African Theology, Departments of Missiology and Systematic Theology, University of South Africa; current Dean of Faculty of Theology, University of South Africa

Jürgen Moltmann
Professor Emeritus, University of Tübingen

Peter J. Paris
Elmer G. Homrighausen Professor of Christian Social Ethics, Princeton Theological Seminary

Norbert M. Samuelson
Grossman Professor of Jewish Philosophy in Religious Studies at Arizona State University

Desmond Tutu
Archbishop of Cape Town Emeritus, Chair of the Truth and Reconciliation Commission in South Africa, and Nobel Peace Prize winner

Edward P. Wimberly
Professor of Pastoral Counseling and Care, Interdenominational Theological Center

Index of Names

Index of Subjects

advocate, 6
Africa
   land issue in, 51
   as too selectively imagined, 49
African
   ANC. *See* African National Congress
   church, 183
   churches, 97
      African-initiated, 98
      independent, 124
   as complex cultural being, 67
   cultural and religious traditions, 87
   culture of social belongingness, 112
   economic structures, 51
   heritage, xvi
      tension between American and, 61
   identity as inextricably linked with
      blackness, 60
   perspectives, 41
   religion
      African Christianity as, 117, 123–25
   spirituality, 99
   theologies, 43
   use of imagery, 43
   value of community, 105
   worldviews
      Christian attack on, 98
   visions of authenticity, 103–06
African American culture, xvi

African American preacher, 130–31
African American religious
   history, xvi
   scholarship, xvii
   thought, xiv, xvi
African American theological institutions
   vii, x, xii
African Canadian Christians, 106
African Christianity as a new African religion, 123–25
African National Congress, 102
Africanity-versus-Christianity problem,
   122
Afro-American Christianity, xvi
AIDS, 7, 117, 118, 119, 144
Albert Schweitzer Fellowship, x
alienation
   professional training as cause, 148
All Africa Council of Churches (AACC),
   96–97, 104–05
American Academy of Religion, 158
American Theological Society, 34, 156,
   181, 182, 187
analogy of being, 85
anthropology, 88, 98. *See also* theological,
   anthropology
anti-Semitism, 12, 18, 22–24, 47, 181.
   See also Judaism
apartheid, 50–51, 94, 99, 114, 119

211